Frankline Ojoo (Adhesives, ceramics, fiberglass, composite rubber), Jenipher Anjalo (Cotton, silk, timber, wool), Wakhu Emily (Metals, paints, smart materials, smart textiles), Wambui Muragu (Manufactured boards, echo materials, steel, stones), Evelyne Ng'ang'a (Aluminium, glass, gypsum, leather).

Your dedication and indefatigable academic enterprise is unfathomable. I have no doubt that you will excel in the disciplines of your choice in the design professions.

MASTER TABLE OF CONTENTS

The outline

Before embarking on the task of compiling this text, the author set the general outlook of the guidelines that were to generally form the content of the book. They included the physical, chemical and aesthetic properties and qualities of materials for design- lead, charcoal, ink, fabrics, plastics, leather, fibres,paint, paper and other substrates, preparation and use of existing materials, experiments with materials and processes to elicit new use to enhance old use.It also planned visits to relevant industries. History of materials and processes for design (graphic design, textile and fashion design, interior design, product design, illustration, architecture & engineering) was gathered through desk research.

Outcomes

The author then set his eyes on the reader and set the expected outcomes. It became the goal that, by the end of interacting with the book, the reader should be able to;

• Identify materials suitable for design
• Test materials for applicable/desirable characteristics
• Apply and/or recommend materials in requisite projects
• Report academically/professionally the deliverables of materials projects

The roles

The author gathered a team of academic researchers with requisite knowledge of desk and library research to collect data on selected topics. They also had to have a background in a design related field. Each researcher was to tackle at least three different materials. Where possible, they were also supposed to do field visits to verify their findings and collect visual case study data in form of Photography to back up their assertions. Each researcher was to;

Research, review and report on findings through presentations, write-ups, discussions and short papers.
The author's task was to;
Introduce, moderate, critic, advice and collate the materials into a coherent format for the target reader.

DESIGN MATERIALS AND PROCESS

Introduction

Generally, design materials can be classified into two broad categories; Natural and Manmade. Natural materials occur in nature either as natural minerals or as plant life. Manmade materials are achieved through chemical manipulation of gases through polymerization.

General Material Classifications

There are thousands of materials available for use in design applications. Most materials fall into one of three classes that are based on the atomic bonding forces of a particular material. These three classifications are:

1. Metallic,
2. Ceramic and
3. Polymeric.

Additionally, different materials can be combined to create a composite material. Within each of these classifications, materials are often further organized into groups based on their chemical composition or certain physical or mechanical properties. Composite materials are often grouped by the types of materials combined or the way the materials are arranged together. Below is a list of some of the commonly classification of materials within these four general groups of materials.

Metals Polymeric

• Ferrous metals and alloys • Thermoplastics plastics (irons, carbon steels,
alloy • Thermoset plastics steels, stainless steels, tool and • Elastomers die
steels)

• Nonferrous metals and alloys
(aluminum, copper,
magnesium, nickel, titanium,
precious metals, refractory
metals, superalloys)

Ceramics Composites

• Glasses •• Glass ceramics •• Graphite •• Diamond
Reinforced plastics
Metal-matrix composites Ceramic-matrix
composites
• Sandwich structures • Concrete

Different materials possess different properties to meet the various
requirements for design purposes. The properties of materials which dictate
the selection are as follows: (a) Mechanical Properties

The important mechanical properties affecting the selection of a material are:
(i) Tensile Strength: This enables the material to resist the application of a
tensile
force. To withstand the tensile force, the internal structure of the material
provides
the internal resistance.
(ii)Hardness: It is the degree of resistance to indentation or scratching,
abrasion and
wear. Alloying techniques and heat treatment help to achieve the same.
(iii) Ductility: This is the property of a metal by virtue of which it can be
drawn into
wires or elongated before rupture takes place. It depends upon the grain size
of the
metal crystals.

(iv) Impact Strength: It is the energy required per unit cross-sectional area to fracture a
specimen, i.e., it is a measure of the response of a material to shock loading.
(v)Wear Resistance: The ability of a material to resist friction wear under particular
conditions, i.e. to maintain its physical dimensions when in sliding or rolling contact
with a second member.
(vi) CorrosionResistance: Those metals and alloys which can withstand the corrosive
action of a medium, i.e. corrosion processes proceed in them at a relatively low rate
are termed corrosion-resistant.
(vii)Density: This is an important factor of a material where weight and thus the mass
is critical, i.e. aircraft components.

(b) Thermal Properties

The characteristics of a material, which are functions of the temperature, are
termed as its thermal properties. One can predict the performance of machine
components during normal operation, if he has the knowledge of thermal
properties. Specific heat, latent heat, thermal conductivity, thermal
expansion, thermal stresses, thermal fatigue, etc. are few important thermal
properties of materials.

Some of these properties are:
(i) *SpecificHeat*: It is the heat capacity of a unit mass of a homogeneous
substance.

(ii) *Thermal Conductivity:* the capability of the material to transmit heat
through it is termed as the thermal conductivity. Higher the value of thermal
conductivity, the greater is the rate at which heat will be transferred through a
piece of given size. Copper and aluminium are good conductors of heat and
therefore extensively used whenever transfer of heat is desired.

(i ii) *Thermal Expansion:* All solids expand on heating and contract on
cooling. Thermal expansion may take place either as linear, circumferential

or cubical. A solid which expands equally in three mutually orthogonal directions is termed as *thermally*

isotropic

(i v) Thermal Resistance: It is the resistance offered by the conductor when heat flow due to temperature difference between two points of a conductor.
(v)Thermal Diffusivity(h): A material having high heat requirement per unit volume
possesses a low thermal diffusivity because more heat must be added to or removed
from the material for effecting a temperature change.

(vi) Thermal Fatigue: This is the mechanical effect of repeated thermal stresses caused by repeated heating and cooling.
(c) Electrical Properties

Conductivity, resistivity, dielectric strength are few important electrical properties of a material. A material which offers little resistance to the passage of an electric current is said to be a good conductor of electricity.

(d) Magnetic Properties

Materials in which a state of magnetism can be induced are termed magnetic materials. There are five classes into which magnetic materials may be grouped: (i) diamagnetic (ii) paramagnetic (iii) ferromagnetic (iv) antiferromagnetic and (v) ferromagnetic.

(e) Chemical Properties

These properties include atomic weight, molecular weight, atomic number, valency, chemical composition, acidity, alkalinity, etc. These properties govern the selection of materials particularly in Chemical plant.

(f) Optical Properties
The optical properties of materials, e.g. refractive index, reflectivity and absorption coefficient etc. affect the light reflection and transmission.

(g) Structure of Materials The properties of design materials mainly depend on the internal arrangement of the atoms on molecules. We must note that in the selection of materials, the awareness regarding differences and similarities between materials is extremely important.

Basis for material classification

The factors which form the basis of various systems of classifications of materials in design, material science and engineering are: *(i)*the chemical composition of the material, *(ii)*the mode of the occurrence of the material in the nature, *(iii)*the refining and the manufacturing process to which the material is subjected prior it acquires the required properties, *(iv)*the atomic and crystalline structure of material and *(v)*the industrialand technical use of the material. Common engineering materials that fall within the scope of industrial design, material science and engineering may be classified into one of the following six groups:

(i) Metals (ferrous and non-ferrous) and alloys
(ii) Ceramics
(iii) Organic Polymers
(iv) Composites
*(v)*Semi-conductors
(vi) Biomaterials
(vii) Advanced Materials

(i) *Metals:* All the elements are broadly divided into metals and non-metals according to their properties. Metals are element substances which readily give up electrons to form metallic bonds and conduct electricity. Some of the important basic properties of metals are:

(a) Metals are usually good electrical and thermal conductors,
(b) At ordinary temperature metals are usually solid,
(c) To some extent metals are malleable and ductile,
*(d)*The freshly cut surfaces of metals are lustrous,
*(e)*When struck metal produce typical sound, and
*(f)*Most of the metals form alloys.

When two or more pure metals aremelted together to form a new metal whose properties are quite different from those of original metals, it is called an *alloy*.Metallic materials possess specific properties like plasticity and strength. Few favourable characteristics of metallic materials are high lustre, hardness, resistance to corrosion, good thermal and electrical conduction. These properties of metallic materials are due to:

(i) the atoms of which these metallic materials are composed and *(ii)* the way in which these atoms are arranged in the space lattice.

Metallic materials are typically classified according to their use in design as under: *(i)PureMetals:*Generally it is very difficult to obtain pure metal. Usually, they
are obtained by refining the ore.
*(ii)AlloyedMetals:*Alloys can be formed by blending two or more metals or at least one being metal.
*(iii) Ferrous Metals:*Iron is the principal constituent of these ferrous metals. Ferrous alloys contain significant amount of non-ferrous metals. Ferrous alloys are
extremely important for design purposes. Such ferrous alloys include;
(a) Mild Steels: These are moderately strong and have good weldability. The production cost of these materials is also low.
(b) Medium Carbon Steels: The strength of these materials is high but their weldability is comparatively less.
(c) High Carbon Steels: These materials get hard and tough by heat treatment and their weldability is poor.
(d)Cast Irons: The cost of production of these substances is quite low and these are used as ferrous casting alloys.
(iv) Non-Ferrous Metals:
These substances are composed of metals other than iron. However, these may
contain iron in small proportion. Out of several non-ferrous metals only seven are
available in sufficient quantity reasonably at low cost and used as common design
metals. These are aluminium, tin, copper, nickle, zinc and magnesium. *(v) Sintered Metals:*These materials possess very different properties and structures as compared to the metals from which these substances have been

cast.

Powder metallurgy technique is used to produce sintered metals.

*(vi) Clad Metals:*A _sandwich' of two materials is prepared in order to avail
the advantage of the properties of both the materials. This technique is termed
as
cladding

Organic materials
The study of organic compounds is very important because all biological
systems are composed of carbon compounds. There are also some materials
of biological origin which do not possess organic composition, e.g.,
limestone.These materials are carbon compounds in which carbon is
chemically bonded with hydrogen, oxygen and other non-metallic substances.
The Common organic materials are plastics and synthetic rubbers which are
termed as *organicpolymers.* Other examples of organic materials are wood,
many types of waxes and petroleum derivatives. Organic polymers are
prepared by polymerization reactions, in which simple molecules are
chemically combined into long chain molecules or three dimensional
structures.

The two important classes of organic polymers are:
*(a)Thermoplastics:*On heating, these materials become soft and hardened
again upon
cooling, e.g., nylon, polythene, etc.
*(b)Thermosettingplastics:*These materials cannot be resoftened after
polymerisation,
e.g., urea-formaldehyde, phenol formaldehyde, etc. They however have good
corrosion resistance.

Inorganic materials
These materials include metals, clays, sand rocks, gravels, minerals and
ceramics and have mineral origin. These materials are formed due to natural
growth and development of living organisms and are not biological materials.
Rocks are the units which form the crust of the earth. The three major groups
of rocks are:

*(i) IgneousRocks:*These rocks are formed by the consolidation of semi-liquid
of liquid material (magma) and are called *Plutonic*if their consolidation takes

place deep within the earth and *volcanic*if lava or magma solidifies on the earth's surface.

(ii) Sedimentary Rocks: When broken down, remains of existing rocks are consolidated under pressure, and then the rocks so formed are named as sedimentary rocks, e.g., shale and sandstone rocks.

*(iii) Metamorphic Rocks:*These rocks are basically sedimentary rocks which are changed into new rocks by intense heat and pressure, e.g., marble and slates. The structure of these rocks is in between igneous rocks and sedimentary rocks. Rock materials are widely used for the construction of buildings, houses, bridges, monuments, arches, tombs, etc. The slate, which has got great hardness, is still used as roofing material. Basalt, dolerite and rhyolite are crushed into stones and used as concrete aggregate and road construction material.

Another type of materials, i.e. *Pozzolanics,* is of particular interest to engineers because they are naturally occurring or synthetic silicious materials which hydrate to form cement.

Rocks, stone, wood, copper, silver, gold etc. are the naturally occurring materials exist in nature in the form in which they are to be used. However, naturally occurring materials are not many in number.

Biological materials

Leather, limestone, bone, horn, wax, wood etc. are biological materials. Wood is fibrous composition of hydrocarbon, cellulose and lignin and is used for many purposes. Apart from these components a small amount of gum, starch, resins, wax and organic acids are also present in wood. One can classify wood as *soft wood* and

hard wood . Fresh wood contains high percentage of water and to dry out it, seasoning is done. If proper seasoning is not done, defects such as cracks, twist, wrap etc. may occur.

Leather is obtained from the skin of animals after cleaning and tanning operations. Nowadays, it is used for making belts, boxes, shoes, purses etc. To preserve the leather, tanning is used. Following two tanning techniques are widely used:

(a) Vegetable Tanning: It consists of soaking the skin in tanning liquor for

several days and then dried to optimum conditions of leather.

(b) C hrome Tanning: This technique involves pickling the skin in acid solution and then revolving in a drum which contains chromium salt solution. After that the leather is dried and rolled.

CHAPTER ONE

DESIGN MATERIALS AND PROCESS

PLASTICS
Abstract

The creative product design industry today faces the challenge of raw materials across the entire world. Among the reasons for this state of scarcity of design materials can be attributed to a steady rise in human population which translates to a higher demand for products, environmental degrading practices like deforestation which means the common source of raw material, wood, is no longer easily available. In the effort of addressing this issue, this paper explorers the use of plastics as a raw material for design. By reviewing the history, properties, sources and application of plastic, this paper recommends its use, citing its cheapness, flexibility, reusability and versatile properties as some of its advantages as a design raw material.

Key words: thermoplastics, thermosetting plastics, polymerization, additives,

moulding

INTRODUCTION

To begin with, it is critical to understand the scope of this paper which actually is a summary presentation of the facts of plastic as a material for design. It is a fact that any discussion on the use of plastic will elicit spirited debate any day. Maina (2011) argues that the deplorable state of the environment has lately become a major issue nationally and internationally, a phenomenal he attributes mainly to polythene (plastics). Holding this as a fact – a negative side of plastic - overwhelming are the achievements that have been derived from plastic as a raw material in the design of day to day products like the basic kitchen appliances. Even as early as five decades back, Yoshioka (1964) observed that plastics had shown their worth. He goes on to point out that man can no longer do without them. —Long considered cheap substitutes for metal, cloth or leather, plastics have now become so highly developed, with inherent special characteristics not found in other substances, that they have become recognized as an entirely separate group of basic materials on which mankind depends.‖ Yoshioka's very statement is echoed In the life-time publication book (1981)

- *working with plastics* which states and I quote; —once plastics was regarded as a cheap substitute for real materials, but today plastics do an assortment of jobs better than any natural substance can do‖. Plastics entry in the worlds list of great materials does not need to be researched further. Plastic as a material for product design has entered every aspect of our lives, from toys for children to the interiors of vehicles, from basic kitchen utensils to building materials, and from plastics medical products like disposable syringe to ideal packaging material for all sorts of commercial and industrial user. The versatile nature of plastic as a material which can possibly take any form, as contributed to its extensive use in many spheres of life not mentioning the easiness with which it is available.

The Early History of Plastics

Swallow (1953) urged that perhaps the earliest plastic ever to be used was horn, citing the fact that homers' craft was very old even during his time. Shallow observed that the techniques of shaping and moulding that were established with very primitive tools long time ago bared quite interesting resemblance to those in use in the early fifty's. To support this he notes that the Worshipful Company of Homers was incorporated in1638. Around 1833, the first plastic derived from natural polymer was realized and was known as cellulose. The first of the cellulose plastics to be produced in this way was nitrocellulose made by the action of nitric acid in cellulose which is the basis of celluloid. This development dates back to the work of Brackenot in France in 1833 and to that of Schoenbein in Germany in 1845 (Yoshioka, 1964).

Yoshioka (1964) also points out that in the 'sixties, Alexander Parkes whilst attempting to produce substitutes for ivory and tortoiseshell, in Birmingham, found that nitrocellulose, when it had been mixed with a certain amount of camphor and alcohol which subsequently evaporated, gave a hard hornlike mass. This became the first known manmade plastic and in 1862 at the Great International Exhibition in London, it was introduces to the world. Called Parkesine at that time, it was an organic material from cellulose that could be molded after it was heated, and it could retain its shape when cooled. Come the late 19th century, an American by the name of John Wesley Hyatt used celluloid to produce billiard balls, and this celluloid became known as the first thermoplastic (Duggal 2007).

According to Yoshioka (1964) the next cellulose derivative to be made was cellulose acetate which is not as dangerously inflammable as celluloid, and soon after World War I, during which it was used in solution as an aeroplane dope, processes were developed for making it into sheet, rod and tube, and later it was produced as a moulding powder, and it occupies today a most important place in the modern injection moulding industry.

Once the structure of cellulose had been established, the synthesis of further derivatives followed fast, and a number of esters and ethers were made, amongst which may bementioned cellulose aceto buty rate, the mixed ester, and more recently ethyl cellulose and cellulose propionate. The uses to which these materials have been put are enormous, and they continue to play a most important part in the plastics industry (Yoshioka, 1964). Further improvements were made to plastics at the turn of the 20th century. In 1909, Dr. Bakeland invented a liquid resin called Bakelite, a thermosetting plastic that was capable of retaining its shape under any condition (Duggal, 2007). Bakelite was used in the manufacturing of military weapons and machines as well as electrical insulators.

According to Yoshioka (1964) the research effort put towards the improvement of plastic as a raw material was recognized in the year 1963, when the Nobel Prize in Chemistry Award was given to Profs Giulio Natta and Karl Ziegler, in recognition of their work on plastics chemistry. Dr. Ziegler did fundamental work on new catalysts which made possible countless varieties of plastics, while Dr. Natta through his research produced new plastic polymers including poly-propylene.

Polymeric Materials

According to Shallow (1951), although by their nature plastics can be very complex, it is possible to under- stand what modern plastics are chemically, and why they possess many of their particular properties, by applying chemical principles which are familiar enough in the case of organic chemicals of low molecular weight, to compounds of very high molecular weight, or as they are called, polymer. Plastics are made by breaking down the components of crude oil into simple molecules made up of hydrogen and carbon atoms, then stringing these units into long molecular chains by a process known as polymerization (Time-life Books inc, 1982).

Polymeric Mechanical Properties

Mott (2010) explains that in order for plastic to be used as a design material, special considerations should be observed in the process of selecting plastic for use in a certain project. A particular plastic is often selected for a combination of properties, such as light weight, flexibility, color, strength, stiffness, chemical resistance, low friction characteristics or transparency.

Thermosets, Thermoplastics

Plastics (or polymers) fall into two main groups: Thermoplastics and Thermosetting plastics. Thermoplastics – these are plastics that always soften when heated and harden again on cooling, provided they are not overheated and thermosetting plastics
– which undergo an irreversible chemical change in which the molecular chains crosslink so that they cannot subsequently be appreciably softened by heat. Excessive heating causes charring (Everett and Alan, 1994).
Thermoplastics can be made 'plastic' and malleable at high temperatures. Modern thermoplastic polymers soften anywhere between 65 $_0$C and 200+

$_0$C. In this state they can be moulded in a number of ways. They differ from thermosetting plastics in that they can be returned to this plastic state by reheating and so are fully recyclable. In table 1, some brief details on different thermoplastic materials used in injection moulding are shown. The list is by no means exhaustive and there are a number of blends of different materials, e.g. PC/ABS, designed to achieve the best performance properties of the two individual components. Within each group of plastics materials different levels of performance are available.

Material Abbr. Properties Typical Applications
Polypropylene PP Good chemical resistance Packaging, containers
PP Homopolymer HPPP Semi rigid, durable Small domestic appliances
e.g. kettles
PP Copolymer CPPP Good gloss, texture possible,
low cost
Large automotive parts,

plates and cups for children and
picnics

Polyethylene PE Good chemical resistance,
PE Low Density LDPE/LLDPE
PE High Density HDPE
flexible or semi rigid

depending on grade.
Weatherproof, good low temperature performance. Non toxic. Low cost

Low Density –Packaging,

containers. High Density
– crates, chemical drums,
gas/water pipe and fittings, kitchenware

Polystyrene PS
General Purpose GPPS Brittle, transparent. Poor UV
stability. HIPS up to 7x impact strength of GPPS
GPPS – toys, packaging,
cosmetic packaging
High Impact HIPS
HIPS – TV cabinets,

refrigerator linings, toilet
seats

Acrylic PMMA Rigid, clear, glossy, good
weather resistance

Lenses, signs, light
diffusers, point of purchase displays
Acrylonitrile ABS Rigid, opaque, tough, good
Butadiene Styrene gloss, texture possible
Domestic appliances, car
fascias, computer housings
Nylon (Polyamide) PA Rigid, tough, hardwearing Gears, bearings,

automotive under bonnet
parts

Acetal POM Rigid, tough, spring like,
good wear and electrical Properties
Aerosol valves, clock

parts, computer printer
components

Polycarbonate PC Rigid, transparent, excellent
impact resistance, good weather resistance, good
dimensional stability
Crash helmet visors,

vandal proof glazing, riot
shields, car headlamp lenses, safety
helmets,
babies' bottles

Acrylate Styrene ASA Rigid, opaque, tough, good
Acrylonitrile UV resistance
Housings, telephones,

automotive door mirrors
and radiator grilles

Styrene Acrylonitrile SAN Rigid, transparent, tough,

resistant to stress cracking Lenses, drinking tumblers, kitchen and picnic
ware, hi-fi covers

Polyvinyl Chloride PVC Drainpipes and guttering,

cable insulation, flooring, roofing, hosepipes
Rigid or flexible grades,

weatherprooof, nonflammable, good impact strength and electrical Insulation

Polyurethane PUR Flexible, clear, impermeable Shoe soles and heels, seals,
gaskets, rollers, wheels
Polyesters PBT, PET Rigid, clear, extremely tough,
wide temperature range Resistance
Drink bottles, business
machine components, transformer parts
Polysulphone PES,PSU,PEE
K
Excellent high temperature
stability, rigid or flexible grades available. High cost
Microwave grills,

chemotherapy devices, surgical equipment, fuel cells

Polyphenylene PPS
Sulphide
Rigid, opaque, non-burning,
good chemical resistance at high temperature
Chemical pumps, medical

and dental equipment, transformer parts, heating element bases

Polyvinylidene PVDF
Fluoride
Strong, tough material with
excellent chemical and heat Resistance
Valves, pumps, bearings in
chemical process industry
Polyphenylene PPO Oxide
Rigid, opaque, glossy,
excellent dimensional stability
TV housings, automotive instrument enclosures
Ethylene
Acetate
Vinyl EVA Flexible (rubber-like), good
low temperature flexibility, good chemical resistance
Handle grips, ice cube

trays, hoses

Table 1: Some commonly used thermoplastics and the areas they are applicable Source: Adapted from:
http://www.tep.org.uk/a2z_glossary/a2z/plastics.htm

Thermosetting plastics, The molecules of thermosetting plastics are heavily crosslinked toform a rigid molecular structure unlike in thermoplastics where the molecules sit end to end. The molecules in thermosetting plastics sit end-to-end and side-by-side and thoughthey soften when heated the first time - which allows them to be shaped - they become permanently stiff and solid and cannot be reshaped. This group of plastics remains rigid and non-flexible even at high temperatures; table 2 shows just examples of some commonly known thermosetting plastics.

Material Abbreviation Properties Typical Applications
Epoxy resin ER
(Epoxide)
Good electrical

insulator, hard, brittle unless reinforced, resists chemicals well.

Melamine MF
Formaldehyde
Polyester resin (PR) PR Stiff, hard, strong, resists
some chemicals and stains.
Stiff, hard, brittle unless
laminated, good electrical insulator,
Casting and encapsulation,

adhesives, bonding of other materials. Used for
printed circuit boards
(PCB's) and surface coatings.

Laminates for work surfaces,
electrical insulation, and tableware.
Casting and encapsulation,
bonding of other materials, car bodies, boats.
resists chemicals well. Urea formaldehyde UF Stiff, hard, strong,
(UF) brittle, good electrical insulator.
Electrical fittings, handles and
control knobs, adhesives.

Table 2: Main thermosetting plastics showing their areas of application Source: Adopted from
http://www.lanfrancdt.co.uk/materials/thermosetting.htm

Plastic Additives

According to deanin (1973) the polymers used in plastics are generally harmless. However, they are rarely used in pure form. In almost all commercial plastics, they are "compounded" with monomeric addi-tives to improve their processabilty and to modify their end-use properties and product performance. In order of total volume used, these monomeric additives may be classified as follows: reinforcing fibers, fillers, and coupling agents; plasticizers; colorants; stabilizers (halogen stabilizers, antioxidants, ultraviolet absorbers, and biological preservatives); processing aids (lubricants, others, and flow controls); flame retardants; peroxides; and antistatics. The applicability of some additives is summarised in Table 3. This is by no means exhaustive but covers the most commonly used additives for plastics.

Additive Applicability
Colour Pigments
Antimicrobials/Antibacterials
Biostabilisers
Antioxidants
Antistatics
Biodegraders
Foaming (Blowing) Agents Small particles of high density colour that can be added to a natural polymer to produce the desired colour. Special effects, such as metallic sparkle, pearlescent, etc are also available

Used in plastic products to kill bacteria. Many NHS hospitals now have plastic items containing this additive to help in their battle against infections such as MRSA

Help prevent the deterioration of plastic material where it may be susceptible to biological attack

Help prevent oxidation – the reaction of the polymer with oxygen. Oxidation can result in loss of impact strength, surface cracks and discolouration

Help prevent the build up of static electric charge. Plastics have a tendency to build up static charge on the surface which can disturb processing and can be an issue for hygiene and aesthetics

Make plastics softer and more flexible and enhance the degradability of the product

These form a foam like internal structure to the moulding.
Lubricants
Fillers
Flame retardants

Fragrances
Impact Modifiers
UV Stabilisers

Useful in reducing sinkage and weight in thick section parts, for Instance
External to prevent damage to the mould or part during

processing. Internal slip agents to make the surface more slippery if required
as a feature of the product
These can include chalk, talc and glass fibres or spheres.

Generally added to improve strength or stiffness.
To prevent ignition or spread of flame in the plastic material.

These are usually added at the initial manufacturing stage with many grades
of flame retardant polymers widely available.
Primarily for products in the home, such as nappy bags.
Improve a plastic material's ability to absorb shocks and resist

impact without cracking. Particularly useful for PVC, polystyrene and
polypropylene
Many polymers degrade over time when exposed to UV light.

UV stabilisers can be added to lengthen the life of a product under these
circumstances

Table 3: Some of the commonly used plastic additives Source: Adopted from
http://www.rutlandplastics.co.uk

Processing Plastics for Aesthetic Articles

According to Domone and Illston (2010) thermoplastics polymers many
readily be processed into sheets or rods or complex shapes in one operation,
which is often automated. Stages such as heating, shaping and cooling will
ideally be a single event or a repeated cycle. Duggal (2007) further explains
that methods used in the fabrication of commercial articles from plastic,
depends primarily on the type, resin used, shape, size and thickness of the
articles. Duggal lists the commonly used fabrication methods to be:

(1) Moulding - which can be put into different classes of compression
Moulding, Injection Moulding, Transfer Moulding, Extrusion Moulding and
Blow Moulding. Compression Moulding, can be employed both for
thermoplastics and thermosetting plastics. Thefluidized material (preheated
pellet) is filled in the mould cavity by hydraulic pressure (Figure 1).
Temperature and pressure is applied till the chemical reaction is complete.
Finally curing is done by heating (thermosetting plastics) or by cooling

(thermoplastics). After curing is complete, mould is opened and moulded material is taken out. Moulding through the force of compression is another very common industrial process. The materials used are melamine formaldehyde, phenol and urea. These materials can be formed into different shapes through applying both

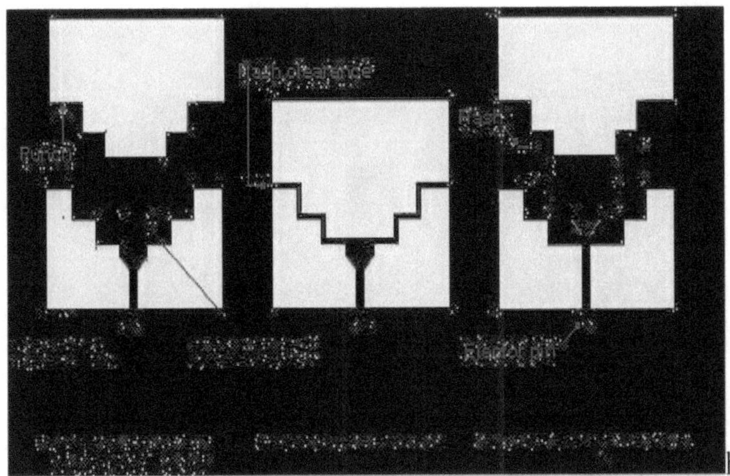

heat and pressure. Other plastics do not have these properties.

Figure 1: Compression moulding of plastic
Source: Adopted from http://resources.jorum.ac.uk

Injection Moulding is best suited for moulding of thermoplastics materials. Plastic powderis fed into a cylinder from a hopper where it is heated. When the mould opens, a screw (Figure 2) or a plunger allows the material to go inside the cylinder from the hopper. The resin melts from the heating zone from where it is sent to the mould cavity through nozzle. The mould is kept cold to allow the hot plastic to cure and acquire shape. Half of the mould is opened to cause ejection of the finished article.

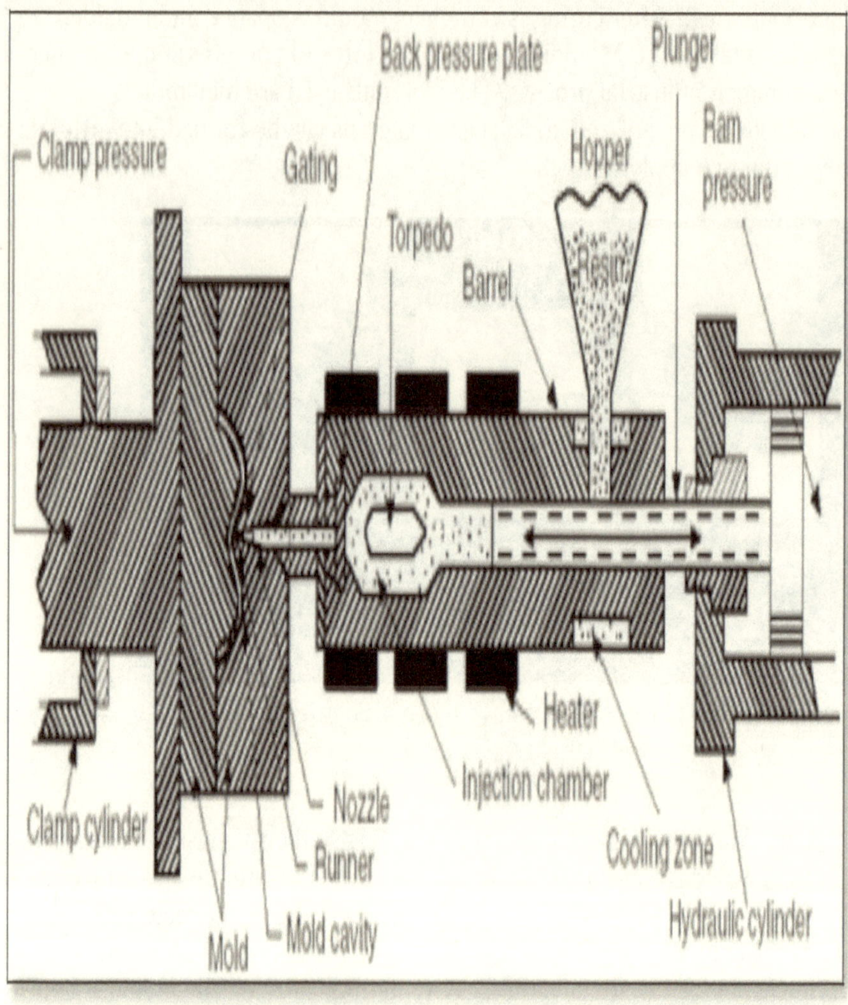

Figure 2: Cross-section of a typical plunger injection-molding machine Source: Adopted from http://www.longmold.com

Transfer Moulding, uses the principal of injection moulding for thermosetting materials. Intricate machine parts are moulded by this method. The thermosetting material powder is heated to become just plastic and injected through a Sprue, as shown in (figure 3), into the mould by the plunger working at high pressure. The temperature of the material rises because of the friction at the orifice (sprue) and the power becomes almost liquid which flows into the mould and in turn is heated to curing temperatures.

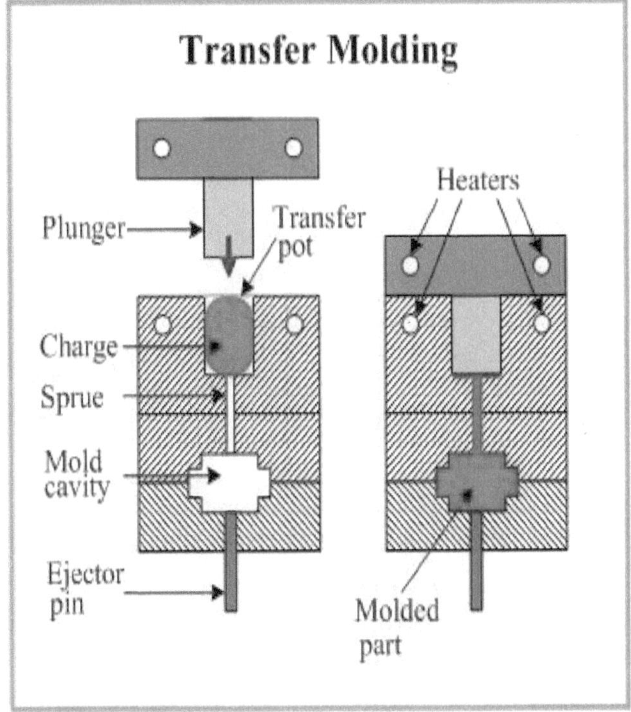

Figure 3: Transfer moulding of plastics
Source: Adopted from http://alexpb.com

Extrusion method, from an engineering view point, is the most important form of plasticmoulding (Domone and Illston, 2010). By this method the powder or granules of thermoplastics polymer are fed from a hopper to a rotating screw inside a heated barrel; the screw depth is reduced along the barrel so that the material is compacted. At the end of the barrel the melt passes through a die to produce the desired finished article. Changing the die allows a wide range of products to be made, such as: profile products, film-blown plastic sheets, blow-moulded hollow plastic articles, co-extruded items and highly oriented grid sheets.

Profile products –with different extrusion dies, many profiles can be manufactured suchas edging strips, pipes, window-frames, etc. However success depends on the correct design of the die.
Film-blown plastic sheet – molten plastic from the extruder passes through an annular die to form a thin tube; a supply of air inside the tube prevents collapse and when the film is cooled it passes through collapsing guides and

nip rolls and is stored on drums. Biaxial orientation of the polymer can be achieved by varying the air pressure in the polymer tube which in turn controls the circumferential orientation. Longitudinal orientation can be achieved by varying the relative speed of the nip roll and the linear velocity of the bubble; this is known as draw-down.

Blow-moulded hollowplastic articles – a molten polymer tube, the Parison, is extruded through an annular die.A mould closes round the Parison and internal pressure forces the polymer against the sides of the mould. This method is used to form such articles as bottles and cold-water storage tanks. The materials commonly used are polypropylene, polyethylene and polyethylene terephthalate (PET). (1) Co-extrude items – a multilayered plastic composite is sometimes needed to withstand the end user requirements. Two or more polymers are combined in asingle process by film blowing with an adhesive film between them. Reactive bonding processes to chemically cross-link the polymers are under development (Domone and Illston, 2010).

(2) Casting– the plastics are muolded without application of pressure. The resin is melted and poured into mould. The casting of plastics is similar to that of cast iron. Since the cast plastic is not so smooth just after casting, they are then polished. This method is most suited to the plastics formed from cellulose acetate and cellulose nitrate.

(3) Lamination– thin sheets of cloth or paper asbestos are impregnated with thermosetting resin. These lamins are then pressed by a hydraulic press. Under temperature and pressure the lamins are bonded together to form one sheet. The laminated plastic exhibit improved mechanical and electrical properties. The thickness of laminated plastics ranges between 0.13 mm – 15 mm. vinyl resins is most suitable for lamination (Duggal, 2007).

Recycled Plastic for Sculptural Art

The figures 4a, b & c show some creative work of Art that is made possible by use of recycled waste plastic. Designers are now creating even clothes from the plastics. This is its conspicuous instance. French designer Frank Sorbier attracted a number of eyes worldwide for this gown (see figure 4c) in 2008/09.

Figure 4 a: On the left shows a plastic chicken figurine, Figure 4 b. in the middle is a plastic horse and Figure 4 c. on the right is a plastic gown.
Source: Adopted from http://oddstuffmagazine.com

CONCLUSION

Plastics are used throughout the world for a broad number of reasons. In Kenya, plastics have replaced almost all types of paper. This is not without adverse effects as observed by Maina (2012). Plastics extensive properties make it one of the most flexible and recommendable design material today, with its application spread across all industrial fields. The commercial success of plastics as a packaging product is due to a combination of flexibility (from film to rigid applications), strength, lightness, stability, impermeability and ease of sterilisation. These features make plastics an ideal packaging material for allsorts of commercial and industrial users. Modern healthcare would be impossible without plastics medical products people tend to take for granted: disposable syringes, intravenous blood bags and heart valves, etc. Plastics packaging is particularly suitable for medical applications, thanks to their exceptional barrier properties, light weight, low cost, durability, transparency and compatibility with other materials. As a result people are living better, longer and have increasingly fulfilling lives. The available technology today that recycles plastic back to oil has given a big breakthrough in environmental concern that made plastic a curse due to its non degradable nature. Very soon this could no longer a concern as this technology gathers momentum and becomes available even to developing nations like Kenya. Nevertheless, much is yet unexplored in the field of plastics chemistry and possibilities seem limitless. As research progresses, more and more varieties of plastics are being produced to satisfy needs as they arise. The qualities of plastics that make them so versatile and so widely applicable are their pliability, strength, corrosion resistance and range of color and textures.

CHAPTER TWO

ESIGN MATERIALS AND PROCESSD

CONCRETES

Abstract

The building industry today, across the entire world, is experiencing a greater demand for expansion of social structures which range from residential/rental houses, hospitals, industrial ware houses, commercial centers, roads, city boulevard, airport run ways, entertainment venues like stadiums, swimming pools just to name but a few. Since time immemorial, the primary construction material - globally - for such architectural projects has always been concrete. The demand for construction of these types of structures in a world that is prone to catastrophic natural occurrences like the recently witnessed earthquakes in Japan and Haiti, tsunami waves in North America ushered a necessitude for deeper scientific relook at materials of construction. This research cuts across the need for new building materials, improvements of the already used materials and new approaches in the building industry. In that view, this paper takes a bias in concrete as the major building block and analyses its nature by looking at its properties and how it is assembled (the processes and the constituent elements) to create the architectural structures as are seen all over the face of the earth today.

Key words: admixture, aggregate, hydration, prestressedconcrete, precast concrete, reinforced concrete, cement.
INTRODUCTION

In an effort to trace the first invention of concrete it is worth to note that this is possible only depending on how one interprets the term —concretell. The building material, which can be called a precursor to concrete, was made-up in about 1300 BC when Middle Eastern builders observed that when they coated the outsides of their pounded-clay fortresses and home walls with a

thin, damp coating of burned limestone, it reacted chemically with gases in
the air to form a hard, protective surface. This wasn't concrete, but it was the
beginning of the development of cement. John Smeaton also used such
materials in 1756 to rebuild the Eddystone Lighthouse off the coast of
Cornwall, England, and a number of others independently discovered the
usefulness of such materials to make concrete during the ensuing 70 years or
so (Nick Gromicko and Kenton Shepard 2000).
According to Bjorn (2003), pure concrete structures are relatively rare in
early buildings history, when cement was used mostly as a mortar to bind
bricks or stones.

Exceptions exist in the Roman Empire where the coffers in the ceiling vault
of the pantheon are cast in concrete using pumice as aggregate. The invention
of cement, an important constituent of concrete is credited to Joseph Aspdin,
which he went on to patented in 1824. He gave it the name portland cement
because the product of Portland cement and aggregate resembled the stone
that came from the peninsula (or island connected to the mainland by a
narrow rocky strip) of Portland on the south coast of England. Today there
are many companies manufacturing Portland cement all over the world but
under different brand names. To be called Portland cement the product must
meet standardspecifications of the American Society for Testing and
Materials, the U.S. Federal government, the Canadian government or other
authority, Concrete Construction (1981). From the period of the discovery of
cement to today, concrete technology has evolved and keeps on advancing
making it possible for the architectural industry to constructs more complex
but secure and strong structures using concrete.

Concrete as a Sustainable Construction Material

According to Anne Balogh (nd), concrete is a friend of the environment in all
stages of its life span, from raw material production to demolition, making it
a natural choice for sustainable home construction. Here are some of the
reasons why, according to the American Portland Cement Association and
the Environmental Council of Concrete Organizations:

(1) Resource efficiency: The predominant raw material for the cement in
concrete is limestone, the most abundant mineral on earth.
(2) Durability: Concrete builds durable, long-lasting structures that will not

rust, rot, or burn.

(3) Thermal mass: Homes built with concrete walls, foundations, and floors are highly energy efficient.

(4)Ability to retain storm water: Paved surfaces tend to be impervious and can block naturalwater infiltration into the soil. This creates an imbalance in the natural ecosystem and leads to problems such as erosion, flash floods, water table depletion, and pollution.

(5)Minimal waste: Concrete can be produced in the quantities needed for each project, reducing waste. After a concrete structure has served its original purpose, the concrete can be crushed and recycled into aggregate for use in new concrete pavements or as backfill or road base, Concrete Network (2001).

Materials based on cement have some general attractions: are of low cost, flexibility of their application – for example, mortals, concretes and grout, variety of finishes obtained, good compressive strength and Protection of embedded steel. On the other hand the following problem areas are of concern to these materials in general: they are of low tensile strength - that is brittle in nature, they are of high density (though lower density types are available) and are susceptible to frost/ chemical deterioration a factor that depends on type. The environmental considerations can be summarized as shown in Table 1 below (Taylor, 2000).

Considerations Assessment
Raw material availability Very good
Extraction Care necessary to avoid damage to landscape
Energy used in manufacturing Cement is a high energy material
Healthy/safety hazards Slight hazard from cement dust. Fresh cement is
caustic – can cause burns
Recyclability Concrete can be crushed to be reused as
aggregate or hard-core
Table 1: Environmental considerations on concretes Source: adopted from (Taylor, 2000)

Constituent Materials of Concrete

Concrete is essentially a mixture of cement, aggregate and water. Other materials added to the mixture are referred to as _admixture'. Figure 2 shows a pictorial representation of the concrete composition.

Cement: cement is the key material in the making of concrete in that it acts as

the pastethat holds other materials together. The cement of interest in the making of concrete have the properties of setting and hardening under water by virtue of chemical reaction with it and are, therefore, called hydraulic cements (Neville, 2000). Seeley (1995) states that other than portland cements there exists several other cements that will produce concretes with more specialized properties. The figure 1 below shows a schematic representation of formation and hydration of Portland cement.
component

O_2 Si Ca Al
component
CaO SiO_2 Al_2O_3
cement
C_3S C_2S C_3A

Figure 1: Schematic representation of the formation and hydration of Portland cement Source: Adopted from Neville (2000)

Aggregates: aggregates are inert granular materials such as sand, gravel, or crushed stonethat, along with water and portland cement, are an essential ingredient in concrete. For a good concrete mix, aggregates need to be clean, hard, strong particles free of absorbed chemicals or coatings of clay and other fine materials that could cause the deterioration of concrete.

According to Domone and Illston (2010), aggregate can be put into three groups depending on their source:
1. Primary aggregate - which are specifically produced for use in concrete.
2. Secondary aggregate - which is a byproduct of other industrial processes not previously used in construction?
3. Recycled aggregate - from previously used construction materials e.g. from demolition. Primary aggregate form by far the greatest proportion of those used.

portland cements
various types of portland cement
Hydration
Gel Cal

Taylor (2000) documents that aggregate are used in concrete for various reasons: one
- they reduce the cost greatly, two - they reduce heat output per unit volume of concrete and therefore reduce thermal stress, three – they reduce the shrinkage of the concrete, four – they help to produce a concrete with satisfactory plastic properties. There are also a number of reasons why _special' aggregate could be used in a concrete and among them are:

Decorative aggregates - for example crushed granite is available in several colours which can be revealed by use of an exposed aggregate finish. Abrasion-resistance concrete - for floors (granite or carborundum aggregates). Improved fire resistance - (limestone, lightweight aggregates such as expanded pulverised fuel ash).
Low density concretes (2000 kg/m$_3$ or less) to decrease foundation loads, especiallythermal insulation and reduce thermal inertia (light weight

aggregates).
High densityconcrete (2600 kg/m$_3$ or more) are required for example for

radiation shelding (barites–barium sulphate – or iron based aggregates).

Water: water is the medium under which a chemical reaction takes place for cement tobe converted from powder into a hardened material with strength and durability. Two major considerations for water in concrete construction are:
(1) Organic contamination; when water is in contact with organic matter like vegetation, it is contaminated with organic acid which can reduce the rate of hydration by increasing the PH value (acidity) of the wet concrete. Also water which appears green with algae can lead to air entrainment which reduces the strength. (2) Dissolved salts; sea water normally contains dissolved salts such as sulphates which react with hydrated cement and result in accelerated hydration which increases the risk of corrosion of the embedded steal.
Admixtures: admixture is the chemical ingredients in concrete other than Portland cement, water, and aggregates that are added to the mix immediately before or during mixing.

Admixtures are used to reduce the cost of concrete construction; to modify the properties of hardened concrete; to ensure the quality of concrete during mixing, transporting, placing and curing and also to overcome certain emergencies during operations.

Figure 2: A

pictorial representation of ordinary concrete constituents Source: Adopted from www.cement.org

Concrete Mix Proportioning

The process of allocating portions of cements, sand, coarse aggregates and water so as to obtain concretes of desired strength and quality is known as proportioning of the concrete mix. According to (Guha, 2006) proportioning of concrete is done in two of either method:
(1) Nominal mix or ordinary mix concrete – this is done by proportioning ingredients by volume batches.
(2) Design mix concrete – this mix is done by proportioning the gradients by weight in the process of the design.

Concrete Operations

When analysis matters to do with concrete operation, it is good to lay a foundation that will help one to understand the processes involved in the construction of concretes. The most important basic knowledge in this context is the states which the concrete will follow immediately the cement, aggregate and water put together. These states can respectively be examined as follows:

• Plastic State, when the concrete is first mixed it islike 'bread dough'. It is soft and can be worked or moulded into different shapes. In this state concrete is called PLASTIC. Concrete is plastic during placing and compaction. The most important properties of plastic concrete are workability and cohesiveness.

• SettingState, concrete then begins to stiffen. The stiffening of concrete, when it is no longer soft, is called SETTING. Setting takes place after compaction and during finishing.

• HardeningState, after concrete has set it begins to gain strength and harden. The properties ofhardened concrete are strength and durability (www.cement.org).

Concrete Formwork/ Moulding

In order for concrete in architectural work to stand out in terms of aesthetic value addition via complex building shapes especially on the interior designs and externals of buildings, the technical aspect of formwork and moulding techniques are employed.

Formwork or shuttering is the materials used to retain concrete in a specific location until the concrete has developed sufficient strength to stay in position hence forming out a particular design according to the formwork layout. A good example is the construction of spiral stair cases of a storey building. According to Buchan, Fleming & Grant (2007), the materials used to construct formwork are generally softwood boards, plywood and sheet steel for working faces, supported on a softwood or steel framework. The figure 3 below shows a 3 dimension stretch work of a formwork for building a spiral stair cases.
Also plastic and other materials are used for construction of moulds especially when the finishing work, see figure 4, is delicate and calls for much details as compared to the construction of pieces like stairs.

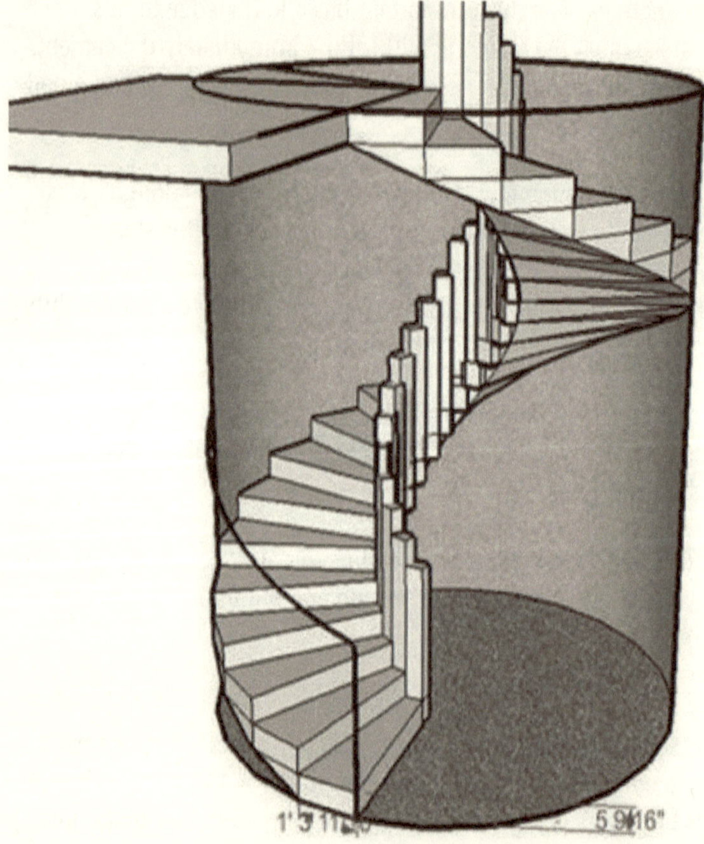

Figure 3: A 3D

Figure 4: Finely finished concrete work of moulding
Source: Adopted from http://www.courtyarddecor.com
Curing: after concrete is placed, a satisfactory moisture content and
temperature (between 50°F & 75°F) must be maintained, a process called
curing. Adequate curing is vital to quality concrete. According to Maldonado,
Zavala and Ballote (2010), the

strength of concrete is inversely proportional to the water cement ratio.
Common Forms of Concrete Structures

The common forms of concrete, while strong in compression resistance, have
structural flaws in that they have low resistance to tension – usually 20% or
less of their resistance to compression for structural application. For building
architectural structures, concrete is mostly used with a number of basic
construction methods, Ambrose and Tripeny (2007). Sitecast concrete - this
type of concrete is formed when wet concrete is deposited informs at the
location where it is to be used. The method is also described as cast-in-place
or in situ construction.

Reinforced Concrete - According to Mc Kaig (1980) concrete is strong in
compression but weak in tensile, and where tension occurs it is usual to
introduce steel bar to provide the tensile strength which the concrete lacks.
When completely surrounded by the hardened concrete mass it forms an

integral part of the two materials, known as "Reinforced Concrete". The steel can be used to resist a given tensile stress much more economically than an equal compressive stress. A bar of any shape will offer equal resistance per square inch to tensile whereas for compression, the steel must be made up of special shapes to provide sufficient lateral rigidity. Even then, the strength in compression is less than the strength in tension. The design of a structure involves a study of its elementary parts such as beams, slabs, walls, columns and foundations. The identification and analysis of the units are more difficult than in steel construction became there is no evident demarcation between slab and beam or girder (Mallick, 1976). According to Sinha (1998) experience has shown that damages occurring to reinforced concrete are more due to errors in detailing than to faulty calculations. In earthquake disasters a structure with proper considerable damage but rarely collapses reinforced detailing may show

than structures without proper reinforcement detailing which may totally collapse.
Fiber-reinforced polymer bar - Since early 1980's fiber-reinforced polymer (FRP) bars have emerged as an alternative type of internal reinforcement for concrete structures exposed to aggressive environments and normally reinforced with conventional steel bars. In addition to improving the durability of reinforced concrete, FRP bars have in structural concrete applications magnetic neutrality of good cutting characteristics are required.

Prestressed concrete - This is a reinforced concrete with the steel reinforcement held under tension during production, to achieve stiffness, crack resistance and lighter construction of components such as beams, slabs, trusses, and other large-span units. By prestressing, less steel is needed and the concrete is held under compression, enabling it to carry much high load before this compression is overcome. Prestressing is achieved either by pre-tensioning (in which the steel is stressed before the concrete is cast) or by post-tensioning (after a concrete has reached adequate strength, allowing the steel to be passed through straight or curved ducts, which are filled with grout after the reinforcement has been tensioned and anchored). This is essentially a factory operation requiring expensive special equipments (jacks, anchorages, prestressed beds, e.t.c) not suitable for low costing houses (stulz and Ronand, 1988).

Precast concrete - according to Foster & Stroud (2000), a precast concrete component may be defined asa component cast in a position other than which it finally occupy in a complete structure and which after removal from forms and maturing requires to be placed and fixed into position. The technique of precasting concrete was for structural purpose was originally applied to the manufacture of floors and roof slabs, but the process has developed to the extent that whole building structures can be erected from factory produced precast components involving beams, columns, roof slabs, floors, walls panels and cladding. Elliott & Kim (2002) observed that what really distinguishes precast concrete from cast in situ is its stress and strain response to external (=load induced) and internal (autogenously volumetric changes) effects. Precast concrete is the highest possible concrete in terms of strength and durability.

This concrete is assembled from precast elements, which when suitability connected together, form a 3d structure capable of resisting gravitation and wind or even earth quake load. The frame work (figure 3) is ideally suitable to buildings like offices, rental units, bridges, stadia, schools and other such building requiring minimal internal obstruction and multifunctional leasable spaces. Precast concrete provides superior fire resistance and sound control for the individual units and reduces fire insurance rates. It is advantageous in that precast structures are built speedily and easily, allows efficient, economical construction in all weather conditions and the product of precasting is created in ideal manufacturing conditions. Although some products are cast outdoors, especially in temperate climates, many precast plants operate indoors where the climate can be fully controlled.

Figure 5: An example of a precast structure; plank beams, and columns Source: Adopted from Journal of Materials in Civil Engineering

Ultramodern Concretes

The need for smart concretes has lead to the invention of new types of concretes which are more flexible, reliable and even cost effective. Some of the concretes that are shaping the future of building industry include: Self-Consolidating Concrete (SCC)

- is highly flowable concrete that can spread into place, fill the formwork and encapsulate the reinforcement without any mechanical consolidation (www.nrcresearchpress.com). Ultra-High Performance _ductile' Concrete (UHPdC) - is cement based composite materialwhich consists of fine granular materials with optimized grading curves, very high strength discrete micro steel fibers and a very low water cement ratio. Ordinary Portland cement, silica fume, fine aggregates, water, steel fibers and high-range water reducing agent are the main ingredient to produce UHPdC (Nematollahil and Saifulnaz, 2012).

CONCLUSION

The ubiquity of concrete as a primary construction material globally posses both challenges and opportunities to the development of new concretes for the useful purpose. The opportunity for effecting widespread improvements in the quality and safety of buildings of all type is certainly a set of issues that could be addressed through better concrete materials. By developing higher strength, better quality, ductile and more durable concrete. Vast material and energy savings can be gained rather quickly. Also by using better the components of concrete as it is formulated today and seeking alternative materials, concrete can be made a less destructive and ecologically problematic material.

In the effort the material most likely to achieve the best results, at least for a short term, are alternative pozzolanic materials engineered to increase the strength and toughness of the material while contributing significantly to its durability through better résistance to water infiltration. As observed by Fernandez (2006) the future of concretes is in high performing concrete, ductile concretes, reactive powder concrete, and smart concrete.

CHAPTER THREE

DESIGN MATERIALS AND PROCESS

BRICKS

Abstract

Even in an advancing world of building technologies, masonry remains a key component of most buildings, even steel-framed and timber framed buildings often have a masonry cladding. The great majority of masonry walling is produced from preformed units: bricks, which are easily handled with one hand, and blocks which are larger units generally requiring both hands. This paper evaluates the brick as a building material that enhances architectural beauty of buildings.

Key Words: aesthetic, bricks, brickwork, clay, firing, drying, kiln, moulding, softmudprocess, shift-mud process.

INTRODUCTION

Originally, bricks were hand-moulded from moist clay and the sun-baked, as is still the practice in certain arid climates. The firing of clay dates back well over 5000 years, and it is now sophisticated and highly controlled manufacturing process; yet the principle of burning clay, to convert it from its natural plastic state into dimensionally stable, durable, low-maintenance ceramic material, remains unchanged (Lyons, 2007).

According to (Duggal, 1998) one of the oldest building material brick continues to be the most popular and leading construction material because of being cheap, durable and easy to handle and work with.

Clay brick is documented as the first man made artificial building material and one of the oldest building materials known. However the properties of clay units depend on the mineralogical compositions of the clays used to manufacture the unit, the manufacturingprocess and the firing temperatures (www.ipcbee.com). Bricks are the only man-made building materials that testify to their use since the early human civilization. With their attractive appearances and superior properties such as high compressive strength and durability, excellent fire and weather resistance, good thermal and sound insulation, bricks are widely used for building, civil engineering work, and landscape design (http://www.claybricks.com). The physical beauty that bricks add to an architectural structure, whether it is the brick wall joint profile with coloured mortar, fences, brick chimney decorations or brick arched doors is one reason why bricks are chosen for buildings. Bricks may broadly be described as building units which are easily handled with one hand. By far the most widely used size at present is the single standard metric brick of actual size 215 x 102.5 x 65mm. According to (Duggal, 1998) the standard brick should be 19 x 9 x 9 cm and 19 x 9 x 4 cm and when placed in masonry the 19 x 9 x 9 cm brick with mortar becomes 20 x 20 x 10 cm the weight of such a brick is 3.0 kg. Other bricks with special shapes (namely Bullnose bricks, Arch bricks, Plinth brick, Soldier bricks, Radial bricks, Cuboid bricks) are possible these days making it even possible for complex decorative brickworks. The elegant cathedral at Evry near Paris in France designed by Mario Botta, illustrates the modern use of brick work. For more than 100 years, clay bricks have dominated the building industry in developed nations as the preferred building units; especially in the UK but more recently other brick types andconcretes have produced strong competition, especially since thermal insulation regulations were tightened and lightweight forms became available (Taylor 2000).

Clay properties and Classifications

Clay, the most important raw material used in brick making, is an earthen mineral mass or fragmentary rock capable of mixing with water and forming plastic viscous mass which has a property of retaining its shape when moulded and dried (Duggal, 1998). According to the (Brick Development Association) 1974, the materials used for clay brickmaking range from soft and plastic surface deposits to hard mudstone, shale, marls, and even some of the softer varieties of slate. The essential requirements are that after being ground, and tempered with water, the material should be capable of taking a good shape – either by moulding, extrusion or pressure – and that the shape should be retained without undue shrinkage, warping or cracking when the bricks are dried and fired.

Purest clays consist mainly of kaolinite with small quantities of minerals such as quarts, mica, feldspar, calcite, magnesite, etc. By their origin clay are subdivided as residual and transported clays. Residual clay, also known as Kaolin or china clay, are formed from the decay of underlying rocks and are used for making pottery while the transported (sedimentary) clays result from the action of weathering agencies. These are more disperse, contain impurities, and free from large particles of mother rocks (Duggal, 1998).

On the basis of resistance to temperatures (more than 1580_0C), clays are classified as refractory, high melting and low melting clays with refractory clays being highly disperseand very plastic. They have high content of alumina and low content of impurities, such as Fe_2O_3, tending to lower the refractoriness. High melting clays have high refractoriness (1350-1580$_o$C) and contain small amounts of impurities like quartz, feldspar, calcium carbonate and magnesium carbonate. These are used for manufacturing facing bricks, floors tiles, sewer pipes, etc. low melting clays have refractoriness less than 1350$_o$C and have varying compositions. These are used to manufacture bricks, blocks, tiles, etc (Duggal, 1998).

Classification of Bricks

Bricks have been classified on the basis of field practice as; first, second, third & forth class bricks, on the basis of use as; common, facing & engineering bricks, on the basis of finish as; sand-faced & rustic bricks, on the basis of manufacture as; man-made & machine-made bricks and on the basis of burning as; pale, body & arch bricks (Duggal, 1998).

Properties and Functional Performances of Brick

Bricks are made from clay by burning it at high temperatures. The action of heat gives rise to a sintering process that causes the clay particles to fuse and develops extremely strong ceramic bonds in the burnt clay bodies. Such bonds are highly stable resulting to bricks that can withstand the severe weathering actions and are inert to almost all normal chemical attacks. Some of the properties are:

Strength Bricks are well-known for their high compressive strength depending on the raw materials used, the manufacturing process, and the shape and size. Aesthetic appeal - Brick possesses the natural and pleasant colours of burnt clay which is as a result of physical chemical reaction during thefiring process. In contrast to colour of stained body, brick colour is permanent and will not be faded during weathering process.
Porosity - In contrast to other moulded or pre-cast building materials, the porosity of brick is attributed to its fine capillaries. By virtue of the capillary effect, the rate of moisture transport in the brick is ten times faster than in other building materials.
Fire Resistance - Brick is inherent with excellent fire resistance. It is a fact

that the non-combustibility of brick helps to promote its use in building
houses against fire.
Sound Insulation Brick wall shows good insulation property due to its dense
structure.
Thermal Insulation Brick generally exhibits better thermal insulation property
than other building materials like concrete. Bricks absorb and release heat
slowly and thus keep the house cool during daytime and warm during
nighttime.
Wear Resistance - The wear resistance of a substance depends on its
particulate bonds. Bricks show high wear resistance because of its extremely
strong ceramic bonds formed by the effect of heat at high temperature.
Flexibility in Applications - Brick is used for an extremely wide range of
applications in an equally extensive range of buildings (see figure 1) and
engineering structures. Durability - Brick is extremely durable and perhaps is
the most durable man-made structural building materials so far. There has
been numerous ancient brick-building standing for centuries as a testimony of
the endurance of burnt-clay brick.

Mortars for Brick Work
Mortar is a material that is plastic and can flow when fresh but sits hard over
a period of hours to days. Its purpose is to fill the gaps caused by variation in
the size and shape of units (bricks) such that the masonry is stable and resists
the flow of air and water. Mortar is compounded from a binder (e.g. cement)
and a filler/aggregate; usually sand (Domone and Illston, 2010).

Figure 1: Buildings extensively constructed out of brickworks
Sources: Adopted from http://www.architonic.com

Various Types of Bricks

There are various types of bricks used in masonry but those with clay content are: Common Burnt Clay Bricks - are fired bricks formed by pressing in moulds or by anextrusion and wire cutting process. Then these bricks are dried and fired in a kiln. SandLime Bricks (Calcium Silicate Bricks) - These bricks are mixtures of sand and hydrated limepressed in moulds and cured in a high-pressure steam autoclave. Bricks of this type are distinguished from fired clay bricks by containing negligible clay and requiring comparatively low temperature treatment during manufacture. They have been used widely in the construction of buildings in the Former Soviet Union since the 1970s (Bailiff and Mikhailik, 2004).

Fly ash Clay Bricks - Fly ash is used along with clay in these bricks. The aim of the present study is to investigate the strength and water absorption characteristic of fly ash bricks made of lime (L), local soil (S) and fly ash (FA), (Rushed et al, 2011). Fire Clay Bricks - Fire clay exists at much depth belowthe surface and is usually mined. Generally, Fire clays contain metallic oxides less than surface clays and have more uniform chemical and physical properties. The future of bricks is that today bricks can be made from a wide selection of materials such as mixtures of cement, sand and aggregates vibrated in moulds and steam cured to make a widely used brick known as concrete brick. According to Lihui, Xiangchao and Jing (2012), the experimental investigation of the preparation process condition of concrete hollow building bricks using the waste concrete as recycled concrete aggregate (RCA) have been reported. A preliminary assessment made by Elinwa (2006), notes that sawdust ash (SDA) can be added to clay when making bricks. Bricks are made with SDA, fired to temperatures of 200°C, 600°C and 1200°C and cured for 1, 4 and 8 days, respectively. Bricks should be free from cracks, chips and warp ages, large particles of lime and organic matter.

First class bricks are suitable for construction of a building

(http://www.gharexpert.com).

Manufacturing of Bricks
According to the Bricks Development Association (1974), methods of brick

manufacture vary depending on the material, but all follow the same basic principles as shown in Figure 3. The raw material is won from the ground; it is prepared and formed into brickshape; finally, it is burnt in a kiln to produce a tough but immensely durable building unit.

Clay Winning (Quarrying and Transporting)

The choice of method of clay winning will depend on the depth, thickness, hardness and physical geology of the clay beds. Laboratory testing of the clays from different parts of the quarry is done to determine the likely characteristics of the layers and clay is mixed according to the required properties of the finished item.

Clay Processing (Clay Preparation)

The processing phases is a stage where heaps of fairly wet clay is being subjected to crushing, grinding and tempering before it can be suitable for shaping/moulding. Clay preparation methods may have to accommodate the physical characteristics of the raw material and special provision may have to be made to deal with certain impurities. Preparation consists of transforming the clay rock into plastic mouldable material by a process of grinding and mixing with water.
Moulding (Brick Forming)

This is the process of giving a required shape to the brick from the prepared brick earth. For creative designs of bricks, different types of moulds should be prepared in relation to where the artistic brick work is to be laid out. The moulding may be carried out by hand as shown in Figure 2; a brick moulder believed to have been used in pyramid construction in Egypt (Campbell, 2012) or by machines for (standard building bricks). According to (Duggal, 1998) the process of moulding of bricks may be the soft-mud, thestiff-mud or the dry-press process. Fire-brick is made by the soft mud process. Roofing, floor and wall tiles are made by the dry-press method. However, the stiff-mud process is used for making the structural clay products.

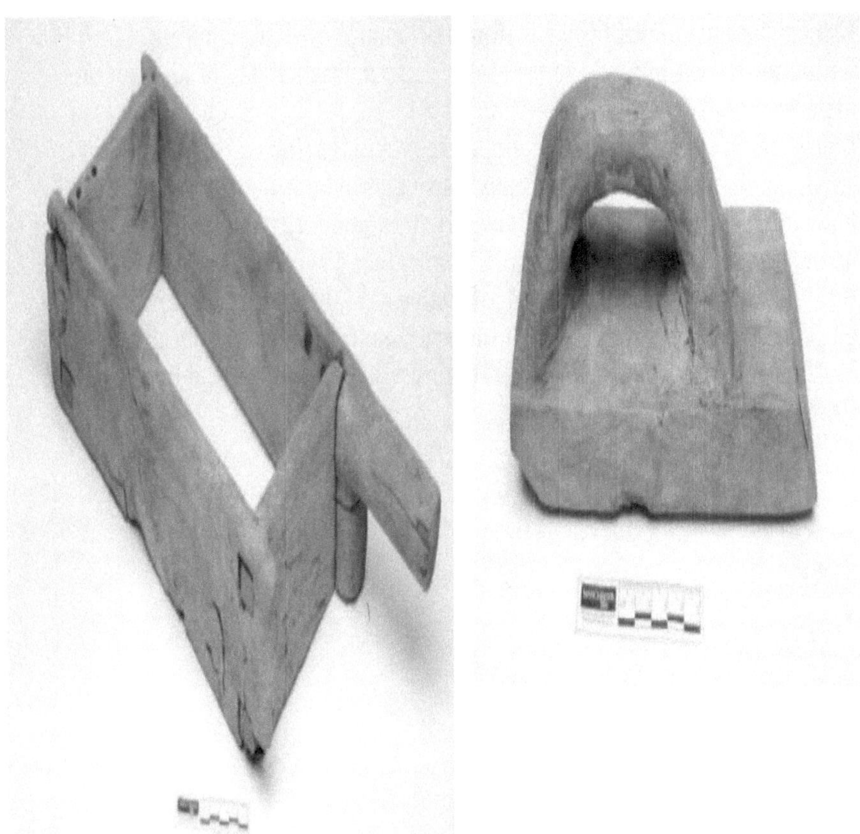

Figure 2: Brick moulder (left) and a plasterer's float (right) used in the construction of the pyramid in Egypt; Source: Adopted from (Campbell, 2012)

Drying: Before the bricks can be fired, as much moisture as possible must be removed orthey will explode in the process of burning in the kiln. According to Duggal (1998) Green bricks contain 7-30% moisture depending upon the method of manufacture. The objective of removing water at this stage is to control the shrinkage and save fuel and time during the burning, also known as firing process.

Firing: Firing constitutes the final stage in the transmutation of raw earth intoaesthetically satisfying, dimensionally accurate, structural unit. Before the firing process, the bricks however must be stacked in such a way as to ensure an even distribution of the hot kiln gases, where the production is mass (The Bricks Development Association, 1974)

Kilns: The burning of bricks is done in a clamp or Kiln; where a clamp is a temporary structure while the kiln is a permanent one. There are several different types of kiln but they can be allocated to two main categories: (1) Intermittent kilns, these are static, usually small kilns and are used for firing small batches of products e.g. Special shapes. The kiln here is loaded with ware and the firing is done followed by unloaded. (2) Continuous kilns, are useful for large scale production. The original circular chamberdesign (see figure 2) was first modified by Hoffman in 1870 to decrease product variability caused by the non uniform geometry of the original design. Hoffmans's Kiln is one of the most common kilns today (Laefer, Boggs & Cooper, 2004).

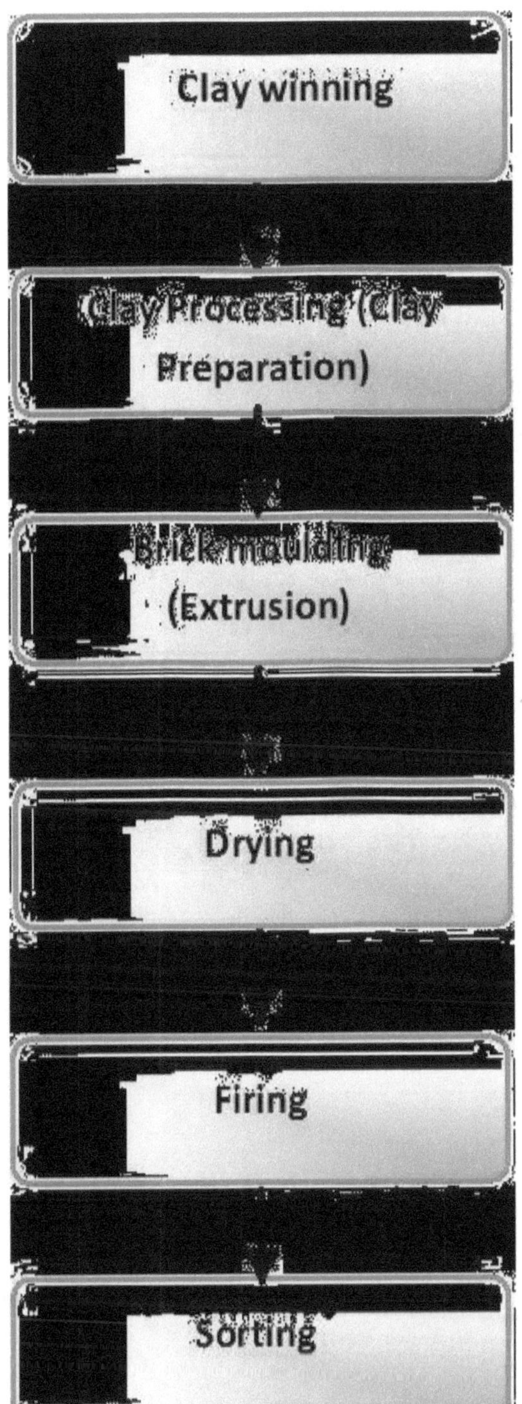
Clay winning
Clay Processing (Clay Preparation)
Brick moulding (Extrusion)
Drying
Firing
Sorting

Figure 3: Flow chart diagram showing the steps in brick making Sources: Adopted from Samuel, 2012

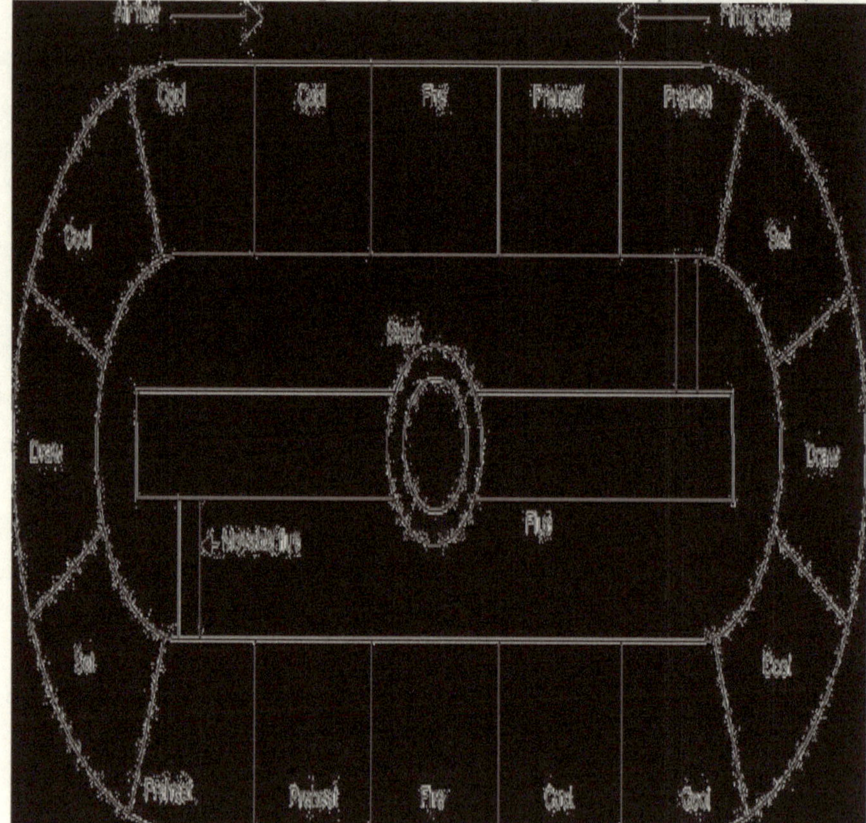

Figure 2: The original chamber Kiln–circular in shape Source: Adopted from Laefer, Boggs & Cooper (2004) Tunnel kiln, In a tunnel kiln dry bricks are loaded onto a fireproof trolley or kiln car asSeen in figure 3 below.

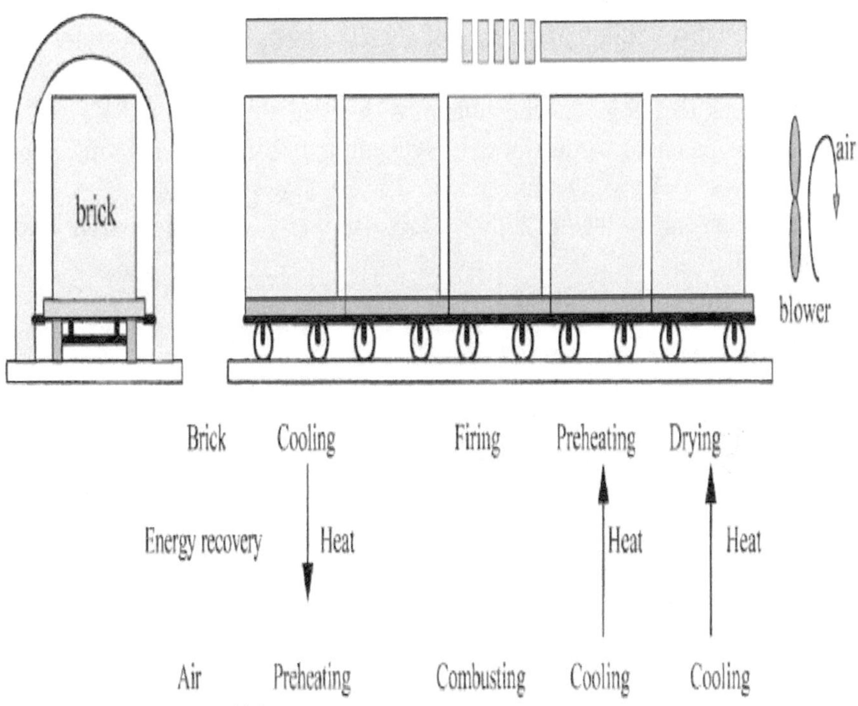

Figure 3: Processes in tunnel kiln
Source: Adopted from Rushad, Kumar, Duggal & Mehta (2011)

Application of Bricks in Design Aspects

Bricks application is determined by the type construction work and for every type of building construction; different types of brick are used. The standard solid bricks are mostly used to create walls of buildings or for fencing. However bricks are used mostly in the decorative work of building example arch constructions and decorative bricklaying.

Brick Arches: - arch construction is a decorative means of spanning openings. True archesare made to curve upwards when looked at in elevation, so that they are always in a state of compression, wedged between abutments as bending under load cannot take place, there will be no tensile stress in the arch (Thorpe, 2010). Decorative brick work: - for breathtaking decorations to be realized using bricks, various special types (figure 4) of bricks are required. Though the bulk of production by brick manufacturers is of plain, basic metric size of 215 x 102.5 x 65 mm, there are other special types of bricks that are manufactured particularly for decorative purposes. Among the decorative features produced by these are: String courses – these are horizontal courses built into the face of a wall to form decorative features. Soldier courses – is a form of string course, when it continues around a building. Dog toothing – is when the bricks are laid 45 degrees to the face line and can be either vertical or flat. Oversailing or corbels – are terms given to the several bricks which project from the face of a wall. Dentil course – provides a decorative feature at the surface of a wall, usually at the eave level (Thorpe, 2010).

Figure 4: special bricks

Source: Adopted from www.northcotbrick.co.uk

Bricklaying

The ability to lay out beautiful patterns using bricks (see figure 5) has no conventional rules which to observe, the rules used are the outcome of experience. Time should be spent by a bricklayer visualizing the job, considering the best methods of approach and using all the skills possible, whether the work is to be covered or highly decorative, for all to see. Another important aspect of brick works is that of cutting bricks which is always difficult but nevertheless possible. This is done using a club hammer and bolster chisel.

Figure 5: Living area retail brick wall interior
Source: Adopted from http://furniture.trendzona.com

CONCLUSION

The physical beauty that bricks add to an architectural structure, whether it is the brick wall joint profile with coloured mortar, fences, brick chimney decorations or brick archeddoors is among the reason why brick – which is documented in this paper as the oldest building material used by men - is chosen for buildings construction even today. Bricks are characterized with attractive appearances and superior properties such as high compressivestrength and durability, excellent fire and weather resistance, good thermal and sound insulation among other advantages. Due to the availability of the clay material, and low cost in production brick is widely used in Africa as the choice material in house construction. In Kenya the best of clay soils are found in Kiambu in central province, Kakuma in eastern province and many other locations with the difference in variations of the quality of clay. Bricks are widely also in massive architectural structures, civil engineering work, and landscape design owing to the fact that they are durable, easy to work with and abundant.

CHAPTER FOUR

DESIGN MATERIALS AND PROCESS

PAPER

Abstract

John Heitman, a professor of chemistry at North Carolina State University once said that people use paper all the time, but they don't think about where it comes from and what it's made of. This fact don't need to be debated because today the world has turned into a commercial global market where packaging of goods (which is done mostly in paper) is one of the most employed method of attracting customers as far as advertising of goods and even services is concerned. Services are also advertised through the paper by use of graphical expressions by way of posters, bill boards, magazines and others. In a time through the industrial evolution of many nations especially in Africa, this paper aims to shed some light on the manufacturing processes that birth out one of the most important material in the world of artistic expressions from painting to graphics design, from industrial packaging to construction of tentative structures.

Key Words: papyrus, paper, pulp, breaching, fibres, mechanical pulp, chemical pulp
INTRODUCTION

Though we may take it for granted, paper is always with us, documenting our world and reminding us of the limitless possibilities of life. Invented by the Chinese 2,000 years ago, paper has been used ever since as a communication medium. Initially, paper was made out of fibres from mulberry bark, papyrus, straw or cotton. Wood only emerged as the chief raw material for paper mass production as recently as the mid 19th century.

The word paper is an English term derived from papyrus a Latin word. Papyrus comes from the Greek (papyros), the word for the Cyperus papyrus plant. Papyrus is a thick, paper-like material produced from the pith of the cyperus plant which traces into use in ancient Egypt. In Egypt and other Mediterranean cultures papyrus was used for writing. It is from Mediterranean that this writing on papyrus technology, spread to Middle East and Europe. Although paper is etymologically derived from papyrus, the two are produced very differently and the development of modern paper is separate from the development of papyrus. Papyrus is a "lamination of natural plants, while paper is manufactured from fibres whose properties have been changed by maceration or disintegration. This paper concentrates on the later with a bias to the manufacturing processes.

Paper was a Chinese technique imported into the Islamic world by Chinese craftsmen

whose artisans also established a paper mill in Baghdad around 794 a move that saw the translations of Greek scientific and philosophical manuscripts into Arabic in the late eighth century, Bloom and Jonathan (2009). A Chinese by the name of T'sai Lun is today credited by many as the father of the modern paper. T'sai experimented with a wide variety of materials and refined the process of macerating the fibre of plants until each filament was completely separate to make the modern paper.

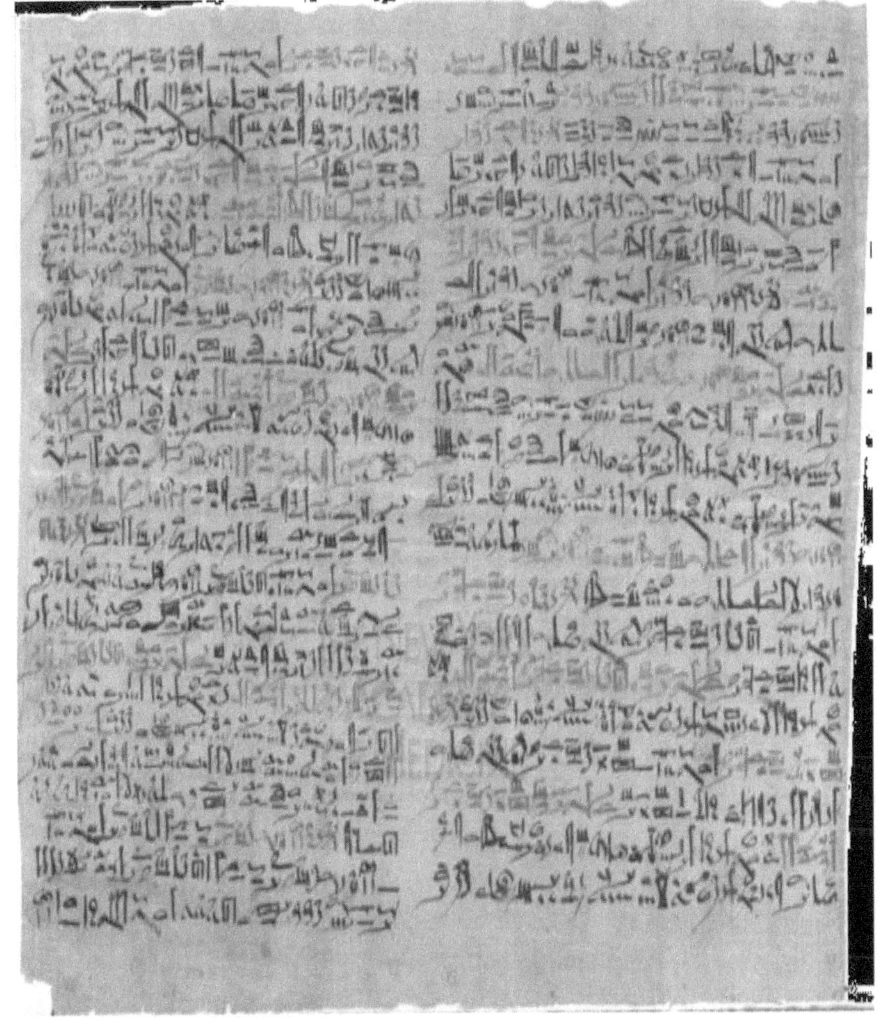

Figure 1: old writings on a papyrus
Source: Adopted from http://writersforensicsblog.wordpress.com

Spread of Papermaking

The spread of paper making can be referred back to the 3rd century when the secret art of papermaking began to creep out of China. The Vietnam was the first to catch the wave of paper making then Tibet followed suit. The technique was then introduced to the Koreans in the 4th century and spread to Japan in 6th. The climax of paper making was captured in the 8thi century when in Japan, Empress Shotuka undertook a massive project which saw the printing of a million copies of prayers (dharani) on individual sheets of paper, with each mounted in its own pagoda. With such a profound inception, it is not surprising that the fine art of papermaking has continued in Japan to this day,garnering deep appreciation and ever increasing sophistication. (http://www.hqpapermaker.com/paper-history). The technology of paper-making was slowly diffused westwards with Spain, France & Italy record papermaking mills in the 12th century. But it was not until 14th century that papermaking locations were recordedin England. From the mid 14th century paper was made in Europe by pulping linen and canvas rags derived from flax and hemp plant fibre. This mix continued until the 18th century, when cotton rags were added to the mix. Rag pulp became an increasingly expensive source of fibre as the demand for paper increased to keep pace with the development of print technology, so around 1850 techniques were perfected for making pulp from trees (Writers services, 2003).

Today, with advancement of technology in both processing mechanics and material chemistry and concerns about environmental impacts, paper making has changed rapidly. Much emphases is now put on the recycling and de-inking technologies with an addition of chemists turning to chlorine dioxide and hydrogen peroxide as pulp breaching alternative due to the recorded effects of chlorine (the traditional breaching agent) on the environment, Especially since the end of World War II, the Paper Industry has experienced a massive wave of technological change that has transformed its basic operating and process management and control systems. Where earlier production processes relied on the craft knowledge of skilled operators and superintendents, newer production processes incorporate sophisticated sensors, information systems, and software-based process controls. This shift, which began in the 1970s, has had far-reaching effects on the industry's fundamental operations.

Pulping, Paper Making Processes

Paper is made from pulp. However, this pulp can be made from two major sources, i.e. from wood and waste materials. According to Chem and Educ (2001) most paper is formed from wood pulp. The main component of wood pulp is cellulose, a polymermade of many glucose molecules linked together. The cellulose molecules and their bonding to each other give paper its properties. The most abundant source of cellulose is trees though trees differ in the value of their fibre for making paper, the fibre of flax, cotton, jute, sisal, Manila hemp, and the like usually comes to the paper industry as a secondary product, after serving other uses. Agricultural wastes - straw, corn stalks, bagasse (sugarcane waste), bamboo, and some other grasses are used for making certain grades. Finally, one of the most important sources of pulp is the fibre recovered from old papers, rags, and cardboard boxes (http://www.britannica.com).

Making Pulp from Wood

Wood pulp currently represents the biggest average of the fibre used to manufacture paper and board worldwide, of which a small percentage is home produced. None of these mills uses mature fully grown trees, but rather small dimension timber, (which is no use to other commercial users such as furniture makers and builders), saw mill waste and forest thinning. In the past the industry used softwoods such as spruce, pine, fir, larch and cedar almost exclusively, but hardwoods such as birch and aspen are gaining in popularity. Fast growing eucalyptuses have been successfully cultivated across the world and provide the papermaker with very high quality pulp. Softwoods provide long strong cellulose fibres and are used to produce papers where strength is a requirement, for example, packaging papers. The shorter hardwood fibres provide bulk, smoothness and opacity and are used to produce fluting medium and printings and writings.

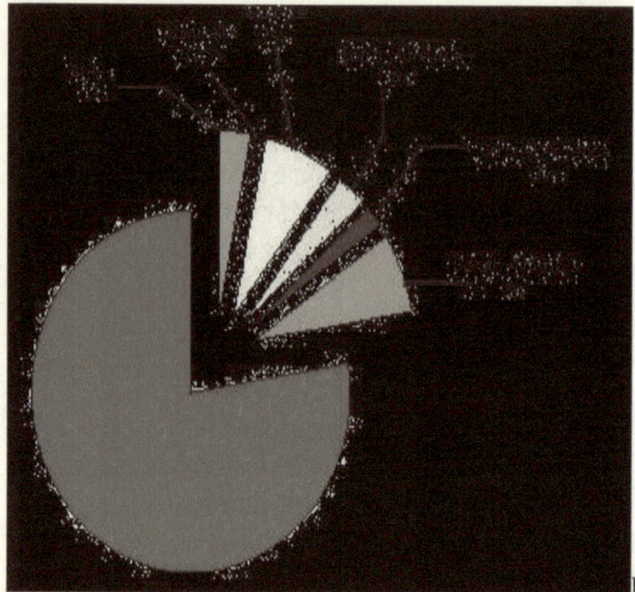

Figure1: Geographical distribution of non-wood cellulose pulp production plants Source: Adopted from http://ethnobotany09.com

Making Pulp from Waste Materials

The global use of waste paper in the production of paper and board is increasing. It reached about 85 million tonnes in 1990. Recycling paper however does not, as many believe, create a perfect cycle allowing paper to be made, used and then made again. For instance there are limits to paper recovery. Paper is lost from the cycle when used for permanent applications like record keeping, destroyed in use or contaminated. Cellulose fibres cannot be recycled indefinitely. Virgin fibres need to be continuously added to the cycle to replace exhausted fibres. Worldwide paper and pulp supply website (2003).

Pulping Process

According to Health Canada (2007) the main objective of the pulping process is to separate cellulose fibre from lignin to free the fibres for papermaking. The two maintypes of pulping processes are mechanical and chemical. Mechanical pulping utilizes heat and mechanical forces to break down the lignin and results in a lightcoloured pulp which requires little bleaching. Chemical pulping uses a mixture of chemicals to separate the cellulose fibres from the lignin.

Mechanical pulp: the wood is processed into fibre form by grinding it against a quicklyrotating stone under addition of water. The yield of this pulp amounts to approx. 95%. The result is called wood pulp or MP – mechanical pulp. The disadvantage of this type of pulp is that the fibre is strongly damaged and that there are all sorts of impurities in the pulp mass. Mechanical wood pulp yields a high opacity, but it is not very strong. It has a yellowish colour and low light resistance.

Chemical pulp: the two major chemical processes are kraft and sulphite pulping. Kraftpulping is carried out in an alkaline medium and releases fibres by dissolving lignin in a caustic solution of sodium hydroxide and sodium sulphide. In contrast, the sulphite process is carried out under acidic conditions and solubilizes lignin through sulphonation using a solution of sulphur dioxide and alkaline oxides such as sodium, magnesium, ammonium, or calcium both chemical processes produce a relatively dark-coloured pulp which requires bleaching. Oxygen delignification, which may be employed as an additional stage in either the sulphite or kraft pulping process, breaks down the lignin further, reducing the amount of bleaching agent required in the subsequent stage. Figure 2 shows a pictorial flow chart of the major phases in the production of paper.

Pulp bleaching

Initially, wood pulp has a brown or brownish colour as shown in figure 3. To obtain the brightness required for white papers, it has to be bleached. During this process of bleaching, the remaining lignin is removed as well. In practical terms, bleaching is a continuation of the chemical cooking process, taking place directly afterward in the pulp mill as an integrated next step of the overall procedure. Bleaching is a complex process, consisting of several chemical process steps, with washing taking place between the various chemical treatments.

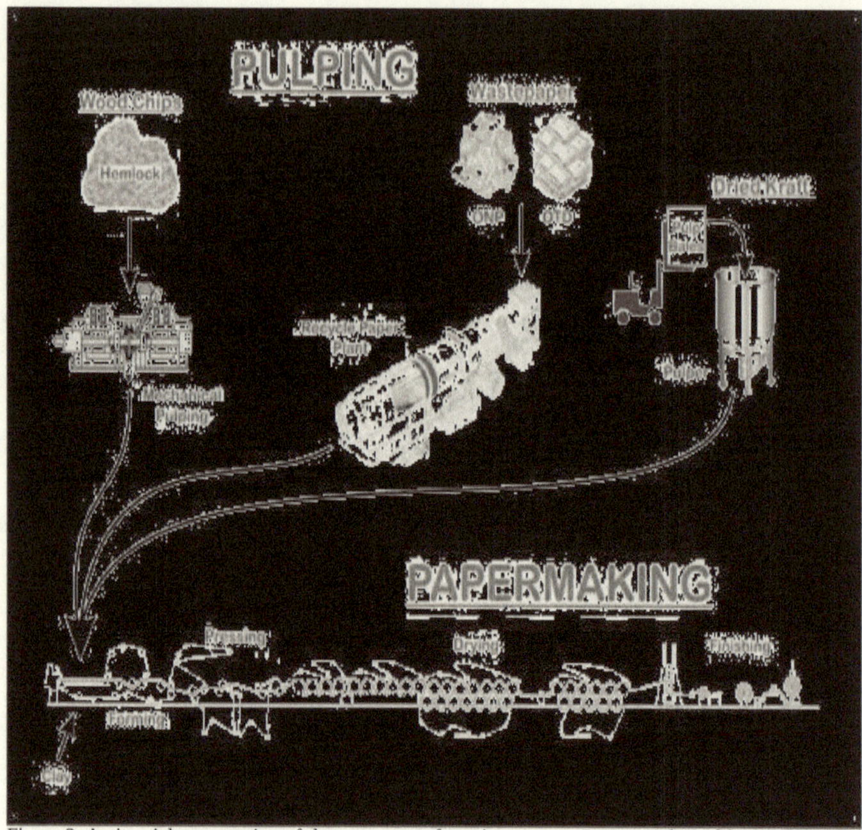

Figure 2: A pictorial presentation of the paper manufacturing process Source: Adopted from YPTALK: the voice of the yellow pages industry (2018)

The wood pulp can be bleached with chlorine / chlorine compounds, ozone / oxygen in different forms as well as hydrogen peroxide. Based on the negative impact of some chlorine containing decomposition products, there are, however, environmental objections against the use of chlorine and chlorine products. Forthis reason, Sappi has long ago switched to chlorine free processes. These processes are referred to as Totally Chlorine Free (TCF), Sappi (2003).

Figure 3: shows the results of a breached paper
Source: Adopted fromSappi (2018)
Producing Paper

In general, although there are many subtleties which affect the quality of a
paper, papermaking in essence is a simple process. Whether using recycled
materials or fresh organic matter, the approach is always to:
(i) first, shred the materials into small strips and then soaking them overnight
to loosen the fibres. (ii) The fibres are boiled for 2-6 hours, as the lose fibre is
stirred every so often. (iii) After the boiling process is accomplished, the
fibres are then washed with fresh water to remove impurities and then small
particles or specks are removed by hand. (iv)The clean fibres content is then
beaten in a blender or by hand till it turns into a creamy pulp. At this stage,
dyes can be added to create coloured papers. (v) The pulp is poured into a
large tub and the fibres are suspended in the water. The artisan dips a framed
screen into the water and with greatskill, lifts it to the surface catching the
fibres onto the screen. (vi)The screens can either be left in the sun to dry, or
be transferred to boards, pressed, smoothed and then dried. Quality Paper
processing – to get paper of quality value, further processing is required to
produce pulp that is white and smooth enough for printing, using wood as the
source material. This process requires boiling the material in sulphuric acid to
generate (and results in a weaker) whiter pulp known as _Sulphite pulp'.
Because sulphite pulp is not an environmental friendly approach, processing

technology has moved on dramatically in the last decade to mitigate the pollution generated by paper mills. Writers services (2002).

Properties of paper
Sappi (2003), a paper making company outlines the properties as follows:

*Ba sis weight:*the basis weight of a paper means the weight in grams per square meter (g/m2) under conditioned circumstances. The entire mass is the sum of fibrous materials, fillers, process materials and water.

*Brig htness:*The brightness (ISO) is a measure for the brightness degree of the paper expressed in percent compared with the brightness standard (magnesium oxide = 100%). The higher the brightness value, the brighter the paper is.

*G loss:*The gloss figure in the data sheets indicates the percentage of reflected light with adefined angle of incidence. A higher gloss leads to stronger light reflections and higher gloss values.

*P PSroughness:*the geometric form of a paper surface is defined as deviation from the ideal flat level. The more the surface approaches the ideal level, the smoother the paper is. The measuring method (PPS) is based on the measurement of air leakage between the paper surface and the even measuring head. In the case of PPS roughness,the average pore depth over a defined circular area is measured. The higher the measured value is, the —rougher‖ the paper surface is.

*Opa city:*the opacity is a measure for the opacity degree of the paper, expressed in percent in relation to the reflected light. Paper which lets a lot of light through is transparent; paper that lets little light through is opaque. The higher the value, the more opaque the paper is.

*Rela tive humidity:*At a given temperature, there is a maximum to the amount of water vapour that the air can absorb. Relative humidity indicates the percentage of this maximum which is actually in the air (i.e. between the sheets of a stack or the windings of a reel).

*p Hvalue:*The value in the data sheets defines the pH value of the surface.

The pH values are indicated on a scale from 0 to 14. The value 7 marks the neutral point which corresponds to distilled water. Values below 7 refer to —increasingly acid‖, values above 7 stand for —increasingly alkaline‖. Papers should have a pH close to the neutral point in order to meet ideal requirements for printing and further treatment.

*Specific volume:*Paper thickness is expressed in micrometer (μm). To compare the thickness of papers with different basis weights, specific volume is used.
Uses of Paper

Paper may be impregnated, enamelled, metallised, made to look like parchment, creped, water-proofed, waxed, glazed, sensitized, bent, turned, folded, twisted, crumpled, cut, torn, dissolved, macerated, moulded, and embossed. It may be coloured, coated, printed or even written on! All these physical characteristics of paper are want affords paper as a design material a room for creative input as an artistic input is required in paper products. Creative design aspects of the use of paper can be found in agriculture industrywhere it is used seed packets and others. In the

building industry we have wallpapers and different types of decorations especially on the ceilings, interior wall designs, window curtains etc. in the world of business paper is a basic requirement and its use ranges from Print out sheets, receipts, circulars, catalogues, filling systems, sales and service manuals, brochures, and letter heading; all of which can afford room for designers creative input. Other area of production where paper plays an important role is in:
Cars - Fascia boards, door and roof liners, filters, the Highway Code, and driving licenses.
Communications - Writing pads, envelopes, newspapers, magazines, greeting cards, calendars, diaries, telephone directories, labels, business and identity cards. Domestic Products - Tissues, paper plates and cups, toilet paper, kitchen towels, table napkins and lampshades.
Education - Books, exercise books, wall charts, flip charts, and report cards.

Finishing

The paper may then undergo sizing to alter its physical properties for use in various applications. Paper at this point is uncoated. However, according to EPA – a *UnitedStatesEnvironmental ProtectionAgency*, Paper is coated for various decorative andfunctional purposes with waterborne, organic solventborne, or solvent-free extruded materials. Paper coating is not to be confused with printing operations, which use contrast coatings that must show a difference in brightness from the paper to be visible. Coating operations are the application of a uniform layer or coating across a substrate. The technology of paper coating is advancing as shown in figure 3.

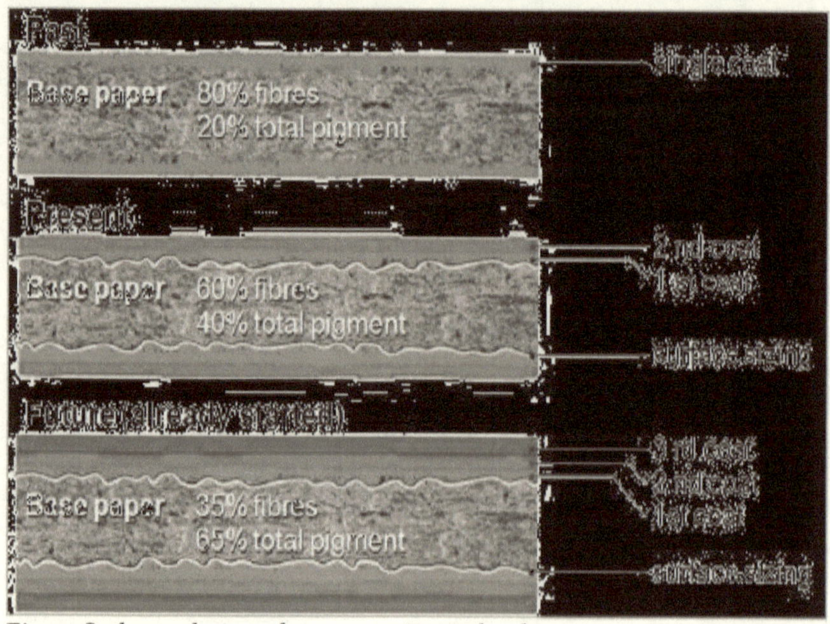

Figure 3: the evolution of paper coating technology
Source: Adopted from http://chempatec-auhorn.com

CONCLUSION

This term paper has explored the processes of making paper one of the day to day used materials across the world and used by almost all the industries. Paper is easily made from waste materials these days because the source of raw material which is trees is becomes scarce by each passing day. However though the mass processing of paper is water consuming today's ever changing technology is opening more options that will see the use of water in paper manufacturing drop drastically. This paper has also explored why paper is one material that affords artistic expressions in the aspect of designs in its various uses. In the packaging industry the paper can be folded into any shape, it can be printed on and cut into various design.

CHAPTER FIVE

DESIGN MATERIALS AND PROCESS

ADHESIVES

ABSTRACT

Bonding different materials together by means of an adhesive may appear to most people as a normal occurrence. In reality, a lot of technology backs the apparently simple action of bonding. Series of technologies has arisen to deal with adhesives and their applications. The diversity of substrates and the continuous introduction of new processes and materials has ensured the continuous expansion of adhesive technology (A. Pizzi, K. L. Mittal, 2003).

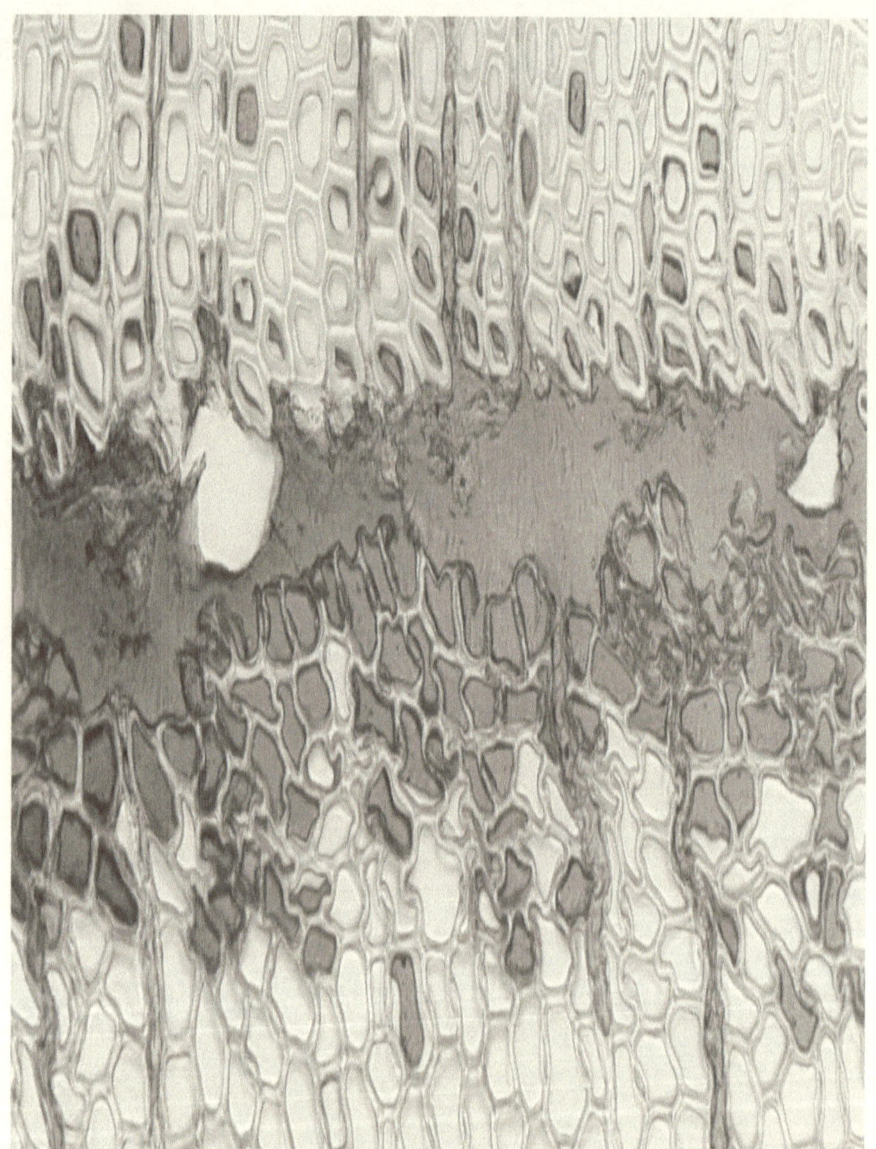

FIGURE 2; Bonding two surfaces together Source: American Forest & Paper Association, Inc. (2007).

The principal attribute of adhesives is their ability to form strong bonds with surfaces of a wide range of materials and to retain bond strength under expected use conditions.

INTRODUCTION
An adhesive is a material used for holding two surfaces together as shown in

figure 2. An adhesive must wet the surfaces, adhere to the surfaces, develop strength after it has been applied and remain stable (Glen A Rowland 1998).

Before synthetic adhesives were introduced in 1930s, adhesives made from natural polymers found in plants and animals were used. These adhesives were made from animal blood, bones, hides, starch, soybeans, dextrin and cellulose. While natural adhesives are still being used, they do not provide the necessary strength and

durability required for today's engineering (American Forest & Paper Assoc. 2007). The raw materials for adhesives are mainly polymeric materials, both natural and synthetic. The best way to classify adhesives is by the way they react after they have been applied to the surfaces to be joined. There is a wide range of adhesives and there has to be a choice depending with materials to be joined.

For a material to perform as an adhesive, it must have four main requirements (Glen A Rowland 1998):

• Be able to wet the surfaces, it must flow out wet over the surfaces that are being bonded, displacing all air and other contaminates present as shown in figure 3.

• It must adhere to the surfaces, after flowing over the whole surface area, it must adhere and stay in position and become —tacky‖.It must develop strength in the process; the material must change its structure to become strong or nontacky but still adherent.

• It must remain stable, should never be affected by age, environmental conditions and other factors.

The basic definition of an adhesive is a material used for bonding that exhibits flow at the time of application.
There are several methods of classifying adhesive, one is a system based on the chemical properties and performance.
Another most important aspect of adhesion technology is preparation of the surfaces for the materials to be bonded together.

THE DIFFERENT RAW MATERIAL TYPES

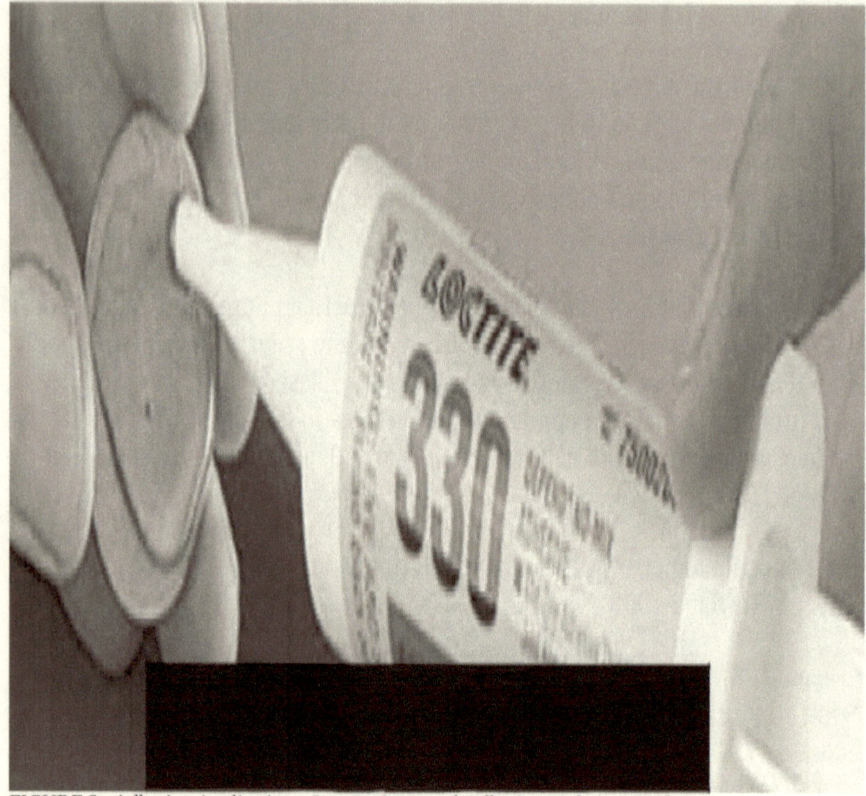

FIGURE 3 –Adhesive Application - Source: Structural Adhesives Selector Guide

NATURAL

Starch and Dextrin:

The materials are extracted from cereals or roots that include wheat, corn and many more. The basic constituent is polysaccharide which yields a chain on glucose units. Variations will occur with the use of different food materials. Adhesives in this category are mainly used in the paper and wood industry (American Forest & Paper Association, Inc. 2007).

Gelatine (Animal, Fish, Vegetable Glues):
They are all proteins which are derived from hydrolysis of either collagen or soya flour or separating casein from skim milk (Glen A Rowland 1998).
Animal glues from bones and hides are used in gummed tape, textiles, book-binding e.t.c.
Fish glues manufactured from skins have been used in rubber gasket to steel

bonding, paper to steel.
Caseirs from skim milk is used mainly in wood to wood binding.
Soya bean glues are used in paper backs.
Blood glues are used in veneering and plywood.
Asphalt and Bitumin:

Consists of high fraction of crude oil and are commonly used as sealers rather
than adhesives except in the bonding of some papers to produce waterproof
building materials.

Natural Rubber:

Rubber is extracted from latex from the rubber tree. The raw latex is tapped,
collected, concentrated and is either sold as latex or it is coagulated and sold
as a solvent dissolution (Richard L. Lehman 2004). Adhesives made from
natural rubber are very tacky and are used in pressure sensitive applications
such as ceramic tile adhesives, flooring adhesives e.t.c.
Resins, Shellac:
Natural resins have been used as adhesives. Shellac is used in mica bonding
to form micaboard and was once used in abrasive. Copal gums are used in
spirit soluble lino cement.

SEMI-SYNTHETIC
Cellulosic:

Cellulose is part of what makes up plants and is a polymer made up of
glucosidic rings joined by oxygen. Cellulosic can be formed to give either
water soluble or solvent soluble polymers.

Cellulose Nitrate: Home handyman adhesive.
Cellulose Acetate: Paper to paper and plastic adhesives
Methyl Cellulose: Leather paste that prevent shrinkage during drying,
Wallpaper paste.

SYNTHETIC
Vinyls: Is one of the many polymers for the coating and adhesive industry.
The number of vinyl derivatives is very huge and all have different
properties. Some are produced as emulsion or solvent. This includes:

• Polyvinyl Acetate: Paper converting, packaging, wood, leather, tile and homehandyman adhesives
• Polyvinyl Alcohol: Paper and textiles
• Polyvinyl Butyral: Laminated safety glass
• Polyvinyl Formal: Adhesive wire enamel
• Polyvinyl Chloride: Pipe adhesives
• Polyvinyl Ether: Pressure sensitive tapes

Acrylics: They can be produced as emulsions or solvent soluble form. They are used as pressure sensitive adhesives for floor, paper lamination, textiles e.t.c

Reactive Acrylic Bases: Reactive Acrylic adhesives are different from the standard acrylics and are final polymers since they are a mixture of acrylic monomers usually with a synthetic rubber. They are catalysed during the bond formation using a free radical mechanism.
The advantages are the fast bond time and their ability to bond a wide variety of substances e.g.

• Used for metal to metal, metal to plastic etc.
• Used in thread locking application.
• Used where fast bonds are required.

Synthetic Rubbers:

Numerous polymers have been developed to match and improve upon natural rubber. Natural rubber has good tack properties but normally not very high strength (Richard L. Lehman 2004). With all rubber adhesives, it is usual to add various resins and other compounding ingredients to give specific properties. The properties allow them to bond variety of substances such as:

• Contact adhesives: Wood, laminates, leather e.t.c. • Pressure sensitive tapes, hot melt adhesives.
• Electrical tapes, sealing tapes.
• Leather, Rubber, Vinyl adhesives.
• Adhesive - sealant in glass to glass, glass to metal bonds.

Aldehyde Condensation Resins:

Some of these resins are the earliest synthetics developed and are used in: Abrasive discs, brake linings, foundry industry, fibre bonding, plywood, particle-board.

Polyester Resin:
Reaction product used for bonding glass fibre, metal to metal and in shoe lasting operations

INORGANICS
Used in bonding paper, some applications of metal to plywood bonds, dental cement and refractory cement.

ADHESIVE TYPES
Adhesives can be classified into three main types:
Chemical Reactive Types: Supplied in low molecular weight form and after application areaction is allowed to take place by use of moisture or heat

Thermoplastic Type: This means they are heated to a sufficient temperature where theywill flow and wet then set and dry to bind o cooling.
Evaporation or Diffusion Types: The adhesive polymer is essential in its final phase however, wetting of the adherent is achieved by dissolving or dispersing the polymers in a suitable solvent.

4 - Different types of adhesives Source: UC Berkeley College of Environmental Design

SURFACE PREPARATION

For effective bonding, the adhesives must intimately wet the surface of each substrate being joined together. A chemical bond must form between the surface of the adhesive and the substrate. Hence the surface of the substrate must be clean, reasonably smooth and chemically receptive to the chosen adhesive as shown in Figure 5. Surface preparation is the process is the process whereby the adherend surface is cleaned or chemically treated to promote better adhesion (Charles R. Frihart, Christopher G. Hunt).

THE MAJOR CHARACTERISTICS OF ADHESIVES:

Adhesives for highly technical applications are designed for both performance and process ability. Adhesives can dramatically differ in characteristics even if their chemistries are similar.Adhesives can be one-component or two-components (resin and hardener) as shown in Figure 5 and have a range of cure temperatures and methods. They can be heat cured, room temperature cured or a combination.

PRO-SET
EPOXY
277 Slow Hardener
PRO-SET
EPOXY
175 Resin

Single or Two Component Adhesives

Two-component adhesives have a longer shelf life and offer lower cure temperatures than single component systems. Advantage of single-component adhesives is that there is no mixing prior to use and they come ready to use. Some may require storage conditions obtain the storage life.

Pot Life

Pot life is the time span in which a two component adhesive must be used after mixing for best results. Once the hardener is combined with the resin, a reaction starts to occur (Epoxy Technology, Inc. 2012). Pot life does not only depend on the adhesive itself, but also on the specific application technique. Depending on the methods (application, process and function)

Viscosity

Viscosity is defined as the resistance of a fluid to flow. It is commonly referred as thickness or flow ability (Epoxy Technology, Inc. 2012). The viscosities of adhesives range from very liquid (low viscosity) to viscous (high-viscosity)

Cure Schedule

The cure schedule is a combination of temperature and the amount of time to which an adhesive is exposed in curing environment for 'complete' curing (Epoxy Technology, Inc. 2012). Depending on the selected industrial cure method (convention oven, tunnel furnace, hot plate e.t.c.), there are different degrees ofhardness. With high temperature curing (High temperature, short drying time) the adhesives hardens almost 100% hence reaching optimal adhesive strength and chemical properties.

Operating Temperature

Most organic compound based adhesives will easily degrade or vaporize under high temperatures.

Lap Shear Strength

The shear force necessary to break a lap joint. An example of a lap joint is an overlapping joint made by placing two pieces of aluminium together with an overlay. The resultant force should determine the strength of the adhesive.

Moisture Resistance

Moisture resistance is the measurement for which a cured adhesive absorbs water. It is measured by exposing the cured adhesive to humidity or submerging in water.

A. Pizzi, K. L. Mittal (2003): *Handbook of Adhesive Technology–Second Edition,Revised andExpanded.www.dekker.com*
American Forest & Paper Association, Inc. (2007). *Adhesive Awareness Guide.www.woodaware.info*
Charles R. Frihart, Christopher G. Hunt. *Adhesives with Wood Materials– BondFormation andPerformance*
Charles B. Vick: *Adhesive Bondingof Wood Materials*
Epoxy Technology, Inc. (2012): *Epoxy Adhesive ApplicationGuide*
Glen A Rowland (1998): *Adhesivesand Adhesion*
Henkel: *Structural AdhesivesSelectorGuide. www.henkelna.com/loctitestructurals*
John Packer (1990): *Adhesives*
Kellar Autumn (2006): *Properties,Principles and Parametersof the Gecko AdhesiveSystem*
Pro-Set Inc. (2005): *Pro-SetAdhesives. www.proseteproxy.com*
Richard L. Lehman (2004): *Adhesives–The CRCHandbook of MechanicalEngineering* UC Berkeley College of Environmental Design: *Materialand ChemicalHandbook*

CHAPTER SIX

DESIGN MATERIALS AND PROCESS

CERAMICS

The word ceramic is derived from the Greek word keramikos, meaning inorganic, non-metallic materials formed by the action of heat. On the other hand Ceramics is defined as name for products made of non-metallic inorganic substances (Russell Giordano, Edward A. McLaren, 2010).

FIgURE 2: an artist working with clay - Source: Student Art Association–art.mit.edu/saa/ceramics

INTRODUCTION

Ceramics is one of the oldest and most endurable forms of art known to human, even the most primitive people used clay pottery (Linda Coreson, Lyla Houglum 2006). Until recently, most commonly known ceramics were traditional clays as shown in figure 2 and 3, bricks, tiles, cements and glass. Ceramics suitability of clay depends on their characteristics such as mineralogy, chemistry, granulometry, plasticity as well as the firing conditions (Aziz Khalfaoui, Mohamed Hajjaji 2010). Many ceramic materials are hard, porous and brittle. The study and development of ceramics over recent decades has involved ways to alleviate problems that rise from these characteristics hence development of advanced ceramics.

Advanced ceramics are materials tailored to possess exceptional properties by controlling their composition and internal structure. Advanced ceramic materials play a key role in the progress of many fields of modern technologies such as communication, information technology, energy, environmental technology, transportation and life science. Techniques previously applied to metals are now considered applicable to ceramics systems (D.A. Taylor 2001).

The advanced concepts fulfil the requirements of increased precision in both design and manufacturing. When used as engineering material, advanced ceramics possess several properties which can be viewed as superior to metal based system. The properties place the group of ceramics in an attractive position in area of performance and effectiveness.

CERAMICS CLAYS

Pure natural clays always have shortcomings. The production process and ultimate use dictates the properties the clay needs to have. Clay can be grouped or classified in several ways (Mayco 2004):

• According to the way they are found in nature.
• By their physical and chemical properties.
• By the way they are used to make finished properties and so on.One of the ways to classify is by the way nature creates clay deposits.

Kaolin or China clay: The clay is almost pure white as primary clay and slightly less whitebut more plastic as secondary clay. The clay contains many impurities, usually calcium, feldspar and iron resulting in clay with finer particle sizes. These clays are a major component of high-fire clay bodies and are frequently used in stoneware to lighten the fired colour.

Ball Clay: These are secondary clays that have been transported to swampy areas whereorganic acids have broken down the mineral particles to ultra-fine size. The clays are extremely plastic and if used alone, they will shrink causing cracks.

Earthenware Clay: Is the most common surface clay found throughout the world andpopular because of it's' versatility. These clays contain high amounts of iron and therefore give fired wares the characteristics terra cotta color. However it does have a greater tendency to chip and the body remains porous after firing.

Stoneware Clay: Tends to contain more impurities especially calcium, feldspar and iron.As a result, it gives the clay fine particle sizes and higher flux content. The flux materials cause the clay to vitrify at lower firing temperatures.

Fire Clay: Fire clays generally contain less flux (especially calcium and feldspar). If firedalone, the clay does not full vitrify even at high fire temperatures

Bantonite Clay: Formed from the decomposition of volcanic ash. Bantonite has the finestparticle size of any natural clay. Very useful as a plasticizer but it must be used inmoderation, too much of it in clay body would result in cracking during the drying process.

Slip Clay: These are naturally occurring clays that have high iron content. At hightemperatures, these clays melt to form a glaze and therefore no additives are needed.

COMPONENTS OF A CLAY BODY

All clay bodies involve combining different clay (many recipes call for several types of clay) with non-clay additives using special equipment as shown in Figure 4. The basic types of additives and purpose for each are (Mayco 2004):

Flux: These materials act as melting agents, helps to lower the maturing temperature

andassist in the formation of glass, it is a very essential binder in all ceramics. Some clay contains higher concentration than others. Feldspar and Iron are the most common.

Glass-Formers: These materials react with fluxes to form glass. The most common glass-former is silica. Pure silica melts at very high temperatures. Proper mix of flux and silica allows glass to be formed at manageable temperatures. The balance must be achieved because too much flux produces a weak glass while too much silica lead to reduced thermal shock resistance.

Refractories: These materials stabilize the body, providing the physical structure orbinding material for the flux and glass-formers to bind together. The primary refractory material is alumina, High in some clay such as fire clay and kaolin.

Fillers: Gritty, granular materials that improve a clay body by enhancing the formingstrength, decreasing shrinkage, providing for drying and greater thermal shock resistance. Common filler is grog, formed from grinding previously fired clay.

Plasticizer: Occasionally, a clay body will need accessory plasticizers to improve themold-ability and flexibility of the clay. The combination and proportion of these ingredients will affect the general properties of the clay.
CLAY MATERIAL PROPERTIES

Every material can be evaluated by objective criteria such as, chemical, electrical, physical characteristics and behaviours. There are two main properties that defines clay, the abilityto be moulded and shaped and how it fires. Some clay are flexible or plastic than others, some can be fired to high temperatures than others (Mayco 2004).

Plasticity: Ability of clay to be moulded and shaped. There are several factors that affectclay's plasticity: The mineral particle size, acidity levels, amount of water e.t.c. The state of clay particles —sticking together‖ or —separating‖ has technical, chemical explanation.
Vitrification: The process under which the clay body experiences chemical and physicalchange during firing. The changes that take place during firing take place in stages (Aziz Khalfaoui, Mohamed Hajjaji 2010). The first stage the clay is fired to red heat and particles are stuck together permanently but the glass forming processes is yet to begin. At this point, the clay body is said

to be sintered and therefore become bisque. Bisque bodies have strength but not as much as vitrified body and are more porous.

As temperatures climb past the sintering stage, the fluxes and glass-formers begin to interact, the particles fuse together, forming glass between and around the mineral particles with almost no airspace. A vitrified body is not porous and is strong and dense.

Porosity: Porosity refers to material's ability to absorb moisture, easily measured onunglazed piece of clay or clay body.

Shrinkage: Shrinkage occurs in all clay bodies as they are dried and fired. The more plastic the clay body, the greater the drying shrinkage. Shrinkage from firing of clay body will depend on flux content, size and quantity of refractory materials. The addition of grog material can aid in reducing the shrinkage.
There are four very important factors required to complete a properly fired piece: Time, Temperature, Air Circulation and Ventilation.

Time: Duration or length the clay piece is subjected to heat in the kiln as shown in Figure5.
Temperature: The degree of heat required to mature the piece. When time andtemperatures are combined, are referred to as —heat work‖.

Air Circulation: Is the way movement of air occurs in the firing chamber.
Ventilation: The removal of the fumes and gases during the firing process. Air circulationand ventilation is apparently independent and is easily confused.

CLAY FIRING

URE 5: A ceramic kiln - Source: www.veniceclayartists.com

CERAMIC PROCESS

Depending with the final product, there are different ways ceramic products
are created:

• Casting.
• Pressing.
• Extrusion.

GLAZING

Glaze is a glass like substance put over clay and when fired, glass-like particles melt to produce a smooth effect. There are many colours and kinds of glazes available. Besides adding beauty to the ware, the glaze makes it waterproof. Glazed ware is less likely to discolour and is easier to clean.

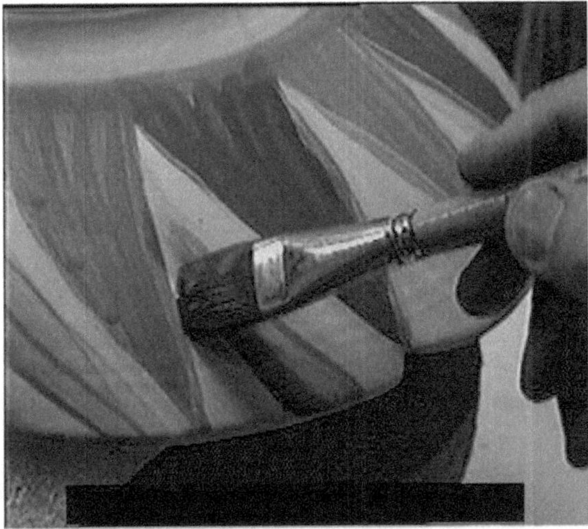
RE 6: Applying glaze using brush -
Source: google.com

Glazes can be flowing or non-flowing. Flowing glazes creep or flow when fired and if two colours are used they will bleed or run together. Non-flowing glazes stay where they are put and are better to use when applying one colour because they do not run together, unless there is desire to achieve special effects.

There are several kinds of glazes (Linda Coreson, Lyla Houglum 2006):
Transparent Glazes: Pick up the details on the ware, you can see through them and theycan be clear or coloured.
Opaque Glazes: Are solid and you can see through them.
Matte Glazes: Have a dull finish with very little shine.
Gloss Glaze: Have a very shiny finish.
Semi-Matte Glaze: Have only a slight shinny finish.

APPLYING GLAZE
Glaze can be applied in several ways: • With a brush as shown in Figure 6. • Sponge.
• Airbrush.
• Dipping.

Most glazing will require at-least three thin coats and it's is important that the pieces are entirely covered with glaze. Too much glaze will cause the glaze to crack or peel during firing.

CHAPTER SEVEN

DESIGN MATERIALS AND PROCESS

FIBREGLASS

INTRODUCTION

Fibreglass is a composite material which is made by combining two materials where one of the materials is reinforcement (fibre) and the other material is a matrix (Resin) as shown in Figure 2. The combination of fibre and matrix provide characteristics superior to either of the materials alone. The term —Fibreglass‖ describes a thermoset plastic resin that is reinforced with glass (Molded Fiber Glass Companies 2003).

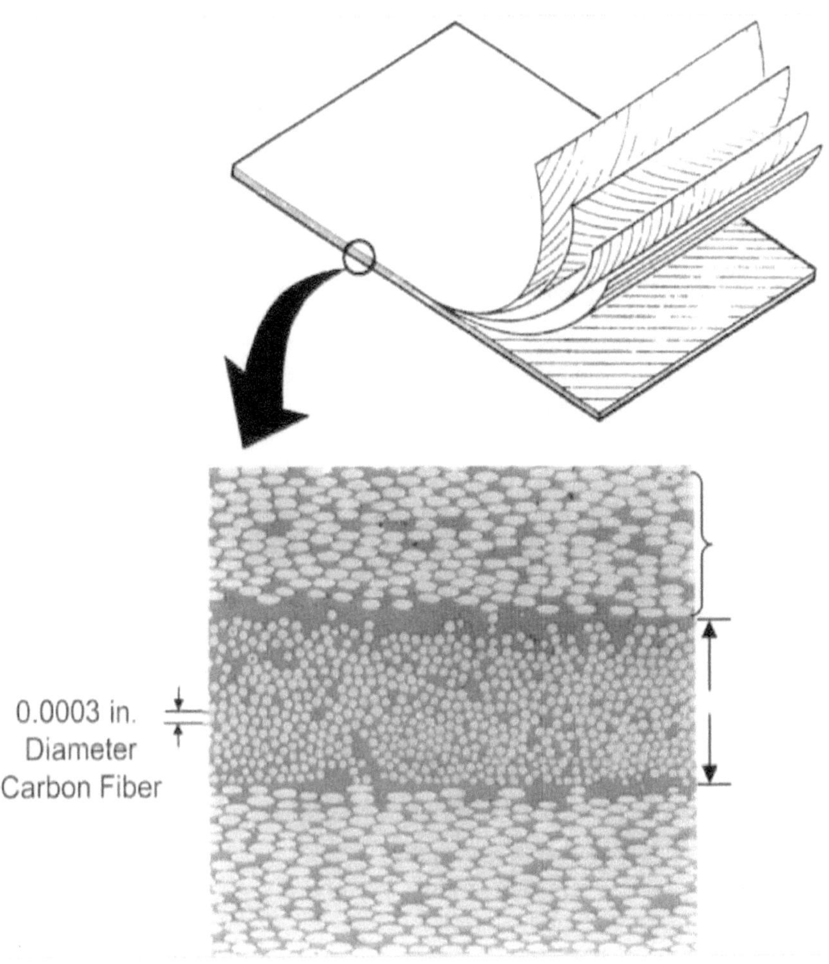

First conceived and manufactured during 1935 in Newark, Ohio. In 1942, fiberglass reinforced composites were first used in structural aerospace parts. In 1960s high strength fiberglass were used in textile products and United States Air Force. Later fiberglass began evolving into a variety of commercial applications (David Hartman, Mark E. Greenwood, David M. Miller, 2006). High strength fiberglass combines high temperature durability, stability, transparency and resilience at reasonable weight. The utility of high strength fibreglass compositions are compared by physical, mechanical, electrical, thermal, acoustical, optical and radiation properties.

It was the first modern composite and is still the most commonly used. It makes up about 65 % of all the composite materials produced today. GRP or

"Glassfibre Reinforced Plastic" consists of two distinct materials, a fibre of glass (ceramic), which is the reinforcement and a polymer resin called polyester, which serves as the matrix. The polyester resin polymer alone is brittle and has a low strength but when fibres of glass are embedded in the polymer it becomes strong, tough, resilient and flexible. It becomes an ideal material to make boats, swimming pool linings, car bodies, roofing and furniture. The other advantage of GRP is that it is very light and has a very good strength to weight ratio. A resilient material is one that returns to its original shape after bending, twisting, stretching, and compression. A tough material is one that has the ability to withstand sudden blows or shocks without breaking. This material can also be bent without cracking.

Fiberglass is a composite material widely used in the automotive industry, cars-kits are often made from fiberglass as are many sports cars. Fiberglass is an incredibly versatilematerial and it comes in several forms. The fiberglass used in the automotive industry is different from insulation fiberglass. It usually comes in a mat, tissue or cloth, although a chopped strand mixed with resin is often used for large applications such as boat hulls.

Fibreglass is a composite material system consisting of fibre reinforcement, plastic resin and additives as shown in Figure 2, combined and processed to meet specific functional performance and manufacturing criteria for a finished product or part. By selecting the right combination of resin and fibres, the designer can create a product or part that meets the most demanding of product specifications.

FRP is short for —Fibre Reinforced Plastic‖ and is the widely used abbreviation for fibreglass. Sometimes FRP is used to mean —Fibre Reinforced Polyester‖, the most commonly used plastic resin. GRP is sometimes used and is the abbreviation for Glass Reinforced Plastic, this being the most common reinforcement used. The terms are all interchangeable.

It takes a combination of different chemicals, to complete this elaborate task of fibreglass production; e.g. unsaturated polyester resins, hardeners and accelerators, titanium dioxide, e.t.c. The unique properties of Fibreglass make it suitable for a wide range of product applications, and also offer advantages that are not found in more conventional constructional materials! (Molded

Fiber Glass Companies 2003 and Sai Raj Kenya)

FIBREGLASS FEATURES AND BENEFITS

FIGURE 3: A fish sculpture molded from fibreglass Source : Sai Raj Kenya

Design Freedom or Flexibility

High degrees of flexibility and the practical uses of Fibreglass are virtually endless, limited only by your imagination. Fibreglass opened up many new avenues for creative designers, its unique physical properties allow it to be easily tooled, molded and manufactured to meet almost any specification as indicated in Figure 3, because there are few constraints on size, shape, colour or finish, this can deliver great styling and appearance whilst being cost effective, and its this design freedom which is the hallmark of composite achievement.

Affordability

This design freedom and the easiness to mould make fibreglass an economical alternative for the manufacture of any component or finished product in any quantity.

Versatility

The lightweight strength of Fibreglass has always made it a popular choice for designers and manufacturers alike, Fibreglass offers distinct advantages for a wide range of products, its reduced weight and maintenance make it attractive on architectural projects,and more industries are discovering the benefits of its versatility, these industries include, construction, leisure, marine, automotive, aerospace, transport, ministry of defence e.t.c.

Strength and Durability

High strength to weight ratio and high flexural strength make Fibreglass an attractive lightweight material, additional reinforcement can be added in specific locations to build in extra strength where load and stress points require it. When used for external applications, Fibreglass can offer a high resistance to environmental extremes, so pound for pound Fibreglass components can provide a better performance over other construction materials!

Appearance

Fibreglass components are gel-coated in their moulds with a choice of flat, semi-gloss or high gloss colour eliminating the need for painting. In highly corrosive environments gel-coats are much more durable than most paints as indicated by Figure 5. Fibreglass products can be manufactured in numerous finishes, textures, and colours, so various surface appearances can be achieved in the mould.

Moulded Look
With sheet steel or wood, you get a plain component; Fibreglass components have a leek contour and a superior moulded appearance complete with required colour.
Corrosion Resistance / Environmentally Tough

Fibreglass is non-corrosive and has a much longer life expectancy when compared to a variety of other construction materials, in highly corrosive environments; Fibreglass is the perfect choice over metal, wood, or plastic. A popular choice where exposure to harsh environments is a concern as indicated with the out-door sculptures in Figure 4, fibreglass can provide resistance to ultra violet light, extreme temperatures, salt air, and a variety of chemicals, because Fibreglass is chemically inert and corrosionresistant it offers an economical alternative to stainless steel.
Sound Deadening

Fibreglass provides superior acoustical properties when compared to plastic or metal, various types of sound deadening material can be laminated in between high strength layers of Fibreglass matt to achieve the preferred level of sound deadening. Fibreglass exhibits a great deal of dimensional stability and the least amount of expansion and / or contraction when compared to other material.

Durability
Fibreglass structures have an exceedingly maintenance requirements; the longevity long life span, coupled with low

of fibreglass is a benefit in critical applications, in a half-century of composite development, well designed fibreglass structures have yet to wear out and are good for outdoor as indicated with flamingo sculptures in Figure 4 .

Low Maintenance

Fibreglass components require very little or no maintenance as they do not rust, rot, orfall to pieces.

HOW ARE FIBREGLASS PRODUCTS MADE

FIGURE 4: Outdoor Sculptures (flamingos) made from fibreglass Source: Sai Raj Kenya

An intricate process, there are essentially seven stages in the manufacture or assembly of fibreglass products (Molded Fiber Glass Companies 2003).
Design Department
Here a specially trained designer designs models that are aesthetically appealing. He is an artist endowed with sculptural talent.
Wooden Model

At this stage, carpenters erect a wooden model which is a complete replica of the proposed product under the keen supervision of the designer. This wooden model is in most cases temporary and dismantled after use.

Fibreglass Model

This model is preferable to wooden in that it is more refined and is intended to be a permanent replica of the product for future use. However in case of unavailability, the wooden model may be used.

Moulding
A molding of either or is undertaken which is painted black to differentiate it from the final product to be laminated in or on it depending on it's design
Laminating

This is the most intricate part. The molding, is polished by use of wax so as to prevent the lamination from sticking to it. The wax forms a cushion whereby the laminate rests and remains independent of the moulding. A paste of the required colour is then pouredover the wax which is mixed with a hardener and a catalyst to speed up the process of solidifying.

Then fibreglass matt is placed whereby the desired thickness determines the number of matts to be used; this is done in conjunction with the application of resin which acts as the bonding agent.

The Drying Stage

Immediately laminating is over, a hardener and a catalyst is added to speed up the drying process. However this is a sensitive stage in that it is essentially controlled by the given locational environmental conditions since most firms prefer their fibreglass production undertaken in an open atmosphere rather than in simulated situations which are quite exorbitant.

If the weather is hot it dries out quickly, if on the contrary it is cold, it may take longer thereby delaying delivery of products to clients. On normal average weather conditions the process may take two to three days and by that time the chemicals have already dried and the curing process is complete, meaning that no more cracks should appear.

The Trimming Department

After drying, a moulding releasing agent is used to separate the moulding from the laminate (final product) and under-sired protrusions are trimmed off. The product is then ground to give it a smooth finish. If there are any cracks due to contractions and expansions in response to weathering, a filler is used to repair and, in the case of car bodies or water tanks e.t.c where there is a visible rough surface, it is not only ground but also a layer of paste is applied to smoothen it mixed with monomer to make it non-sticky [the resin is always sticky.] If there are un-coloured spots, they are painted to give a uniform elegant finish.

Signage, Signs, shop interiors & kiosks
Architectural, fascias & cladding, interior/exterior detail
Automotive, wind deflectors, high tops, body kits
Aviation, cowlings, wheel spats, components
Communications, mobile phone mast enclosures
Construction form work, lift shaft liners
Engineering covers, guards, housings
Exhibition components, stands, themed pieces
Hygiene, shower trays & cubicles, baths
Leisure theme park rides, flumes & slides
Marine boat hulls &, associated components
Specialist applications lining, fabrications & prototypes
Transportation seats, covers, bodywork
And much more! To The User
The end product is then delivered to the client and in case of a car body part, it is fixed to the car and sent back to the owner.

FIGURE 5: A finished fibreglass product Source: Google.com

APPLICATION

Fibreglass can produce mouldings from various material combinations to suit the desired application, it's a fire retardant, chemical resistant or Mouldings that can withstand environmental extremes therefore makes it appealing as shown in Figures 5 and 6.

6: A Fibreglass molded Kiosk Source: Sai Raj Kenya

CHAPTER EIGHT

DESIGN MATERIALS AND PROCESS

COMPOSITE LUMBER

ABSTRACT

More than thirty years ago in Japan, where green awareness is firmly instilled in culture, an engineering company EIN Engineering invented and developed a substitute for wood made from softwood waste and recycled plastics (Einwood, WPC Corporation 2010). This material had the appearance and qualities of a rare wood species while at the same time offering an eco-friendly alternative as indicate in Figure 1.

In 1994, the American Forest Service recognised the need for recycled content material in construction. For the last several years, they have been involved in research products for the most effective way to build a house with minimum waste (Christine L Balogh 1996).

The first area looked at in this research was the roof system components which include engineered wood made of recycled wood products, supplemented by solid wood structure elements for more durable material. Loose-fill cellulose insulation was made from wood mixed with fiberized waste plastic. The tiles for the roof included recycled paper fibre and concrete made from recovered construction materials (Christine L Balogh 1996).

The siding of the house was to be covered with recovered wood fibres along with plastics and inorganic binders. The interior wall was made from 100% recycled materials. Boards made from recycled material could provide sound insulation for the house.
The foundation of the house was constructed from materials exhibiting resistant properties. Particle board and composite lumber was used in this process. Countertops and cabinets were manufactured with wood waste, mixed paper and plastic to increase durability and strength.

INTRODUCTION

Composite Lumber can be described as mix of wood fibres and waste plastics turned into durable material. Composite is a material formed with two or more components, combined as a macroscopic structural unit with one component as continuous matrix and other as fillers or reinforcements. The matrix is the material that holds the reinforcements together and has lower strength than reinforcements. In plastic based composites, the polymers act as

matrix and fibres of wood are fillers.
Recycled wood/plastic composite lumber is one of the prime uses for recycled plastic trash bags and waste wood fibres. The composite material is used to produce building products such as door, window frames, and exterior panels. Manufacturers claim that products produced with recycled wood/plastic lumber are more durable than conventional material

Recycled wood/plastic composite lumber typically consists of a 50/50 mix of wood fibres from recovered saw dust and waste plastics, PVC, and others. The material is formed into both solid and hollow profiles as indicated in Figure2.

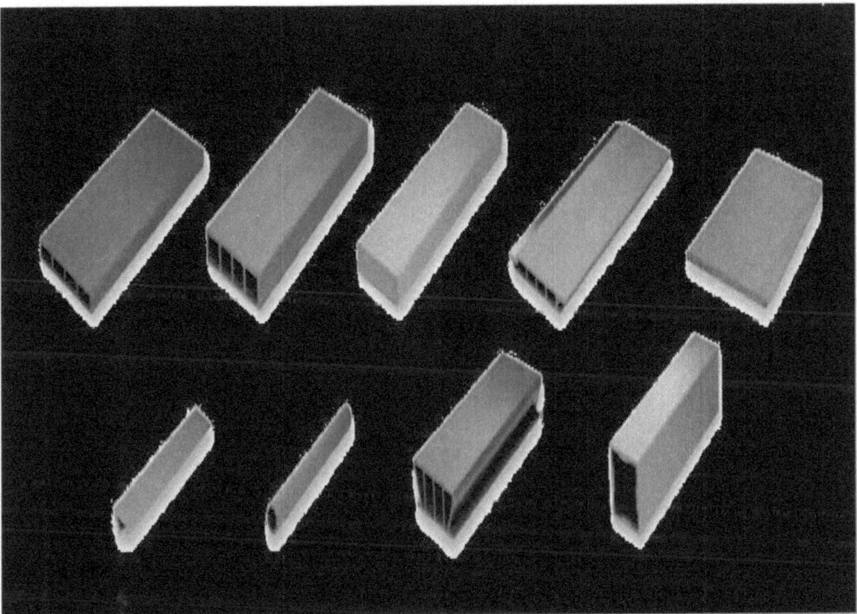

FIGURE 2: Various Products from Composite Lumber
Source: Einwood, WPC Corporation (2010)

Recycled wood/plastic composites are typically more rigid than 100 percent recycled plastic lumber because the wood fibres act as reinforcement. In addition, the plastic binds the wood together to resist moisture penetration and degradation from fungal rot.
USES OF COMPOSITE LUMBER

FIGURE 3: A building made of Composite Lumber, Source: Einwood, WPC Corporation (2010)

Recycled wood/plastic composites are commonly used as building products:
Building Products

This is the largest market for composite lumber which include exterior walls,
floor tiles (interior and exterior) as shown in Figure 3, garden furniture,
exterior windows and doors e.t.c.

Infrastructure
In the United States, it's used in marine use and railroad crosstie
Transportation
Automotive and highway application; used as panels for interior of door panels, roof headliners and seat backs. Highway applications include road signs, fence posts e.t.c.
Playground equipment
It is an important material where durability is an important performance attribute.
MANUFACTURING OF COMPOSITE LUMBER

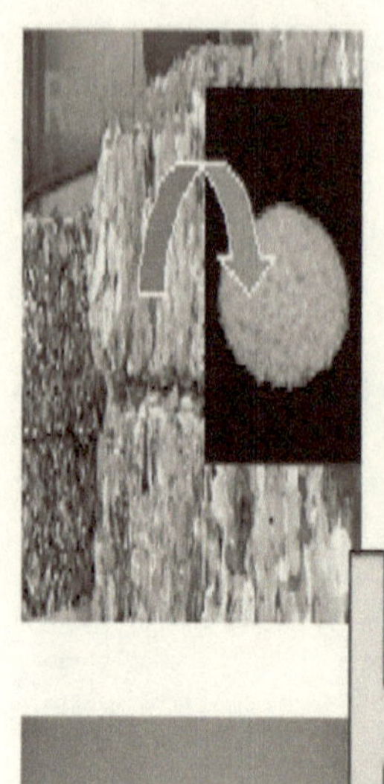

Sawdust (wood-flour)

Mixing/Compounding

WPCs panel (Final product)

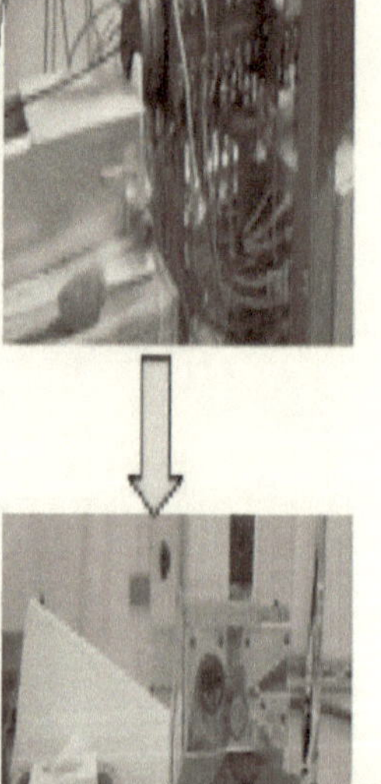

Wood-plastics Pellets

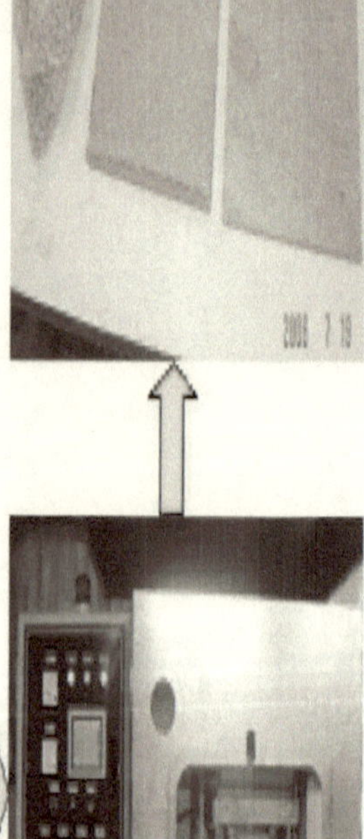

Hot/Cold pressing of pellets

The prepared wood flour is dried in an oven to remove the moisture. Similarly the plastic granules are dried to remove the moisture. Then the wood flour is compounded with the recycled plastic granules as indicated in Figure 4. The manufacturing of the thermoplastic based composite is usually through a two-step process:

• Compounding of wood filler and plastic with coupling agent or other additives.
• Extrusion moulding, injection moulding or compression moulding of the compounded mixture to produce a panel type product. Proper mixing of woodfiller with polymer and additives are important to manufacture consistent composites.

ADVANTAGES/ BENEFITS

FIGURE 5: The _wood' doesn't seem to absorb water, Source: Einwood, WPC Corporation (2010)

Infinitely Versatile

Composite lumber made from recycled wood fiber and plastics can be used to make various building products, including decking, railings, door and window frames and exterior molding. Suitable for any climate and lend itself to multitude of different uses both outdoors and indoors.
Easy to Install

The calibrated boards, accessories and fixing clips reduce laying times. Using standard tools, even the inexperienced installer can produce straight, neat cuts without a problem.

Environmental Friendly

Composite lumber does not contain the toxic chemicals used for preservation. And by using recycled materials, the production of composite lumber contributes to environmental sustainability.

In addition to their benefits in terms of environmental impact, composite building materials, made with recycled saw dust and woodchips and plastic from discarded shopping bags, plastic bottles and other wastes, have some performance advantages (Robert H. Falk 1993).

Durability

Manufacturers claim that composite lumber can be more durable than conventional material. Composite lumber is more resistant than 100 percent plastic products since the wood fibers act as reinforcement. With its plastics content, composite lumber resists:

• Moisture penetration as indicated in Figure 5.
• Insects such as termites
• Fungal rot that causes degradation

Straightness

Composite lumber is straight, does not splinter, and resists warping like other plastic products and in addition can become more flexible in hot weather and more rigid in cold weather than other decking materials.

Affordability

The cost of composite lumber products is generally competitive with high-end traditional wood products, but more expensive than standard treated wood products. But in taking into account that composite lumber doesn't require sealing or painting, and is durable, the maintenance cost can be lower than traditional wood products.

Stability
They are strong enough for applications such as load bearing deck boards. They tends to have significantly greater dimensional stability and a lower coefficient of expansion than solid plastics (Kamal Babu Adhikary 2008).

CONCLUSION

Composite Lumber has become a premium material especially in architecture because it easily adapts to any style and has superior qualities. The material is able not just to withstand extremes of temperature, but will resist insects like termites (prone in Western parts of Kenya), continuous high humidity, stagnant water e.t.c. With the mentioned advantages the material can be used for outdoor flooring, which the traditional wood cannot survive. If adapted more in the construction and manufacturing industry, would save so much of our quickly disappearing forests hence making the material environment friendly.

Dyes and colour can also be added in the composite to give them unique colours that are long lasting compared to paints. Unfortunately, no one has started the production of this kind of material in Kenya, while the process seems straight forward.

CHAPTER NINE

DESIGN MATERIALS AND PROCESS

COTTON

ABSTRACT

Cotton is a high value agricultural commodity which provides income for more than 100million farmers worldwide. 150 countries are involved in the import and exportation of cotton. It is the most preferred natural fiber in the world. All parts of the cotton plant are useful and it has hundreds of uses. No other fiber comes close in duplicating all the desirable qualities combined in cotton. In addition to the fiber which is used in textile manufacturing, cotton seed is used to produce oil, seed mill and seed hull. India, USA and China are the largest producers of cotton in the world. The major damage to cotton comes from insect pests mainly ball worms. (Boopathi M and Ravikesavan February 2009.)

Figure 1: Cotton in its ball
This paper seeks to explore the qualities, properties, history, manufacture and use of cotton with a general overview. All the material in this paper has been obtained from studies, books and papers previously written and published. No primary data was collected.

INTRODUCTION

The Dictionary of American History 2003 defines cotton as a shrubby plant that is a member of the Mallow family. Its name refers to the cream-colored fluffy fibers surrounding small cottonseeds called a boll. The small, sticky seeds must be separated from the wool in order to process the cotton for spinning and weaving. De-seeded cotton is cleaned, carded (fibers aligned), spun, and woven into a fabric that is also referred to as cotton. Cotton is easily spun into yarn as the cotton fibers flatten, twist, and naturally interlock for spinning. Cotton fabric alone accounts for fully half of the fiber worn in the world. It is a comfortable choice for warm climates in that it easily absorbs skin moisture.

HISTORY OF COTTON

The earliest evidence of the use of cotton as a textile fiber is from India and the date assigned to this fabric is 3000 B.C. There were also excavations of cotton fabrics of comparable age in Southern America. Cotton cultivation first spread from India to Egypt, China and the South Pacific. Even though cotton fiber had been known already in Southern America, the large scale cotton cultivation in Northern America began in the 16th century with the arrival of colonists to southern parts of today's United States.

According to the Columbia Encyclopedia 6$_{th}$ edition 2012, the largest rise in cotton production is connected with the invention of *the cotton gin*(a machine for separating
seed from fiber) by Eli Whitney in 1793. With this new technology and thereafter the mechanization of textile production in the Industrial Revolution, it was possible to produce more cotton fiber than wool and flax textiles which resulted in big changes in the spinning and weaving industry, especially in England. Today, cotton is grown in more than 80 countries worldwide.

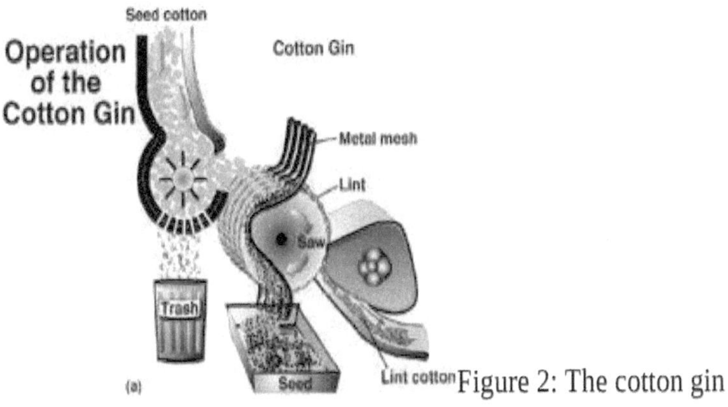

Figure 2: The cotton gin

The Dictionary of American History 2003 states that cotton was used for clothing in present-day Peru and Mexico perhaps as long as 5,000 years ago. Cotton was also grown, spun, and woven in ancient India, China, Egypt, and Pakistan, around 3000 b.c.

COTTON IN KENYA

Mwasiagi, Huan and Wang, (2008) in their paper state that cotton can be grown in all regions of Kenya and especially in the semi-arid area where few other commercial crops are viable. They say that the Kenyan cotton-processing industry has an installed capacity of over 120 000 bales of cotton lint per year, which is able to meet half of the national demand for cotton products. Kenya has consistently produced less than 30 000 bales of cotton lint annually since 1990, so the country is a net importer of the commodity, causing adverse strain on its foreign exchange reserves.

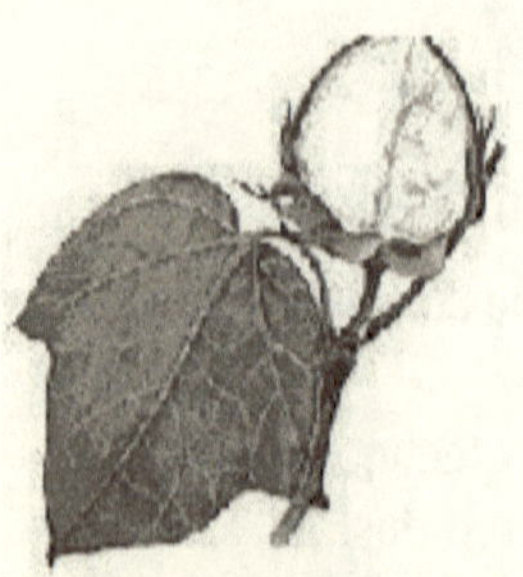

The cross-section of an unopened flower.

According to Mutua, Hagen, Kuria (2011), cotton farming in Kenya has been on the decline for the past two decades. However it is slowly picking up after years of neglect and disillusionment among farmers from continued synthetic competition and importation of cheap second hand clothes as well as diminished profitability. The main factors that influence cotton yield are government policies, crop husbandry methods and cotton price.

Crop husbandry methods such as land preparation, the type and quantity of fertilizers used, and weed and pest control methods have been reported to have a primary influence on cotton quality and yield.

While prediction of cotton yield using satellite forecasting is gaining popularity, especially in the main cotton-producing countries, there are other, less-affluent countries where the cotton-growing industry struggles to survive, and a cheaper yet effective forecasting method is still needed. Such a method will serve as an interim measure for a struggling cotton-growing industry to rationalize itself and achieve a requisite level of competitiveness. In one study carried out by Mutua and Kuria, they identified that there are three cotton-growing regions in the Kenya: eastern/central (e/c), coastal (c) and western (w). Data volumes from a given cotton region correlated with the amount of cotton grown in that region. Their respective percentages of cotton lint production for the eight years from 1996 to 2003 were 54%, 15% and 31%.

PRODUCTION OF COTTON

The Columbia Encyclopedia, 6th ed. 2012 states that until recent years the United States was the world's leading cotton producer and second only to Great Britain in the manufacture of cotton goods. China now is the leading cotton-producing country, followed by the United States and India. Other important cotton producers are Pakistan, Brazil, Uzbekistan, and Turkey. China and India are the leading cotton manufacturers, followed by the United States, where cotton mills have relocated from New England to the Southern cotton-producing states. Historically, all cottonproducing nations have depended on cheap labor; although mechanical cultivating and picking devices have long been known, they have been widely used (especially in the United States) only since World War II.

Figure 4: Cotton shrubs

In the Middle East, cotton is a very important fiber crop. From the early Islamic period onward, cotton acquired new significance in the nineteenth century as the region's paramount export crop and most important raw material link. Egypt took pride of place in the development of the cotton industry as the earliest and the largest producer of cotton for export to date. Cotton developed as the major cash crop of the Sudan from 1925 onward with the development of new irrigation projects. Turkish production expanded after World War I and boomed in the 1950s when the Korean War raised world commodity prices. The same circumstances turned cotton into Syria's biggest cash crop. Israeli and Afghan production expanded in the 1960s. (The Encyclopedia of the Modern Middle East and North Africa 2004)

MANUFACTURING PROCESS

Producers of natural fibers are dependent on raw materials and often held hostage to nature. It is not easy for them to quickly increase or decrease output based on consumer demand. Most producers sell their fiber to mills or wholesalers for resale and seldom have any direct involvement after the fiber is sold. Manufactured fibers can be made from regenerated natural materials, or they can be synthesized from chemicals. Because many of these processes may be petroleum-based, such producers may be affected by events concerning the oil industry, (The Dictionary of American History. 2003). About 30% of world cotton production is harvested by machines. Australia, Israel and USA are the only countries where all cottons are picked by machines. Fifteen percent of world cotton production is ginned on roller gins and almost all rest of cotton is saw ginned in most countries.

After cultivation, cotton is harvested at the farm, and goes through multiple processes. Before processing, there are 3 stages; *ginning spinning,*and *weaving*. After weaving, cotton typically fabric passes through several processing stages.

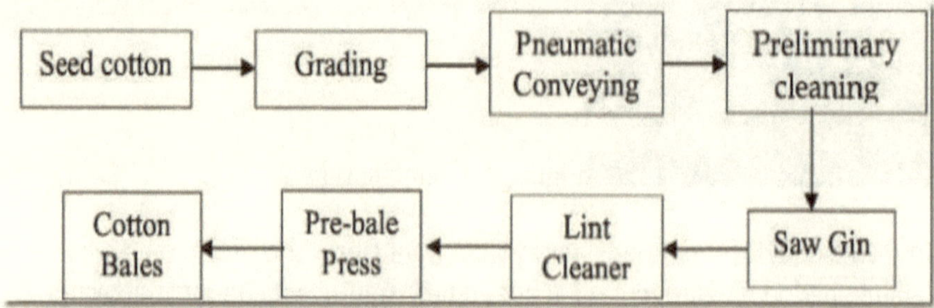

Figure 5: The Ginning Process (Above)
After some stages the fabric can be directly used in the final product, for example unbleached cloth is used in grain bags. Typical stages are; Singeing, Desizing, Scouring, Bleaching, Mercerizing, Dyeing, and Finishing. (http://www.organic-naturenews.com/facts-about-cotton.html)

Figure 6: Cotton ready for harvest (below)

The Dictionary of American History (2003) states, the processing of raw cotton by modern methods begin with the breaking of compressed bales (average weight 478 pounds). Bale breakers, openers, and pickers loosen and blend the tufts of cotton and remove impurities. Carding engines complete the cleaning process, eliminate short and broken fibers, and separate and align those remaining into soft, ropelike "slivers." To obtain high-quality yarn, combers process fine (thin) cotton into slivers, removing as much as 20 percent of the shorter fibers. Drawing frames begin the process of attenuating and twisting the slivers and enhance their regularity by drawing them between rollers and arranging them in parallel rows. A series of machines collectively known as "speed frames" conclude the preparation of cotton for the spinning frames, principally by further drawing out and twisting the material into a rope called "roving" and adding strength to the fibers by making them cling to each other more closely. In the spinning stage, frames equipped with ring spindles draw and twist the fibers into yarn while winding them on a bobbin. The process is continuous, with drawing, twisting, and winding taking place simultaneously. During the preparatory and spinning processes cotton suffers a loss in weight of 9–12 percent. In comparison, man-made filament fibers spun into yarn on cotton textile machinery incur a negligible loss. Approximately two thirds of man-made fibers come from chemical producers already processed as filament yarn.

The Dictionary of American History (2003) continues to state, Machines process cotton yarns into fabrics by knitting, tufting, and weaving. Knitting consists essentially of interlacing a single strand of yarn into a series of interlocking loops. Modern knitting mills produce literally hundreds of items of cotton and cotton-blended apparel. They also convert considerable quantities of cotton yarn into a variety of tufted products on tufting machines and consume them in various nonwoven constructions, in which machines bond fibers together with adhesives. Manufacturers continue to channel the greatest proportion of cotton yarn into broadloom weaving, where additional preparation is required depending on whether it is destined to be warp (longitudinal) or weft (transverse) yarn. Weaving, conducted on high-speed automatic looms, involves the interlacing of yarn at right angles so as to form a fabric.

It goes on further to say that upon leaving the weave shed most unbleached gray goods undergo one of many finishing treatments. Initially, the fabric passes in succession through a series of scouring, washing, and bleaching units before being dyed and printed. Textile engineers have developed a wide range of mechanical and chemical processes to render the fabric more useful and fashionable. Mechanical processes can stiffen, glaze, and improve the texture of the cloth. Chemistry can also provide additional strength, such as fire retardance and abrasion and wind resistance, or it can impart various qualities desirable in apparel, such as permanent press, crease resistance, and shrinkage control, as well as a silk like sheen and the puckering quality of seersucker.
QUALITY CONTROL

Cotton growing is a long, involved process and growers must understand the requirements of the plant and keep vigilant lookout for potential problems. Pests must be managed in order to yield high-quality crops; however, growers must use chemicals very carefully in order to prevent damage to the environment. Defoliants are often used tomaximize yield and control fiber color. Farmers must carefully monitor moisture levels at harvesting so bales will not be ruined by excess water during storage. Soil tests are imperative, since too much nitrogen in the soil may attract certain pests to the cotton. Expensive equipment such as cotton planters and harvesters must be carefully maintained. Mechanical planters must be set carefully to deposit seed at the right depth, and gauge wheels and shoes must be corrected to plant rows at the requisite spot. Similarly, improperly adjusted machinery spindles on harvesting machines will leave cotton on the spindle, lowering quality of the cotton and harvesting efficiency. A well-adjusted picker minimizes the amount of trash taken up, rendering cleaner cotton.

PROPERTIES OF COTTON

Cotton is a comfortable fiber that can be used all year round. According to Kadolph it is the fiber most preferred for many interiors and warm weather apparel especially when the weather is hot and humid. Grades of cotton range from low, medium to high quality grades like Egyptian cotton, Pima, Supima, American Egyptian and Sea Island cotton. She continues to state that there are 39 grades of cotton. Grade refers to the color of the fiber and the absence of dirt, leaf matter, seed particles, motes and tangles of fiber called neps. Today, organic cotton is also available where the cotton plant is grown without the use of commercial pesticides and fertilizers.

Cotton fabrics have a pleasant matte luster, a soft drape and a smooth hand. They are very comfortable to wear due to their soft hand and other characteristics. Cotton fabrics have excellent absorbing capabilities. Garments absorb perspiration, thus keeping the person more comfortable. "Absorbent" cotton will retain 24-27 times its own weight in water and is stronger when wet than dry. This fiber absorbs and releases perspiration quickly, thus allowing the fabric to "breathe". Cotton can stand high temperatures and takes dyes easily. Chlorine bleach can be used to restore white garments to a clear white but this bleach may yellow chemically finished cottons or remove color in dyed cottons. Boiling and sterilizing temperatures can also be used on cotton without disintegration. Cotton can also be ironed at relatively high temperatures, stands up to abrasion and wears well. (Fiber facts 2012) CHEMICAL PROPERTIES OF COTTON

Cotton swells in a high humidity environment, in water and in concentrated solutions of certain acids, salts and bases. It is attacked by hot dilute or cold concentrated acid solutions. It is not affected by cold weak acids. The fibers show excellent resistance to alkalis. There are a few other solvents that will dissolve cotton completely. One of them is a copper complex of cupramonium hydroxide and cupriethylene diamine Cotton degradation is usually attributed to oxidation, hydrolysis or both. Cotton can also degrade by exposure to visible and ultraviolet lightCotton fibers are extremely susceptible to any biological degradation (microorganisms, fungi etc.)

CLASSIFICATION OF COTTON FIBER

According to Kadolph (2011) Grading and classing of cotton is done by hand and by machine HVI (high-volume instrument) systems. Cotton classification describes the quality of cotton in terms of staple length, grade and character. Some of these classifications are explained below as described by Swicofil.com.

Fiber length is described as "the average length of the longer one-half of the fibers (upperhalf Mean length)" This measure is taken by scanning a "beard‖ of parallel fibers through a sensing region. The beard is formed from the fibers taken from the sample, clasped in a holding clamp and combed to align the fibers.

Length uniformity *or* uniformity ratio is determined as "a ratio between the mean lengthand the upper half mean length of the fibers and is expressed as a percentage".

Fiber strength: measured in grams per denier (g/d) or centi-newton per tex cN/tex. It is determined as the force necessary to break the beard of fibers, clamped in two sets of jaws, (1/8 inch apart). The breaking strength of cotton is about 3.0~4.9 g/denier, and the breaking elongation is about 8~10%.

Micronaire measurements reflect fiber fineness and maturity. A constant mass (2.34 Grams) of cotton fibers is compressed into a space of known volume and air permeability measurements of this compressed sample are taken. These, when converted to appropriate number, denote micronaire values

Color of cotton samples is determined from two parameters: degree of reflectance (Rd) and yellowness (+b). Degree of reflectance shows the brightness of the sample and yellowness depicts the degree of cotton pigmentation. The color of the fibers is affected by climatic conditions, impact of insects and fungi, type of soil, storage conditions etc. There are five recognized groups of color: white, gray, spotted, tinged, and yellow stained. As the color of cotton deteriorates, the processability of the fibers decreases.

Trash: measurement describes the amount of non-lint materials (such as parts of cottonplant) in the fiber. Trash content is assessed from scanning the cotton sample surface with a video-camera and calculating the percentage of the surface area occupied by trash particles. The values of trash content should be within the range from 0 to 1.6%. Trash content is highly correlated to leaf grade of the sample.

Leaf grade: provided visually as the amount of cotton plant particles within the sample. There are seven leaf grades (#1-#7) and one below grade (#8). Preparation: the classer's interpretation of fiber processability in terms of degree ofroughness or smoothness of ginned cotton.

Extraneous matter: all the material in the sample other than fiber and leaf. The degree of extraneous matter is determined by the classer either as "light‖ or "heavy". Neps: a small tangled fiber knot often caused by processing. Neps can be measured by a nep tester and reported as the total number of neps per 0.5 grams of the fiber and average size in millimeters. Nep formation reflects the mechanical processing stage, especially from the point of view of the quality and condition of the machinery used.

TYPES OF COTTONS

According to —the fabric tree.com‖ some of the types of available cottons are as follows:
Batiste - very fine, soft, usually sheer cottons, often used for handkerchiefs, nightwearand children's dresses.

Broadcloth - closely woven fabric. If you look closely, you'll see tiny crosswise ribs. Calico - plain woven cotton usually printed with tiny floral designs. Cambric - tightly woven cotton, usually in solid colors, such as cambric blue. Used in apparel, especially casual shirts.
Canvas - heavyweight cotton, used for items that require strength, such as tote bags, knapsacks, and slipcovers.
Chambray - finely woven cotton, usually with white and another color. The white is very subtle, used in the crosswise (warp) yarns. A chambray shirt,

for instance is usually pale blue, but if you look closely you will see the white yarn. Chino - popularized by the GAP! This is cotton twill that has been pre-shrunk andmercerized. Most often used for sports pants and other sports wear. Chintz - highly glazed cotton with a rich glossy finish. At Cranston, we call this"Cransheen finish." Chintz adds a decorator touch to home furnishings, and is also great for dressier apparel.

Corduroy - cotton pile that has been cut and woven with wide or narrow ribs.

Denim - the workhorse of cottons! Very strong and similar to Chambray, in that it isoften made with white filling.

Duck - another strong, durable cotton, used for projects that are meant to last, i.e. travel accessories, slipcovers, awnings, etc.

Flannel - very soft cotton, usually with a nap. Used often in baby wear. For childrenand baby apparel, make sure it is flame retardant.

Gabardine - can be cotton or wool. This is the twilled fabric that spans the seasons, and is often used in jackets, skirts and pants.

Gingham - yarn-dyed woven cotton, usually seen in the form of checks.

Khaki - strong cotton weave -used in uniforms and other items that require strength. Lawn - cotton lawn is a fine, crisp, combed cotton fabric, used in children's wear,night wear and traditional quilting.

Madras - originally from India. Real madras is hand-loomed and dyed with vegetabledyes. Patterns are usually stripes or plaids.

Muslin - very basic plain woven fabrics. Depending on the type, muslin can be coarseor fine, dyed or unbleached. The unbleached variety is often used for pattern making or test garments.

Percale - finely woven cotton, often used for sheets. The higher the thread count, the softer the hand.

Piqu - cotton that has been woven with a raised, cord or weld effect. Also calleddobby weave.

Poplin - usually heavier weight cotton that has a very fine rib running from selvedgeto selvedge.

Sateen - cotton that has been woven with a satin weave.

Seersucker - crinkly cotton fabric, most often used in summer sportswear.

Terry - woven on knitted cotton pile with loops on one or both sides. Because of itsabsorbency it is very often used for toweling.

Voile - crisp, sheer, lightweight cotton, used for formal wear.

APPLICATION OF COTTON

The Dictionary of American History 2003 says that the cotton plant is a source for many important products other than fabric. Among the most important is cottonseed, which is pressed for cottonseed oil that is used in commercial products such as salad oils and snack foods, cosmetics, soap, candles, detergents, and paint. The hulls and meal are used for animal feed. Cotton is also a source for cellulose products, fertilizer, fuel, automobile tire cord, pressed paper, and cardboard.

Kadolph (2011) states that the major end-uses of cotton include: Apparel - in a wide range of wearing apparel: blouses, shirts, dresses, children wear, active wear, separates, swimwear, suits, jackets, skirts, pants, sweaters, hosiery, neckwear. Home Fashion - curtains, draperies, bedspreads, comforters, throws sheets, towels, table cloths, table mats, napkins. Medical and cosmetic applications - bandages, wound plasters.

CARE OF HANDLING OF COTTON FABRIC

Kadolph suggests that white cotton articles should be washed in the washing machine at 60°C, whilst colored cloths, especially if dark, should be washed at lower temperatures. Normally it should be ironed on the right side. Dark articles should be first ironed on the inside and then on the outside, with a cloth, to avoid that the heat of the iron shine the cloth. White articles can be starched to give more consistency to the cloth and avoid it creasing easily.

CONCLUSION

Kadolph (2011) states that Cotton is a natural fiber many environmentally sensitive consumers believe it is a good choice. Although cotton is a renewable resource, it cannot be produced without some environmental impact. The chemicals used in the harvesting and manufacture of cotton destroy the ecosystem once they get in contact with soil and water. With the continued production of GM cotton we reduce the use of pesticides therefore reducing its impact on the environment.

CHAPTER TEN

DESIGN MATERIALS AND PROCESS

SILK

ABSTRACT

Silk is a natural protein fiber containing about 70-75% of actual fiber fibroin secreted from two salivary glands in the head of the silkworm larva, and about 25-30% sericin, a gum which cements the two filaments together. It has a high natural luster and sheen of a white or cream color and has a reputation as a luxurious and sensuous fabric, retains its shape, drapes well, caresses the figure, and shimmers with a luster all its own. Silk is naturally hypoallergenic, yet is still breathable; it absorbs moisture and reduces humidity, which makes it cool in the summer and warm in the winter. While silk is one of the strongest fibers, it can be weakened by perspiration, deodorants and sunlight. Silk is absorbent so it dyes easily, but some dye colors tend to bleed and fade in water and during stain removal procedures. This paper will explore the history properties manufacture and use of silk. No primary data was derived from this study.

INTRODUCTION

Silk is a natural protein fiber that is similar to wool in that it is composed of amino acids arranged in a polypeptide chain but has no cross links. It is produced by the larvae of a moth. It is universally accepted as a luxury fiber such that The International Silk Association of the United States emphasized this by the slogan —Only silk is silk‖. Silk has a combination of properties not possessed by any other fiber: it has a dry tactile hand, isunique in luster, and has good moisture absorption, lively suppleness and draping qualities and high strength. It is a solid fiber with a simple physical structure. (Kadolph 2011) According to Kadolph, the beauty and hand of silk and its high cost are probably responsible for the development of the manufactured fiber industry. It is the physical nature of silk that some manufactured fibers attempt to duplicate.

HISTORY OF SILK

According to Thinkquest.org (2012) The Chinese has used silk since the 27th century B.C. Silk is mentioned by Aristotle and became a valuable commodity both in Greece and Rome. During the Roman Empire, silk was sold for its weight in gold. The Chinese d omesticated silk worms and fed them with mulberry leaves. They unwound the silkworms' cocoons to produce long strands of silk fiber. Farm women in China at that period were supposed to raise such silkworms as one of their chores.

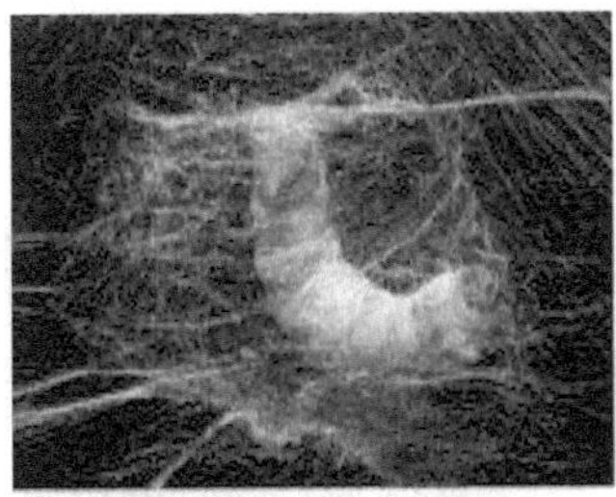

Figure 1: Silkworm spinning cocoon

Silk was used in China and exported along the Silk Road (the ancient trade route linking China and the Roman Empire). This trade brought China great wealth, but the Chinese did not give away the secret on how silk was formed. Christian monks finally broke China's monopoly of the silk production by smuggling silkworm eggs out of the country, and soon other countries started to produce their own silk.

Thompson (2004) states, Silk became an important textile product and luxury commodity in the Middle East from antiquity. Silk textiles came into the Middle East by trade from India and China while Indian and Arab merchants sailed the Indian Ocean. Chinese merchants sent the fine cloth along the famous 4,000 mile (6,400 km) Silk Road—through central Asia and northern Iran to Europe.

According to the article by Joanna Shaw (August 2004) Silk has been called the cloth of kings, yet it is born from a lowly worm. The "Secrets of Silk" exhibition at the Textile Museum showed how the tiny Bombyx mori silkworms make cocoons for their change from caterpillars to moths, and then produce two fine threads of silk from glands on either side of their heads. Astonishingly enough, the threads can be more than a mile long.

PRODUCTION OF SILK

According to Kadolph (2011), the production of cultivated silk is known as sericulture. It begins when the silk moth lays eggs on a specially prepared paper. When the eggs hatch, the caterpillars or larvae are fed fresh, young mulberry leaves. After about 35 days and four moltings, the silk worms are 10000 times heavier than when hatched and are ready for to begin spinning a cocoon (chrysalis case). A straw frame is placed on the tray and the silkworm starts to spin the cocoon by moving its head in a figure eight. The silkworm produces silk in two glands and forces the liquid silk through spinnerets opening its head. The two strands of silk are coated with water soluble protective gum sericin. When the silk comes in contact with the air it solidifies. In 2 or 3 days the silkworm will spin approximately 1mile of filament and will completely encase itself in a cocoon. The silkworm then metamorphoses into a moth. Usually the silkworm is killed (stifled) with heat before it reaches the moth stage.

Kadolph goes on to say that if the silkworm is allowed to reach the moth stage, it is used for breeding additional silkworms. The moth secretes a fluid that dissolves the silk at one end of the cocoon so that it can crawl out. These cocoons cannot be used for filament silk yarns and the staple silk produced from them is less supple.

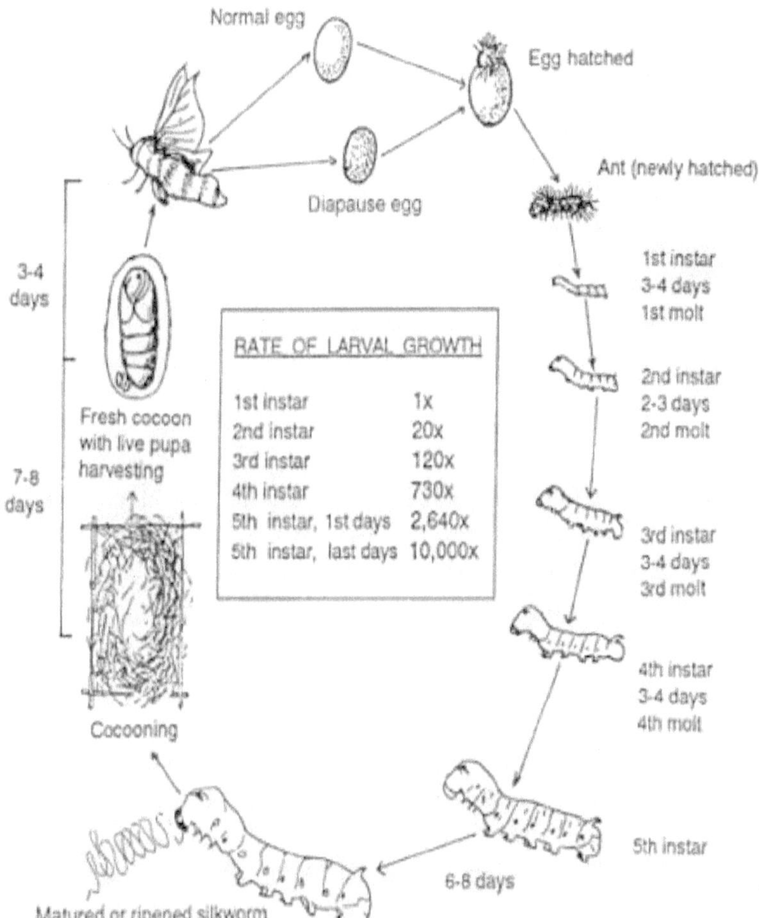

Figure 2: The Life cycle of a silkworm (below)

To obtain filament silk, the cocoons that have been stifled are sorted for fiber size, fiber quality and defects and thereafter brushed to find the outside ends of the filaments.

Figure 3: Silk cocoons

According to the National Sericulture Institute in Thika, Kenya, Several filaments are gathered together and wound into a reel. This process is called reeling. Each cocoon yields about 1000 yards of usable silk filament. This is the raw silk or silk in the gum. Several filaments are combined to form a yarn. Uniformly reeled filament silk is the most valuable. As the fibers are combined and wrapped onto the reel it can be twisted to hold the filaments together. This process is called throwing. The resulting yarn is called *thrownyarn*. The type of yarn and amount of twist determine the fabric produced. The simplestthrown yarn is a single which three to eight yarns are twisted together to form yarn. There are many kinds of natural silk which are commercially known and produced. Among them Mulberry silk is the most important and contributes as much as 95% of the world production. There are other two types of wild silkworm that produce silk in Kenya; Gonometa and Aphe.

According to the New Agriculturalist (2007) Pamela Onyango, a breeder of silkworms for the production of silk under ICIPE's guidance says she initially reared silkworms in her grass-thatched house, having learnt the skill of egg production from a silk farming group in Buseni, Uganda. To form the cocoon, she explains, silkworm larvae feed on mulberry leaves before climbing onto a twig placed nearby, where they spin their silken cocoons. The silk formed is a continuous-filament fiber. These single filaments are combined to form yarn, which is drawn under tension through several guides and wound onto reels.

Finally, the yarn is dried, and the raw silk is packed according to quality. Silkworm waste can be collected and used as manure for mulberry plants.

She adds that there is a high demand for silk. Silk fabrics are produced in several weights. Higher numbers describe heavier fabrics. They are graded for their degree of evenness, fiber or yarn size and freedom from defects. Grade A is the highest grade which amounts to only about 10percent of silk produced.

Mbahin, Raina, Kioko, and Mueke (2012) in their paper state that In Kenya, Kakamega forest is well known for the production of wild silk. It is a supplementary activity for income generation for communities that mainly depend on subsistence farming. It helps assist in the conservation of the wild silk moth and its habitat. PROPERTIES OF SILK

Kadoldph (2011) describes Silk is a solid fiber. That it is the only natural filament fiber and these fibers are very fine though wild silks are slightly coarser.

She states that aesthetically silk can be dyed and printed in different colors. It is adaptable to a variety of fabrication methods and is available in many fabric types for interior and apparel use. Its luster is soft with an occasional sparkle. This luster has been the model for many manufactured fibers. Silk fabrics have a smooth appearance and a luxurious hand. It is not slippery as many synthetic fabrics.

When it comes to durability, Kadolph states that silk is one of the strongest natural fibers. It is not as elastic as wool because there is no cross linkage to retract the molecular chains. Therefore when it is stretched even a small amount, it does not return to its original length but remains stretched. It may lose about 20 percent of its strength when wet. Silk has good absorbency and it may develop static cling because of the smoothness of the fibers and yarns and the fabric weight.

Silk products are comfortable as they are poor conductors of heat. Weight of a fabric is important in heat conductivity - sheer fabrics are cool whereas heavy fabrics are warm. Weighted silk is not as durable as regular silk and wrinkles more rapidly. Thinkquest.org (2012) states that Silk fibers do not shrink as its molecular chains are not easily distorted. It has moderate resistance to wrinkling. It swells a small amount when wet. Fabrics made from true crepe yarns shrink if laundered due to the yarn structure and not the fiber content. Dry cleaning solvents do not damage silk. Dry cleaning is normally recommended for silk items because of yarn types, dyes with poor fastness to water or fabric construction methods.

Pure dye silk should be ironed damp with a press cloth. Silk is resistant to dilute mineral acids and organic acids. It is weakened and yellowed by exposure to sunlight and perspiration. For this reason, interior textiles of silk should be protected from direct sunlight. Weighted silk will deteriorate even under ideal storage conditions. Historic items often exhibit a condition known as shattered silk which is not reversible.

TYPES OS SILK

According to the article on MCOT online news (2011) Japan is known for its high quality silks. India produces hand woven wild silks with a pronounced texture. Thailand's hand woven iridescent silks are created by using two yarn colors in weaving the fabric. Over 30 countries produce silk therefore there is a wide range of silk qualities and types in the market.

Silk noels (silk waste) is staple silk produced from cocoons whose filament broke or themoth was allowed to mature and come out. It comes from the inner part of the cocoon. It is degummed and spun into a yarn like any other staple fiber. It can be blended with another fiber and spun into a yarn. It is less expensive, less durable, more likely to pill and is of low quality than filament silk.

Duping silk results when two silkworms spin their cocoons together. The yarn is irregularin diameter with a thick and thin appearance. It is used in linen like silk fabrics as shantung.

Wild silk production is not controlled. The silkworms feed on oak and cherry leaves inthe wild and produce fibers that are much less uniform in texture and are most often brown in color. Yellow, orange and green also occur. Researchers are investigating the feasibility of producing fabrics from these naturally colored silks. Tussah silk is the most common type of wild silk. It is coarser, darker and cannot be bleached. It cannot be found in white or light colors. The term raw silk is sometimes used incorrectly to describe these fabrics. Pure silk and pure dye silk describe 100 percent silk fabrics that do not contain any metallic weighting compounds.

APPLICATION OF SILK

Silk has a drape, luster and texture that may be imitated by synthetic fibers but cannot be duplicated exactly. Because of its unique properties and high cost, it is used primarily in clothing and interior products. It is extremely versatile hence can be used to create a variety of fabrics as sheer, brocades and velvet. Because of its absorbency, it is appropriate for warm weather wear and active sportswear. It is also appropriate for cold weather wear due to its low heat conductivity in form of underwear, socks and leggings. Silk blends are important in interior textiles for use in upholstery, wall covering fabrics and wall hangings because of their soft luster and drape. Occasionally expensive handmade rugs are made from silk. Bed sheets of silk feel warm, soft and luxurious next to the skin. The texture and drape of wild and duping silks make them ideal for covering ceilings and walls. Silk is also used in the medical field for sutures and prosthetic arteries and iron based scaffolds and grafts. The scaffold provides support for regenerating ligaments, tendons and other bodily connective tissues. It has been successful in restoring full functionality following some injuries.

As its special properties, silk protein has been used in many beauty and skin care products such as solid soap, liquid soap, water spray, and moisturising cream. Incomes from selling these products, which are available in Mahasarakham University in Thailand, will support further studies related to growing mulberry for raising silkworms instead of depending on budgets allocated from the government. The developed technology and knowledge could be passed on to communities to add value to silk farmers' products. In addition to beauty products, the centre also produces silk products for health applications; for example, mulberry tea and crispy rice snacks made from silkworms. This is stated by the MCOT online news (2011)

Spider silk produced by some species of spider can be magnetized, conducts electricityand is stable to high temperatures. This is because they are exceptionally strong, elastic and are lightweight. It is difficult to produce quantities of this spider silk for research because spiders are territorial and they kill each other before spinning much silk. Spider farms are not possible. Possible applications of this silk would include civil engineering, road construction, protective clothing and bone and tendon repair in the medical field.

SUSTAINABILITY AND ENVIRONMENTAL CONCERNS OF SILK

Kadolph (2011) states, that Silk is a natural fiber and renewable resource. Sericulture uses leaves of the mulberry tree. These trees grow in regions where the soil may be too poor to grow other crops or in small and irregular places. The trees help retain soil and contribute to the income of small farms. Since the mulberry tree is deciduous, leaves are only available for part of the year hence silk production is limited to one generation each year.
Silkworms are susceptible to disease and changes in temperature. Research is being undertaken to produce disease resistant varieties and induce an all year round production by controlling internal environments. Some animal rights activists avoid purchasing or using silk products. This is because silk worms are killed before they have matured in order to harvest the filament.

Figure 4: Spider silk
The alternative is to use wild silk which is harvested after the moth leaves the cocoon. This silk is lower in quality. Silk production makes extensive use of water and other chemicals to clean the fiber and remove sericin. The waste is discharged into the ground water system without any treatment.
Environmental regulations are minimal in some parts of the world and disposal of chemicals is done with little regard for the environment. Although not all silk products require dry cleaning, many do Dry cleaning solvents may harm the environment and their use and their use and disposal are restricted.
Silk production is concentrated in areas where cost of production is low.
When the world prices of silk drop, these regions suffer. Child labor may also

be used in producing silk as it is labor intensive. Mechanizing this production may affect the regions that have relied on hand labor to produce it.

CONCLUSION

Sericulture is an ancient science, and the modern age has not brought great changes to silk manufacture. Rather, man-made fibers such as polyester, nylon, and acetate have replaced silk in many instances. But many of the qualities of silk cannot be reproduced. For example, silk is stronger than an equivalent strand of steel. Some recent research has focused on the molecular structure of silk as it emerges from the silkworm, in order to better understand how new, stronger artificial fibers might be constructed. Silk spun by the silkworm starts out as a liquid secretion. The liquid passes through a brief interim state with a semi-ordered molecular structure known as nematic liquid crystal, before it solidifies into a fiber. Materials scientists have been able to manufacture durable fibers using liquid crystal source material, but only at high temperatures or under extreme pressure. Researchers are continuing to study the silkworm to determine how liquid crystal is transformed into fiber at ordinary

temperatures and pressures (Avizienis, A. 1996).

CHAPTER ELEVEN
DESIGN MATERIALS AND PROCESS

TIMBER

ABSTRACT

Materials have played an important part in our civilization both political and cultural. Eras have been named after important materials. Human civilizations would not have advanced without such materials as wood, ceramics glass and iron. Materials are chosen either pragmatically for their utility and availability or formally for their appearance and ornamental properties. Decisions about building and architecture continue to determine material choice. Today, materials are part of a design palette from which compositional and visual surfaces are created. This paper seeks to explore the

History, Properties, Quantities, Sources and Application of Timber as a Design material.

INTRODUCTION

According to Desch (1973) Timber is arguably the original building material and retains importance especially in the construction industry. This is because of its versatility, diversity and aesthetic properties. There are hundreds of available timber species which vary widely in their properties and their appearance. Within any one species there is often a wide variation between trees growing in different climatic conditions and on different soils, and between parts of trees. Their variability presents problems in economic conversion and utilization. Increased knowledge of properties of timber has improved its performance and manipulation. This has caused timber to continue to satisfy requirements and performance in a wide range of uses as a structural material, component and decorative material. Despite its complex chemical nature, timber has excellent properties which lend themselves to human use. It is readily available, economic and amendable to fabrication into an infinite variety of sizes and shapes.

According to Lyons (1997) Selection of timber depends upon factors such as strength, moisture movement and dimensional stability. The availability of species, sizes and sections varies widely from place to place and time to time. Natural durability and ease of preservation, together with appearance are other factors to consider. Environmental issues raised by the current and future demands for timber can be resolved only by sustainable forest developments.

ANATOMY OF TIMBER

Lyons (1997) describes the tree as a complex living organism that can be considered in three main sections: the branches with their leaves, the trunk and the roots. The characteristic that separates trees from other plants is that they have a single main stem and a trunk (or bole). The timber user is interested primarily in the trunk. The trunk has an outer covering that protects the wood from extremes of temperature, drought and mechanical injury (bark). It grows outwards around a leading shoot by adding new rings of timber. Usually one ring is added each year (growth ring)

Richardson (1993) states, the more rapid the growth, the wider the growth rings. When comparing species, the wider the *growth ring*, the less dense and strong the timber. In fast grown softwoods the wood is generally of low density and inferior quality. Whereas in fast grown hardwoods the wood tends to have a high density and superior quality. According to Desch (1973)The food conduction and storage functions of trees are fulfilled by the outer, more newly grown layers of cells referred to as *sapwood*,while the inner layers are known as the *heartwood*.The rings consist of minute tabular or fibrous *cells* tightly cemented together and each ring has two parts: *early wood* (spring wood)and the *late wood*(summer wood) - it grows slowly and is often denser, darker and narrower than the early wood.

Figure 1: Growth rings

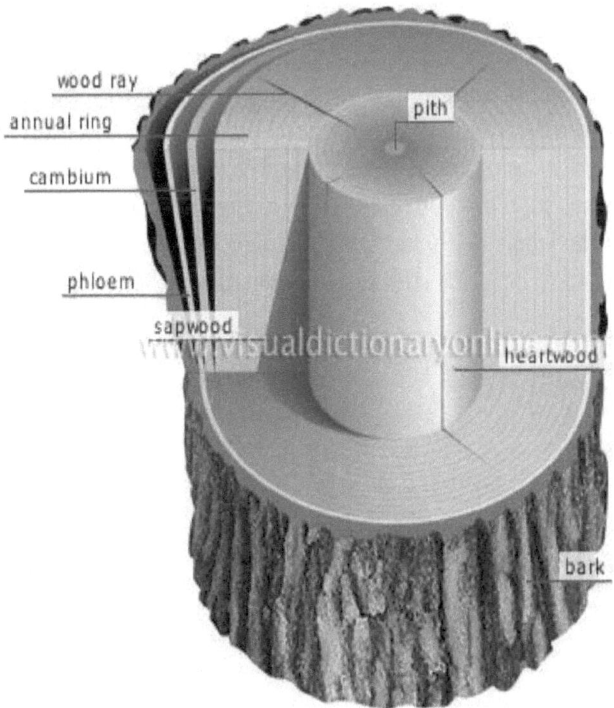

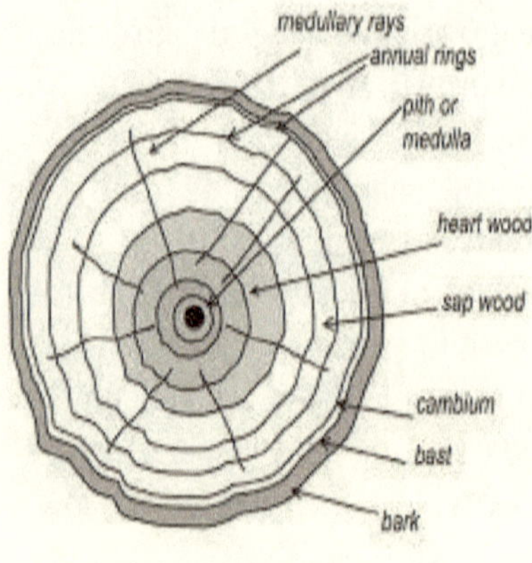

Figure 2: Cross section of a tree.

Timbers in which early wood contains larger pores than the late wood are called *ringporous* and those which the pores are equal in size in both zones are called *diffuse porous.*As most trees mature, for each new ring which is added forming a band of *sapwood*, reserve materials such as starch are extracted from an inner ring and aheartwood core is formed. In most species, sapwood is lighter in color and is more attractive to fungi and certain insects. Desch continues to state that the *grain*refers to the general direction or arrangement of the fibers and other wood elements (or cells), but it can sometimes be used to describe structural or ornamental features of timber.

Figure 3: Transverse sections showing full sets of rings (Above)

CLASSIFICATION OF TIMBER

Desch (1973) states, some trees belong to more primitive plant types than others, giving rise to different classes of commercial timber. Commercial timbers fall into two main groups, the softwoods and the hardwoods, and the trees that produce these different classed of timber are themselves quite distinct.

HARDWOODS AND SOFTWOODS

These are biological terms which do not always relate to hardness. Not all hardwoods are hard. (Balsa is very soft.)
Hardwoods

Taylor (2000) describes these as *angiosperms*and are from broad leaved trees which are mostly deciduous although others are evergreen as the oak trees. They have a more complex cell structure than softwoods and grow much slower. They are the densest and most durable timbers. Some contain resin and /or oils which interfere with hardening of paints as teak. Their cost varies with species, quality, availability and dimensions. Narrow and short stock costs less while extra long lengths and in some species wide boards are more costly. Hardwoods grow in temperate climates such as UK and shed their leaves in winter. They may be used where durability is beneficial as window sills and doors or in high quality joinery.
Softwoods

Taylor (2000) states, that softwood are known as *gymnosperms*and are not all soft. Some softwood is very hard. They are all derived from coniferous trees which are mainly evergreen. They grow relatively quickly hence their wood is generally soft, of low density and easy to work on. They are more economical than hardwoods though less durable. They are the more widely used woods for general structural purposes. They include pines (redwood), firs and spruces (cedar and cypress) Cedar wood contains natural resins which make it unattractive to fungi and insects therefore it has very good durability.

PROPERTIES OF TIMBERS

Density

According to Everett (1970) Density is the mass of unit volume. Found by dividing the weight by the volume. The heaviest wood is found at the base of the tree and it gradually decreases in density in samples from successively higher levels in the trunk. The weight of wood tissue is about the same for all species.

Thermal Insulation

Desch (1973) states, that timber is a good insulator. In many situations the ability of a substance to resist the passage of heat, electricity and sound is of great importance. Dry wood is one of the poorest conductors of heat. The reaction of timber to heat has as important bearing on its suitability as a fire resistant material. Wooden doors are often effective in preventing the spread of a fire for a considerable period.

Acoustic Properties

According to Desch (1973), acoustic properties are important in musical instruments and in building construction. Wood, whose elasticity is destroyed by fungal decay, will give a dull sound when tapped, in contrast to the clear ring of sound wood. The cellular nature of wood is such that when wood is fixed it does not easily vibrate. For this reason wood is valued as a flooring and paving material.

Behavior in fire and the energy value of wood.

Desch (1973), states that moisture in timber absorbs some heat but it is easily ignited at about 220 to 300 degrees centigrade. Treatment with flame retardant chemicals, by impregnation or by surface coatings, reduces the rate of spread of flame but timber will carbonize if untreated. Charcoal is wood fuel in an alternative form. It has higher fuel value than ordinary wood. Its advantage is mostly economic. Wood and charcoal can be used as a source of producer gas for internal combustion engines.

Chemical resistance

Everett (1970), states that compared to metals, wood has a good resistance to alkali and weak acids. Inorganic salts from the soil or damp masonry probably pay a minor role in the decomposition of wood. Wood darkens when exposed to light and suffers photo degradation mainly due to visible wavelengths in sunlight.

Strength

Lyons (1997) states that timber has a high strength weight ratio in tension and compression and is elastic. It is able to sustain greater loads for a short while than it can over long periods. Its strength increases with density, particularly within species. Strength reduces as moisture content rises. Different parts of a tree have different strengths. This strength is reduced by the particular defects contained in each piece of timber. Direction of the grain also affects the strength. All forms of warping reduce its strength.

EFFECTS OF MOISTURE IN TIMBER

According to Richardson (1993) the properties of wood are profoundly influenced by the presence of water. Drying timber from green (freshly felled wood) to the normal seasoned condition reduces its density, consequently shrinking and increasing its strength properties, thermal insulation, resistance to decay and suitability for impregnation, painting and gluing. Unless it is hermetically sealed on all sides, timber acquires high moisture content when part of it is in contact with water or damp material. Being hygroscopic, it takes in or gives off moisture vapor until it reaches equilibrium with the humidity of the surrounding atmosphere.

Movements

Richardson (1993) continues to state that timber shrinks when it is dried. This process can be reversed by re-wetting it. The swelling or shrinkage with changes in moisture content is known as movement. Moisture movements occur when there is variation in size in response to moisture changes as a result from changes in atmospheric humidity or direct wetting. In the longitudinal direction the movement is generally very low. The movement between the radial and tangential direction can be largely attributed to the fact that early or springwood shrinks less.
Stresssetting is when the movement of timber is restrained by compression or tension.

Itbecomes set in sizes which are permanent for the particular combination of atmospheric humidity and temperature prevailing at the time of stress setting.

*Dis tortions*can occur from the application of external forces during shrinkage as timberdoes not shrink equally in all directions when it dries. The distortions become aggravated by defects such as knots or wood reactions. They include cupping, spring and bow, twist, end split and compression failure.

Fiber saturation point

This refers to the variation in moisture content that is attributed to the chemical structure of wood. The loss of bound water reduces the separation between adjacent cellulose chains which causes shrinkage as well as progressive changes in the physical properties. (Richardson 1993)

Seasoning

Taylor (2000) describes this is the controlled reduction of the moisture content of timber to a level appropriate to its end use. Correctly seasoned timber should not be subject to further significant movement once in service unless a leak has occurred. It is also immune to fungal attack, is stronger and has low density therefore easier to transport or handle. It is also easier to work, glue, paint or preserve than wet timber. Seasoning does not confer immunity from subsequent infection of the timber should there be prolonged exposure to damp conditions. Some insects thrive in green timber and are eradicated by this process as the wood dries out. The methods below are as explained by Desch (1973).

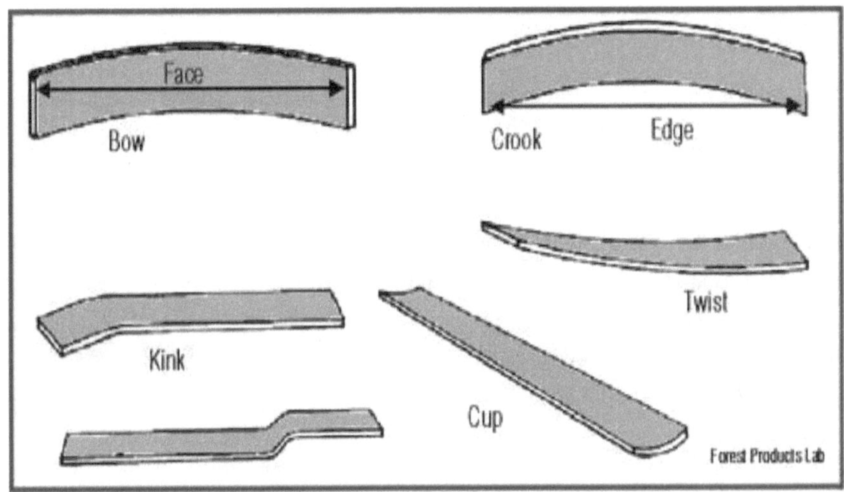

Fig 4: Distortion of timber

Air seasoning: - This is a natural process. Timber is protected from rain and the groundand stacked so that air can circulate freely around all surfaces and so that the

risks of degrade and of attack by fungi and insects are minimized.

Kiln seasoning: - Artificial means are used to achieve moisture contents needed forjoinery and furniture in modern buildings. This may follow air seasoning. It involves adherence to a precise schedule of humidity and temperatures, achieving a

moisture content without significant degrade.

Wa terseasoning: - Logs are kept under water to preserve them from attack by fungi andinsects. Ring porous hardwoods are sometimes immersed in running water to wash out the sap which is attractive to Lyctus beetles.

DEFECTS FOUND IN TIMBER

Everett (1970) states that these are features which develop in the living tree or soon after it is felled, which may detract from the usefulness of the timber. Conversion effects, Seasoning defects and deterioration defects occur thereafter.

Other defects which occur at later stages as described by Everett are:

*Brittle hear t (soft-pith, soft and spongy or punky heart)*is found at the centre of manytropical trees. It can be detected by raising the grain with the pint of a knife. It should be avoided where strength is of importance

Sapwood is more attractive to insects than heart wood. It is usually considered to spoilthe appearance of unpainted joinery. It is discolored by fungi.
Wide growth rings indicate rapid growth resulting in thin walled fibers or smallerportions of the denser latewood.

React ion wood has the effect of throwing the heart off centre, bending the trunk orbranches. *Upsets*are fibers that have been damaged by shock or crushing during growth or felling.

*Fissures*include checks, splits shakes and resin pockets.

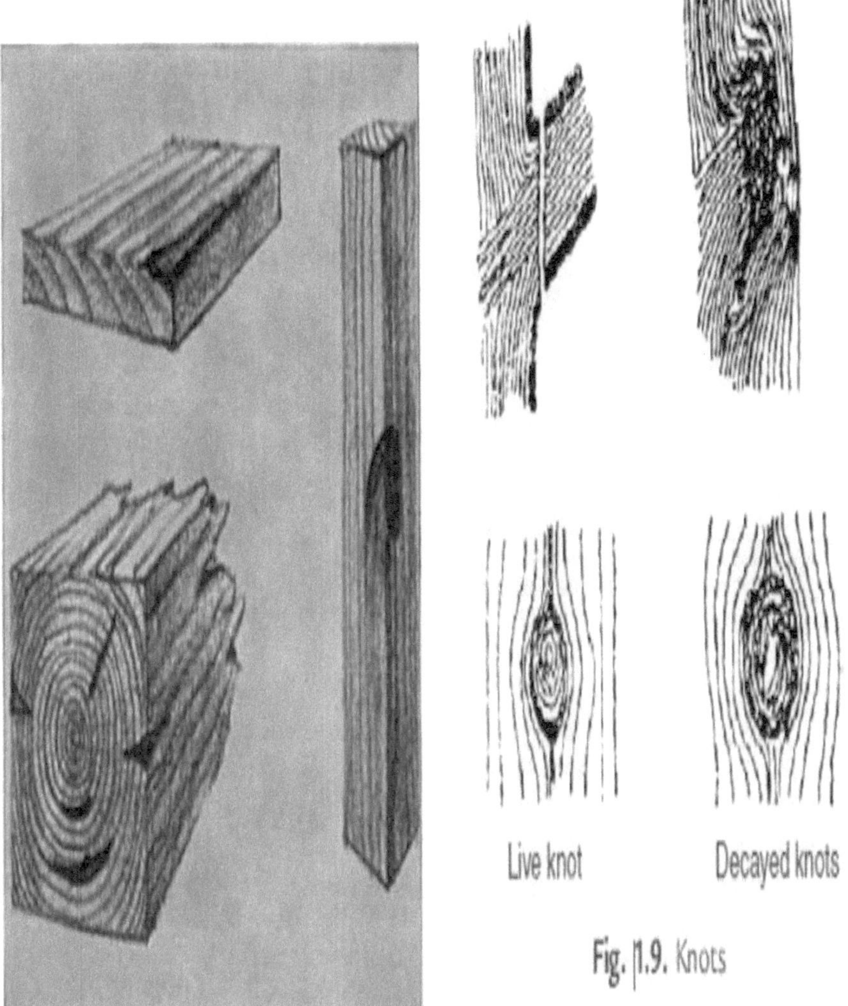

Figure 5 & Figure 6: Common timber defects. *Knots* are the part of the branch which became enclosed in a growing tree.
Fungal decay at its early stages, it shows as whitish streaks or patches.

Insect damage -Occasional exit holes of pin bores are not generally regarded as defects in structural timber and are accepted in joinery which is to be painted or which is out of sight.(For painted joinery, it is often economical to remove defects such as dead knots and resin pockets and to replace with plugs or patches.)

DURABILITY OF TIMBER

Taylor (2000), states that timber has remarkably good resistance to deterioration by atmospheric exposure. It is virtually unaffected by rain, frost, and acids which damage other types of materials. The main mechanisms of deterioration in wood other than during seasoning, involve it being used as food by fungi and by insects. These digest the cellulose fibers converting them to food.
In favorable conditions, timber remains in good conditions indefinitely. The major causes of deterioration of timber as explained by Everett (1970) are:

Weathering is the result of effect from exposure of timber externally such as loss of color.
Other effects include change of color caused by algae, moulds and chemical fumes. Another effect is cracks resulting from constant wetting and drying. Fungi are simple plants without leaves or flowers consume ready-made organic matter.
As they increase they leave white matrix on the wood, causing mould and stain.

Fire -Timber is combustible. Its surfaces char in fire. The timber beneath the charred layer does not lose significant strength. Timber has low thermal conductivity which, combined with the protection from the charred surface material, insulated the interior from rapid rise in temperature and loss of strength.

Insect - damage from beetles which during their larval stage bore through timber mainly within sapwood. This causes loss of mechanical strength.
CONVERSION OF TIMBER

Richardson (1976) describes this as the cutting of logs into sawn wood before seasoning it. The manner in which logs are sawn is usually considered to be relatively unimportant. Re-sawing and reshaping after conversion is called manufacture. He describes the basic methods of cutting as:
Sawing: This depends on the direction of the growth of rings. Peeling: For producing piles for plywood.
Slicing: Of thin decorative veneers.
Cleaving/Splitting: As used before development of tempered steel saws.

DISTORTION OF TIMBER (CONVERSION DEFECTS)

Everett (1970) gives the following examples of the different types of distortions found in timber and their causes:

Sloping grain occurs because of the cone like form of the tree. A slope occurs relative tothe surface of the converted timber and contour markings on a flat sawn board.

Wane is the loss of the square edge of the cut timber owing to the incorporation of thebark or curved surface of the trunk. A degree of wane is acceptable in structural and floor timbers.

Raised grain is when the early wood bands recover and raise the latewood bands abovethe surface after the late wood bands were forced into the early wood bands during conversion, in plain sawn boards.

PRESERVATION OF TIMBER

There are three classes of wood preservatives according to Desch (1973)They are Taroil group of wood preservatives (derived from coal or wood), Water soluble salts (Zinc chloride, Sodium fluoride and magnesium silicofluoride) and Organic solvent wood preservatives(Refined paraffin and other petroleum products.). Volatile substances, fumigants and sterilization are other methods of preserving wood.

Timber is treated with toxic chemicals to protect it from attack by both fungi and insects (insecticides and fungicides). Success in preservation depends on the timber species, the size and condition of the specimen and the resulting depth of penetration and the amount which is retained. Processes vary from superficial treatments of limited protective value, to pressure impregnation. Lyons (1997) lists some as: Brush and spray (liquid is flooded on the surface to absorb as much as possible.) Deluging, dipping and steeping (using organic solvents),Hot and cold open tank method, Pressure impregnation, Diffusion process, Plug inserts and Injection (drilling holes in intervals.)

TIMBER PRODUCTS

Richardson (1976), states that a wide range of products is manufactured from wood material. Physical properties of the products reflect a combination of the subdivision of the wood. Many building products are manufactured from small timber sections or by products that would be otherwise wasted. The product range includes but is not limited to plywood, fiberboard and particle board. They are described below.

Plywood

This may be sliced for decorative end uses or peeled. It consists of cementing or fastening together a number of sheets with the grain of the successive pieces. Some may run clockwise others diversely. The crossing of the wood gives it strength, protects it against splitting and preserves it from liability to expansion or contraction. Figure 7 & 8: Normal plywood (left- below) and Hardwood plywood (right- below)

Particle board (Hardboard)
The bulk of it is wood but wool or hemp shives are also used. Five types of hardboard re recognized:

Fig: 9 General purpose hardboard (above) Figure 10: Interior –structural hardboard

Figure: 11 Interior – non- structural (above) Figure: 12 Exterior – structural (above)

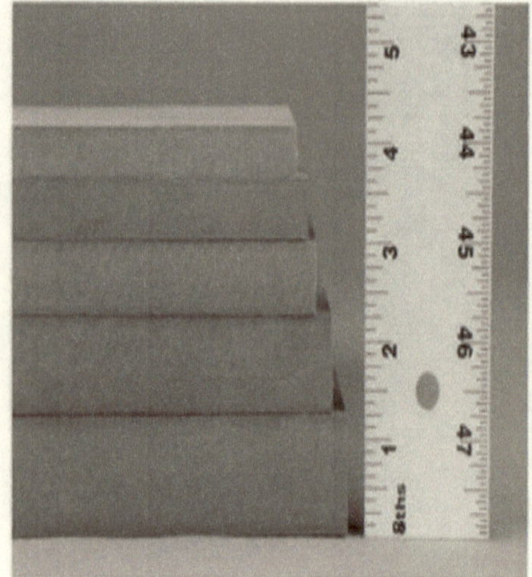

Figure 13: Exterior – non- structural hardboard (below).
Fiber building boards
There are two broad distinctions and they are manufactured from pulped wood: Soft boards (below) Insulation boards (below).
Figure 14: Reinforced gypsum board wood Figure 15: Fireproof building board
Heavier hardboard also exists, which are subdivided into medium, standard and tempered hardboards.
CONCLUSION

According to Africa speaks.com, through improved protection and management of the remaining forests, through well-targeted socioeconomic development programs, and through policy and institutional reforms, deforestation can be brought under control. The technologies and approaches needed to implement policies are known. All people need to renew their commitment to live in harmony with the environment through sustainable development.

CHAPTER TWELVE

DESIGN MATERIALS AND PROCESS

WOOL

ABSTRACT

Wool is a natural fiber made from the fleece of sheep. Talk about wool and it
conjures up a picture of cozy warmth. However, wool is not uniform among
all sheep. Sheep live in a wide variety of climates and conditions, and
develop their wool to suit the conditions under which they live or are bred.
Today there are different grades of wool for different uses. There are coarse
wools for carpets, soft fine wools for undergarments, highly crimped wools
for bulky woolen yarns, wools with very long fibers for strong fine worsted.
This paper will explore the history, production, characteristics and uses of
wool as a material.

INTRODUCTION

Yates (2002), states that the most prevalent protein fiber is the fleece of
sheep. Various breeds of sheep are domesticated and bred for the qualities of
their wool and ability to thrive in specific geographic regions. The natural
crimp or waviness of the wool fiber, its roundness and the scale like quality
of its outer layer make wool beautifully springy, loft and resilient. It naturally
regains its shape making it maintain any finish applied to it during
manufacturing, without accepting wrinkles or creases created by normal use.
According to Hallet and Johnston 2010, wool can be satisfyingly soft, warm,
cozy and sensuous or rugged, tough and functional, while its inherent
drapability allows its finest fibers to appear lustrous, sleek and elegant.

HISTORY OF WOOL

Hallet and Johnston 2010 have stated that our relationship with this fiber is
almost as old as civilization itself. Wool's unique thermally responsive and
insulating qualities remain as relevant today as at any time in history. The use
of felted wool can be traced as far back tens of thousands of years. With
inspiration from the way fleece appears naturally on the back of an animal,
primitive cultures worldwide developed process of wetting, massaging and
pressing wool to produce dense, matted felt (blanket) that could be cut or
manipulated into varying thickness or molded into shape.

Figure 1: Sheep grazing

According to Fiber Facts (2012), Wool was probably the first animal fiber to be made into cloth. The art of spinning wool into yarn developed about 4000 B.C. and encouraged trade among the nations in the region of the Mediterranean Sea. The first wool factory in England was established in 50 A.D. in Winchester by the Romans. It is believed that the Romans invented the carding process to brush, tease and comb the fibers into alignment for a smoother spinning and weaving of the yarn. It is also believed that they started the selective breeding of sheep to provide better and finer qualities of wool. In 1797, the British brought 13 Merino sheep to Australia and started the country's Merino sheep industry. There are 40 different breeds of sheep in the world producing a rough estimate of 200 types of wool with varying standards. The major wool producers in the world are Australia, Argentina, China and South Africa.

Kadolph (2011) stated that wool was one of the more widely used textile fibers before the Industrial Revolution. Sheep were probably among the first animals to be domesticated. Because of the initial high cost of wool products, many consumers consider them to be investments. These factors have encouraged the substitution of acrylic, polyester or wool/synthetic blends in many products.

MANUFACTURING PROCESS

According to Hallett and Johnston 2010, sixty percent of all global wool is destined for the clothing market. Australia is the largest producer of wool by far with majority from Merino breeds. New Zealand is the second largest producer mainly from cross bred varieties.

Shearing

Kadolph (2011) states, that Merino Sheep produce the most valuable wool. Good quality fleece weigh 15 to 20 pounds each. Merino wool is 3 to 5 inches long and very fine. It is used to produce high quality long wearing products with a soft hand and luster and good drape. Sheep are generally sheared once a year. The fleece is with power shears that look like barber shears. A good shearer can handle 100 to 220 sheep a day. The fleece is removed in one long piece with smooth strokes beginning at the legs and belly. After shearing, the fleece is folded together and bagged to be shipped to the market.

Kadolph continues to state that an alternative to shearing has been developed
where both a chemical feed and injection is fed to the sheep. When digested,
the feed additive makes the wool brittle and several weeks later the wool can
be pulled off the sheep. The injection causes the sheep to shed the fleece a
week or so later. Both alternatives decrease shearing costs. Newly removed
wool is known as raw wool or grease wool. It contains impurities as sand,
dust, grease, and dried sweat. When removed, clean or scoured wool is
produced. The grease is purified to lanolin and is used in creams cosmetics,
soaps and ointments.

Wool classes

Prior to spinning, wool is separated and graded to different categories known
as wool classes. Kadolph says the following about *Grading*and *Sorting*wools
of the same character together. Grading evaluates the whole fleece for
fineness and length while in sorting a single fleece is separated into sections
of fibers of different quality. The best wool comes from the sides, shoulders
and back while the lower legs have the poorest. The quality of the wool
determines its use. Fine wool works well as a worsted fabric while coarse
wool is good for carpets. Hallet and Johnston 2010 say that the diameter of
the fabric is measured in microns. This determines the classification category.
Anything under 25 microns is used for light clothing. Medium grades are
used for heavier outwear and coarse grades for rugs. Finesse, crimp, fiber
length cleanliness and color are other key ingredients of considered. This also
depends on the breed of sheep and the end purpose of the wool. Wool is
blended with less expensive fibers to reduce the cost of the fabric or extend
its use.
Some terms of wool as explained by Gale and Kaur (2004) are:

She ared wool: removed from live sheep,
Pulled wool: taken from pelts of meat-type sheep.
Recycledwool: recovered from worn apparel and cutters' scraps.

Lamb'swool : from animals less than 7 months old. (It is finer and softer and
has onlyone cut end. It is normally labeled as such.)
Virginwool: wool that has never been processed. (Using the single term wool

implies
itis a virgin wool.)
Reprocessed wool: The unused scrap fiber and fabric accumulated during
themanufacturing process.

Re cycledwool: recycled from used wool fabrics.
Felting: Wool produced from wool fibers that are not woven or even spun
into yarn. (The matted fibers are wet out and then dried, flattened and pressed
into a uniform thickness).

Carding,combinganddrawing

Yates (2004) states that until wool had been scoured and cleaned it is called
grease wool. Scouring removes the grease and debris from the wool prior to
spinning. Scoured wool is usually about 70 percent of the weight of grease
wool. *Carding*(the fibers are passed through a series of metal teeth that
straighten and blend them into slivers and removes residual dirt and other
matter left in the fibers) *combing*and

drawing, (the sleeker slivers are compacted and thinned) are what form the
spinning process which includes spinning itself. These are carried out in a
spinning mill.

According to Yates, wool like all staple fibers has variations in length and
fiber quality. The short staple wool when carded and spun is called *woolen*.
Tweed fabrics, flannel and melton are typical woolen fabrics. Longer staple
wool which yields softer a grade is combed after carding and spun on
different equipment then piled to yield *worsted* yarns. Suiting, gabardine and
sateen are some examples of worsted yarns.

Hallet and Johnston (2010), state that Drawing and finisher drawing may be
applied to woolens and worsteds to further improve the evenness and
regularity of the yarn prior to final spinning. Woolen spun yarns go through
condensers to separate the multiple sheets of fiber into predetermined weight
strands. *Wool yarncount*refers to the number of hanks of yarn that is possible
to spin from one pound of clean wool. The finer the count, the more wool it is
possible to obtain from one pound. The number of hanks produced gives the
wool count. The finer the wool count the finer the fabric is to the touch. E.g.

Super 120's fabric is woven from finer yarns than super 110's fabric.

Spinning

Figure 2: Wool spinning into yarn

The final stage of the spinning process is the application of twist to the yarn, giving it greater tensile strength and added flexibility in preparation for the subsequent knitting or weaving processes.

Figure 3: Wool yarn
Hallet and Johnston (2010) state that adding a twist achieves many effects as
does twisting several colors or shades of a color together. Twisting a Lurex
yarn with a traditional yarn gives it an element of shimmer that takes a
traditional woolen or worsted fabric into another dimension. Once the yarns
have been spun they are ready either to be knitted or woven into fabric.

Weav ing
The Columbia Encyclopedia, 6th ed. (2012) states that the wool yarn is
woven into fabric. Wool manufacturers use two basic weaves: the *plain*weave
and the *twill* Woolen yarns are made into fabric using a plain weave which
produces a fabric of a somewhat looser weave and a soft surface with little or
no luster. The napping often conceals flaws in construction. Worsted yarns
can create fine fabrics with exquisite patterns using a twill weave. The result
is a more tightly woven, smooth fabric. Better constructed, worsteds are more
durable than woolens and therefore more costly.

Figure 4: Woven yarn
Finishing
The Columbia Encyclopedia continues to state that after weaving, both
worsteds and woolens undergo a series of finishing procedures as follows:
fulling(immersing the fabric in water to make the fibers interlock), crabbing
(permanently setting the interlock), *decating* (shrink-proofing) and
occasionally, *dyeing*. Although wool fibers can be dyedbefore the carding

process, dyeing can also be done after the wool has been woven into fabric.

SOURCES OF WOOL

Hallet and Johnston (2010) state that sheep breeds are classified in three main groups as follows: Exotic wool sheep, Fine wool sheep e.g. Merino. Indigenous hair sheep as Thin tailed ,Fat tailed e.g. Maasai sheep (Red Masai) and Fat rumped e.g. Blackhead Persian, Somali sheep

Merino

Merino originated from Africa but was developed in Spain then spread to other parts of the world. It is important for fine wool production in range areas because of their hardiness, excellent flocking instinct and efficiency in utilization of low quality forage.

Figure 5: Merino sheep (above)

Although pure breeding of the merino is still done, cross breeds with dorpers and hampshires produce offspring with fast growth rates and quality mutton. The offspring are ready for the market in 5 – 6 months.

Southdown

These are the smallest and oldest of the medium breeds. They provide quality wool and provide fat lamb. They have a fast growth rate and can afford to lamb at weaning. They are also highly prolific with about 125 – 150% lambing rate. But the very small body size limits the final weight of fat lambs and the fleece produced is light. Because of their size cross breeding is not encouraged and the breed is dying in Kenya.

Figure 6: Southdown sheep

Dorper

The dorper breed was developed from a cross between black head Persian and Dorset Horn. By 1950 the first consignment of Dorper had arrived in Katumani Research Station. Rams were sold to Eastern Province.

Figure 7: Dorper Sheep
This is an improved hair sheep and it is important for mutton in marginal areas. They are hardy and produce quality meat. They have a faster growth rate and fertility compared to the indigenous. One limitations of the breed is the deposition of too much subcutaneous fat. The Red Masai is also an improved hair sheep used to cross breed with the Dorper.

RedMasai
This breed is popular in south west Kenya and north Tanzania. They are important for mutton in marginal areas because they are hardy. The coat color is distinguished.

These are good milkers and have high fertility. The size has large variations. Areas that need improvements in crossbreeding are size, fertility, fat distribution from the tail and behind the neck and growth rate.

Figure 8: Red maasai sheep

Somalish eep
Somali sheep are fat ramped mainly found in Somali, North Eastern Province of Kenya and Sudan. They are hardy; the skin quality is higher than other indigenous hair sheep and is important for mutton production.

Figure 9: Somali sheep
SPECIALITY WOOLS

According to fiber facts (2010), different breeds of sheep produce wools with different characteristics but the fiber is simply identified as wool. Luxury wools are considered to have special more desirable attributes than standard wool varieties. They include lamb's wool, merino, Shetland wool, Icelandic wool (double layered) and Karaul wool (from Persian lamb) and Rambouillet (French merino).The term wool legally includes fiber from animals as sheep, angora, cashmere goats, camel, alpaca, llama and vicuna. Fiber facts (2010) describe these specialty wools as follows:

Mohai r is made from the hairs of the Angora goat. It is durable, warm, extremelylightweight, and lustrous with a soft hand. It is the most resilient natural textile fiber, and is often combined with other fibers in the production of apparel and home fashion items. The finest grade of mohair is Kid Mohair, obtained from the first shearing of a young angora goat. Kid Mohair possesses the unique feature of natural wicking properties that takes perspiration away from the skin, preventing bacterial build up and odor.

Figure 10: Mohair

Angora

There are two types of Angora. One from goat hair, the other is from rabbit hair. When talking about Angora, it is usually describing rabbit hair. There are 4 different angora rabbit breeds, English, French, Satin and Giant. The wool harvested from these rabbits is lightweight, silky, fine, and very soft. It is 7 times warmer than wool, and is ideal for baby clothes, winter underwear, sweaters and mittens. Only a small amount of wool can be harvested from these adorable creatures, angora is often combined with other fibers to minimize the high cost of this luxurious fiber

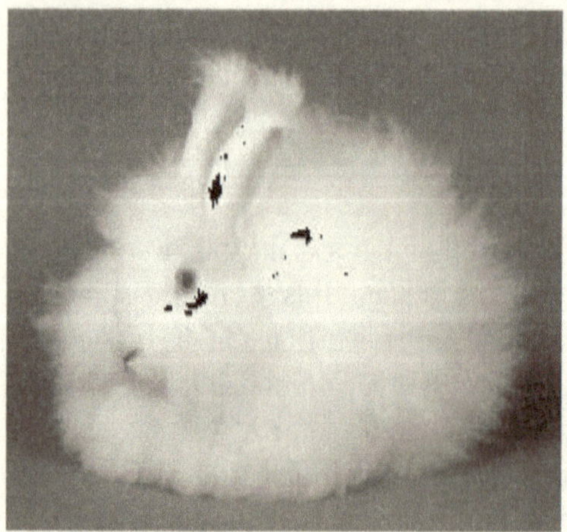
Figure 11: Angora

Camel hair,Alpaca,Vicuna andLlama

Yarns made from the fibers of these animals are very soft, lustrous, lightweight and warm. The down hairs of the Llama produce a soft yarn also suitable for apparel. Alpaca is used for the manufacture of warm, luxurious apparel. Camel hair comes from the extremely soft and fine fur from the undercoat of the camel. Camel's hair can be used alone but is most often combined with fine wool for overcoating, top coating, sportswear and sports hosiery Vicuna is the world´s most valuable fiber. The vicuna is small and wild and belongs to the Camel family. It yields the finest animal fiber in the world. Its fiber is rare and very expensive.

C ashmere

Cashmere is also known as the fiber of kings. It is produced from the fine, soft undercoat of hair of the Kashmir goat. Sixty percent of the world's supply of cashmere is produced in China, Mongolia and Tibet, and the remainder from Turkey, Afghanistan, Iraq, Iran, Kashmere, Australia and New Zealand.

Figure 12: Llama

Cashmere yarn is extremely soft, lightweight, yet very warm. It is very luxurious and possesses excellent drape. As each Kashmir goat is capable of producing an average of only 4-6 ounces of underdown per year, Cashmere is hence very expensive

PHYSICAL STRUCTURE OF WOOL

Pepper, Dan in his book —wool‖ How products are made, describes the physical structure of wool as follows:

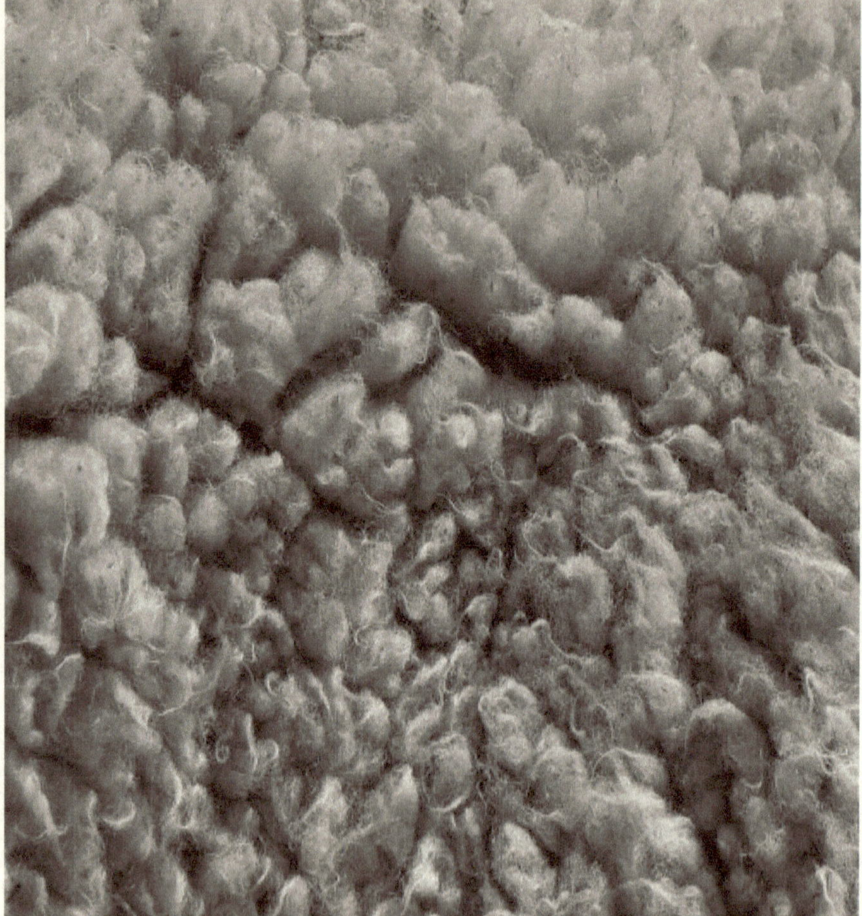

Figure 13: Texture of wool

L ength: Describes the diameter of wool fiber varies from 10 to 50 micrometers. Thelength of Merino fibers ranges from 1 and a half to 5 inches, depending on the animal and the time between shearing. Some sheep breeds produce coarse long wools used in specialty and hand crafted fabrics. Merino lamb's wool may average 15 micrometers in diameter.

Medu lla: This characteristic is rarely found in fine wools. The medulla comprises a seriesof cells (similar to honeycombs) that provide air spaces, giving wool its thermal insulation value. Wool, like residential insulation, is effective in reducing heat transfer.

C ortex: Is described as the main part of the fiber and is made up of long flattenedtapered cells with a nucleus near the center. These cells are responsible for the unique 3 dimensional crimp of wool. These cells are of two different types with different properties which react differently to moisture and temperature. In naturalcolored wool, these cells contain melanin. Wool can be compared to a giant molecular spring. In natural-colored wools, the cortial cells contain melanin, a colored pigment.

C uticle: This is the outer layer. It is a protective layer of scales arranged like shingles orfish scales. When two fibers come in contact with each other, these scales tend to cling and stick to each other. It's this physical clinging and sticking that allows wool fibers to be spun into thread so easily.

Chemicalcomposition

Wool fiber is a cross linked protein called Keratin. The same protein found in horns, hooves and in human hair and finger nails. It consists of carbon, hydrogen, oxygen, nitrogen and sulpher. These combine to form 17 different amino acids.

PROPERTIES OF WOOL

Wool can be satisfyingly soft, warm, cozy, sensuous or rugged, tough and functional. Its inherent drapability allows its finest fibers to appear lustrous sleek and elegant. Kadolph explains some of the properties of wool with the examples below:

A esthetically, wool contributes loft and body to fabrics. It has a matte appearance. Shorter wool fibers are sometimes blended with longer wool fibers and specialty wools like mohair to modify the luster or texture

Wool fabrics are *durable*. They have excellent flexibility. They can be bent back 20000 times without breaking as compared with cotton's 3000 times.

When stress is put on the fabric, the crimp fibers elongate as the molecular chains uncoil. When stress is removed, the cross links pull the fibers back almost to their original positions.

When it comes to *comfort,*wool is a poor conductor of heat so warmth from the body is not easily lost. The wool fibers trap air hence keeping the body heat close to the body. Wool provides superior comfort to outdoor enthusiasts. For comparison, a winter blanket of wool is heavy and warm. An equally thick blanket of cotton would be even heavier but not as warm.

The *appearance retention*of wool has to do with its resilience. It resists wrinkling and recovers quickly from wrinkles when wet. Wool maintains shape fairly well during normal use too. When wool fabrics are dry-cleaned they retain their size and shape well but with hand washing, special care needs to be observed to avoid shrinkage. Wool carpets maintain an attractive appearance for years.

Wool does not soil easily and removal of soils is relatively easy. Grease and oil do not spot wool fabrics as readily as they would other fibers. They also do not need to be washed or dry-cleaned with every use. It is important to layer wool garments with washable ones next to ones skin to decrease odor pick up. Chlorine bleach, (an oxidizing agent) damages wool by dissolving the fiber. Wool is sensitive to alkalis as strong detergents and it is attacked by moth larvae and other insects. The use of moth balls is discouraged due to the toxic nature of these substances; hence storage of wool items should be such that they will not be accessible to moths. Wool is very popular with interior designers as it is known to be flame resistant. It burns very slowly and is self extinguishing. However when used in buildings, flame retardant finish may be applied to meet public building code requirements.

APPLICATION OF WOOL

Gale and Kaul (2004) state, that once yarns have been spun they are ready to be knitted or woven into fabrics. Specialist knitting factories and weaving mills will use selected yarns to produce the woolens, worsted fabrics or knitwear. Upholstery, woven tapestries, handcrafted items, fire safety blankets, carpets, tailored suits and foundation pads under heavy machinery are some uses to which wool can be put to. The Wool Bureau has adopted symbols to adopt the promotion of wool. The Woolmark$_R$ is used on all woo l products that meet their quality specifications. And Wooblend$_R$ mark is used for blends with at least 60precent wool.

WOOL IN KENYA

According to Spinnersandspinners.org (2012), Wool trade organizations have invested in fiber technology and proactive marketing campaigns to regain the market share originally lost to manmade materials. In Kenya, Nanyuki spinners and weavers boasts of bringing beautiful African designs of Carpets, Shawls, Cardigans, Throws, Pullovers, Scarves and Bedcovers into many contemporary homes from its spinning and

weaving. Large scale sheep farmers around Nanyuki supply them the wool. Acquiring of raw materials has become the biggest challenge because many of the suppliers have taken to selling their wool to bigger companies who are able to pay very high prices. Also the suppliers are exporting their wool to other countries, especially South Africa where there is great demand for it and a bigger profit margin.

ENIRONMENTAL CONCERNS AND SUSTAINABILITY OF WOOL
Gale and Kaur (2004) have stated that looking to the future wool's defining strength is reliability and quality. With the many lifestyle issues that fabrics and fashion must strive to address, research into its relevance is of

importance. Today natural fiber and synthetics can blend harmoniously from both a fiber and social point of view. Wool care in the past meant careful hand washing, a dedicated cleaning agent and towel drying. Today consumers can enjoy the beauty of woolen products while caring for them in much the same way as many other fibers.

Some ecological considerations that need Gale and Kaur suggest that need to be looked into are: Correct grazing for the flocks to minimize soil erosion and overgrazing, Clean water: unpolluted drinking sources, Predator friendly environment: well trained sheep dogs, Healthy veterinary practices: correct types of medications for the sheep, Soil chemical control, Livestock chemical control and Carbon footprint: distance of travel from primary source to final destination

Hallet & Johnston (2010) state new generation wool technology is now about adding enhancements to give alternative fibers an aspect to wool. For example, adding 2 percent Lycra will give fine wool suiting a _memory' while Lurex can liven up a flat worsted suit fabric. The options are endless. Modern interpretations of wool can give provide the designer with a broad, tactile vocabulary that can express a wide range of design requirements from classic, traditional and authentic themes to the most futuristic explorations in performance fabrics.

CHAPTER THIRTEEN

DESIGN MATERIALS AND PROCESS

METALS

Historical Background of Metals

Metals consulate the backbone of modern industrial capacity, After the Stone Age and into the middle of the 19_{th} century the important aspects of technological innovation were based on the development of new metallic alloys and their applications in new tools and machines. The bronze and iron ages overlapped by a thousand years as iron and then steel were to become the dominant modern materials. Bronze was discovered around 3500BC, iron

1500BC, although these dates vary significantly depending on the region of the world under consideration. Arthur Lyons (2008)

The seven metals of antiquity were copper, tin, gold, silver, iron, lead and mercury. These were the only known metals until well into the 13_{th} and 14_{th} centuries when antimony, arsenic, bismuth and zinc were discovered. In the centuries since, many more have been added to the list so that now there are 86 known metals. Of these only 10 are regularly used in architectural applications; iron, copper, lead, tin, zinc, nickel, tungsten, titanium, chromium, and aluminium. Other metals are also used in small amounts for various alloys. L. Aicheson (1960)

Beginning in the mid-19_{th} century, developments in alloying, processing and production, and an elementary understanding of metallurgy, quickly accelerated the intensity of research and the quick application of various metals.

Demand for metals was very strong during the 20_{th} century, with a growth rate constituently averaging around 3 percent per year. Recently, however, the demand for metal ore in developed regions has leveled off or actually dropped slightly. This can be attributed at least in part, to the continuing _decarbonization' of advanced economies. (Arthur Lyons 2008). Recovery of metals and recycling has become a major source for all ferrous and many nonferrous metals. A metal is an element, compound, or alloy that is a good conductor of both electricity and heat. They exist in nature as compounds like oxides, carbonates, sulphides and phosphates and are known as ores (S.K Duggal 2007)

Categories of metals
Ferrous

Researchers have come to the conclusion that ferrous metals are those that contain iron. They may have small amounts of other metals or other elements added, to give the required properties. They also agree that ferrous metals are magnetic and give little resistance to corrosion. Examples are cast iron, wrought iron, mild steel, carbon steel, and high steel. The following is a list of ferrous metals that gives the composition, properties and uses of the different ferrous alloys.

MildSteel

Mild steel is the most commonly used ferrous metal. It contains about 0.15 to 0.30% carbon and the rest is iron. As mild steel has low carbon content, it cannot be hardened and tempered, however, it can be case hardened. It is malleable and ductile and bends easily. Mild steel is used in the manufacture of nuts, screws, bolts, girders and other general metal products.

Carbon Steel

Carbon steel, also known as tool steel or cast steel is an iron alloy with 0.5 to 1.5% carbon. The major property of carbon steel is its toughness. It can be hardened and tempered and is fairly ductile. Carbon steel is mainly used in the manufacture of tools like drills, chisels, shears and hammer heads. It has a smooth skin of black oxide and becomes hard and brittle on heating. Fig 1. Shows an example of a fabricated carbon steel.

Figure 1.Carbon steel fabrications
Source: http://periodictable.com
Castiron

Cast iron is another commonly used ferrous metal. It is made up of 2 to6% of carbon and 94 to 98% of iron .It is hard and strong but quite brittle. Cast iron has a high compressive strength and is resistant to oxidation .It can be classified into different varieties like gray cast iron, malleable cast iron and white cast iron .Cast iron is normally used in the manufacture of heavy crushing machinery, machine tool parts, brake drums ,car cylinder blocks, machine handles and gear wheels, plumbing material, etc.

StainlessSteel

Stainless steel, also known as corrosion steel, is an alloy of iron, nickel and chromium. The important property of stainless steel is its high resistance to corrosion. It is tough and resistant to stains, hence, called stainless steel. It is commonly used in kitchen cutlery and cookware, medical instruments. Kitchen, draining, boards and pipes, Fig 2 shows an example of a kitchen whose appliances and surfaces are made of stainless steel.

Figure 2: Stainless steel kitchens
Source: http://periodictable.com/items/Garnierite

Wroughtiron

Wrought iron contains less than 0.008% carbon. As it is almost 100%pure iron, it is highly resistant to corrosion and oxidation. It is strong and tough, yet, fibrous and ductile. Wrought iron can be welded, machined and plated easily. It used to make ornamental gates and railings. See fig 3.

Figure 3: A glass coffee table with a wrought iron stand that looks like a tree branch

Non-Ferrous Metals

These are metals which do not contain any iron. They are not magnetic and are usually more resistant to corrosion than ferrous metals. Examples are aluminium, copper, lead, zinc and tin, nickel, titanium, precious metals, refractory metals super alloys

Pure Metals

A pure metal only consists of a single element. This means that it only has one type of atom in it. The common pure metals are:-aluminium, copper, iron, and lead, zinc, tin, silver and gold. See Figures 4 and 5.

Figure 4(left). Sink made from copper and Figure 5 (right) shows an Aluminium chair

Precious metal / noble metals

A precious metal is a rare metallic chemical element of high economic value. Chemically, the precious metals are less reactive than most elements, have high luster and high electrical conductivity. Figure 6 shows the difference in appearance of these metals.

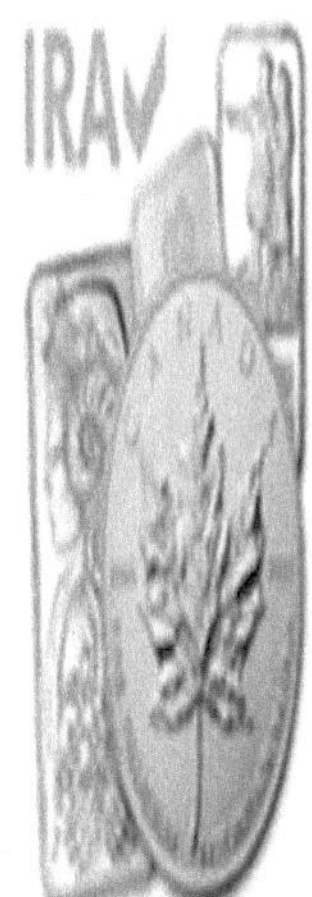

Gold Silver Platinum Palladium Figure 6: Precious metals, Source: http://www.apmex.com/

Alloys

An alloy is a mixture of two or more elements in solid solution in which the major component is metal. Most pure metals are either too soft, brittle or chemically reactive for practical use. Combining different ratios of metals as alloys modifies the properties of pure metals to produce desirable characteristics. The aim of making alloys is generally to make less brittle, harder, and resistant to corrosion, or have a more desirable color and luster (Kreith and Yogi Goswami, 2004).

Alloys can either be ferrous or non-ferrous Examples of Ferrous alloys include steel, stainless steel, cast iron, tool steel, alloy steel make up the largest proportion both by quantity and commercial value. Iron alloyed with various proportions of carbon gives low, mid and high carbon steels. Examples of non-ferrous alloys are aluminium, titanium, copper, and magnesium.

Structure and Bonding

Metals typically consist of close packed atoms. see figure 7, meaning that the atoms are arranged like sphere. Two packing motifs are common one big body centered cubic wherein each metal is surrounded by eight equivalent metals. The other main motif is face – centered cubic where the metals are surrounded by six neighboring atoms. Several metals adopt both structures depending on the temperature.

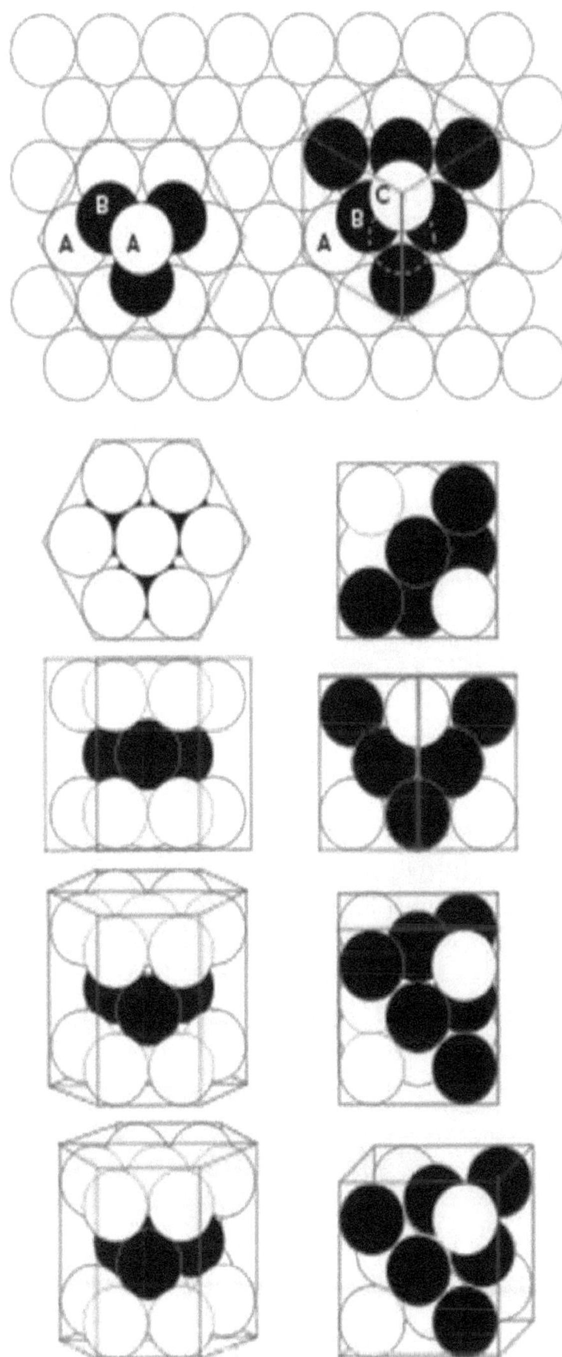

Figure 7: Structure and Bonding Close – packing of spheres Source:
http://en.wikipedia.org/w/index.php?

In a metal, atoms readily lose electrons to form positive (cations). Those ions
are surrounded by de-localized electrons, which are responsible for the
conductivity. The solid thus produced is held together by electrostatic
interactions between the ions and the electron cloud, which are called
metallic bonds

Properties

Pure metals are little used in engineering: They rarely possess the required
properties and some are difficult to produce in the pure state. Hence metals
are commonly used in form of alloys. The following are the general physical,
chemical, Electrical and Mechanical properties of metals that researchers
have found out. S.K Duggal (2008) starts by describing that most metals are
hard, shiny, they feel heavy (dense) and they melt only when they are very
hot. Lumps of metal will make a bell-like sound when

1 2 3 4

Obtaining the
metals from mines and pits etc.
Separation of the mineral into ore (metal) and gangue (impurities e.g.
sand, mud and other elements). Obtaining the pure metal from the mineral
(reduction
process)
Final treatment: They better the Properties of and/ or change the
physical form of the metals.

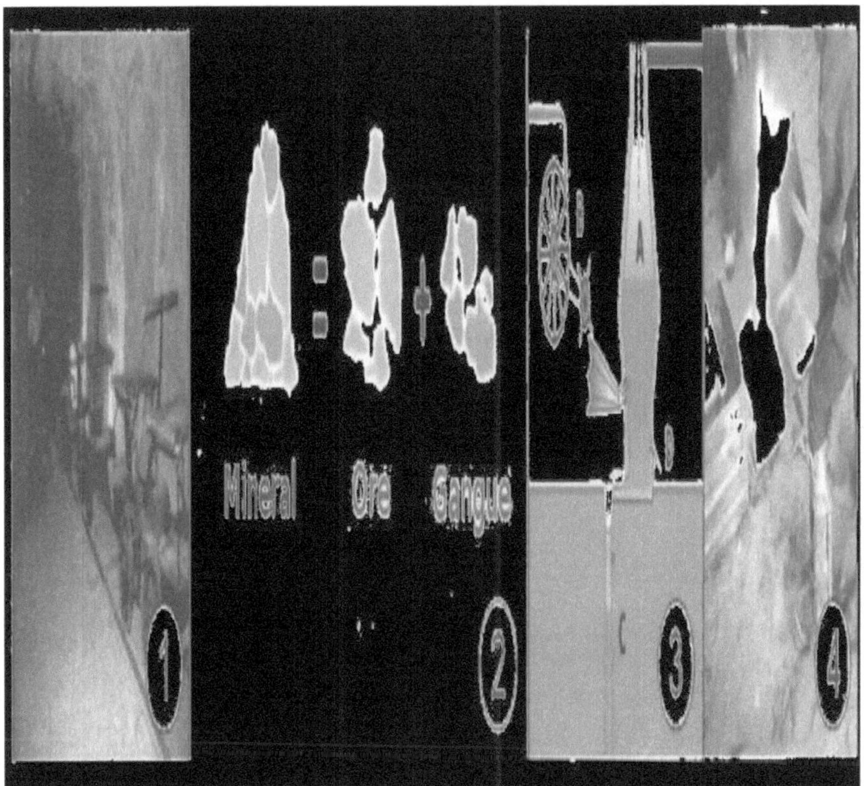

they are hit with something heavy (they are sonorous). John Fernandez (2006) adds that heat and electricity can easily pass through a metal (conductivity).

He further explains that a lump of metal can be beaten into a thin sheet (malleability) or can be pulled into thin wires (ductility). Most researchers agree that metal is hard to pull apart (high tensile strength) or smash (high compressive strength) and that If you push on a long, thin piece of metal, it will bend, not break (elasticity). They also

agree that metals have the ability to support impacts without breaking (Tenacity), Metals are relatively hard materials, (Density) Metals characteristically shine (Metallic

shine) after being recently cut, except mercury all metals are solid at room temperature. Not all metals have these properties. Lead, for instance, is very soft, and heat and electricity do not pass through iron as well as they do through copper. Allan Everette (1998).

Methods of extracting metals

Metals either exist naturally or can be extracted from their ore in one of three ways firstly by roasting the ore in oxygen, secondly, through the process of carbon

reduction, thirdly by the process of electrolysis and lastly through recycling of metals.

Ted, Kretchen, (2011). The way that a metal is extracted from the earth really depends on where the metal lies in the reactivity series of metals. The reactivity series on the table below gives the common metals positions in a periodic table see figure 8.

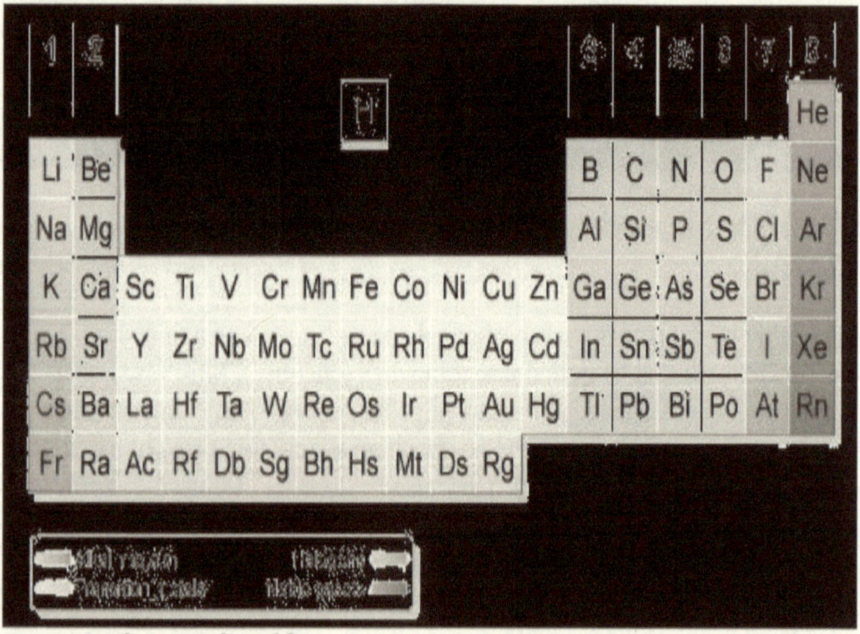

Figure 8: The periodic table
Source: http://www.bbc.co.uk/schools/gcsebitesize/science/

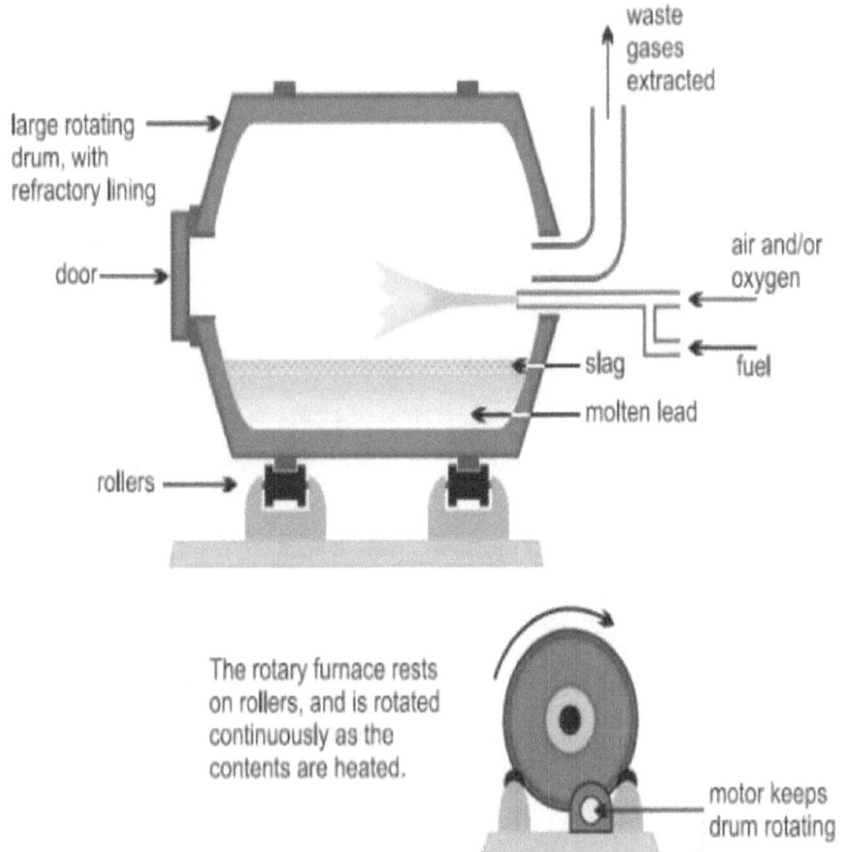

Figure 9: Extracting metals by Roasting in oxygen

Naturally occurring metals

Copper, silver, gold and platinum are the four most unreactive metals. This means that they do not form compounds and can exist as simple lumps of the metal in the rock. They can be found native. These are easy to extract since they can be mined. Also, you can even find pieces of gold in streams. More reactive metals are not found in lumps and must be extracted from the rocks in which they occur. Rocks containing metal compounds are called ores.

Roasting Metal in oxygen or Blurstfurnace

For all the extraction processes, the rock must first be dug up, crushed, and the impurities removed so that a pure ore remains. The ore of a metal is actually a compound. It is frequently the oxide of the metal, e.g. iron ore is the compound iron oxide, but it can also be other compounds. The more reactive a metal is, the more difficult it is to extract from its ore. Metals with quite a low reactivity can be extracted by roasting the ore in air. The oxygen in the air reacts with the compound, releasing the metal. Copper and mercury ores can be treated in this way to extract the metal. Allan Everette (1998). See figure 9.

Carbon reduction

Metals with a medium reactivity can be extracted using a process called carbon reduction. Here, the element carbon is used to separate the metal from the ore. Although carbon is not a metal it can act like a metal in a displacement-type reaction. The carbon can come in and take the place of the metal in the ore compound. This will only work with metals which are less reactive than carbon - which is everything from zinc downwards. The most common example of this is iron extraction. The reduction part means that the ore is reduced by using carbon, so that the metal loses oxygen and gains electrons, (Habashi, F. (1973).

Electrolysis

This is a process principally used to obtain and or purify non-ferrous metals; this process is used for extracting metals with a high reactivity, i.e. the metals from aluminium upwards in the reactivity series. In this process the ore has to be made into a liquid: this can be done by either melting it or dissolving it in a solvent as shown in figure 10. In this state there exists a mixture of metal ions and non-metal ions, all of which can move around freely. The metal ions are positive and the non-metal ions negative. An electric current is then passed through the liquid by means of a positive electrode, the anode, and a negative electrode, the cathode. See figure 10. This requires a lot of electricity

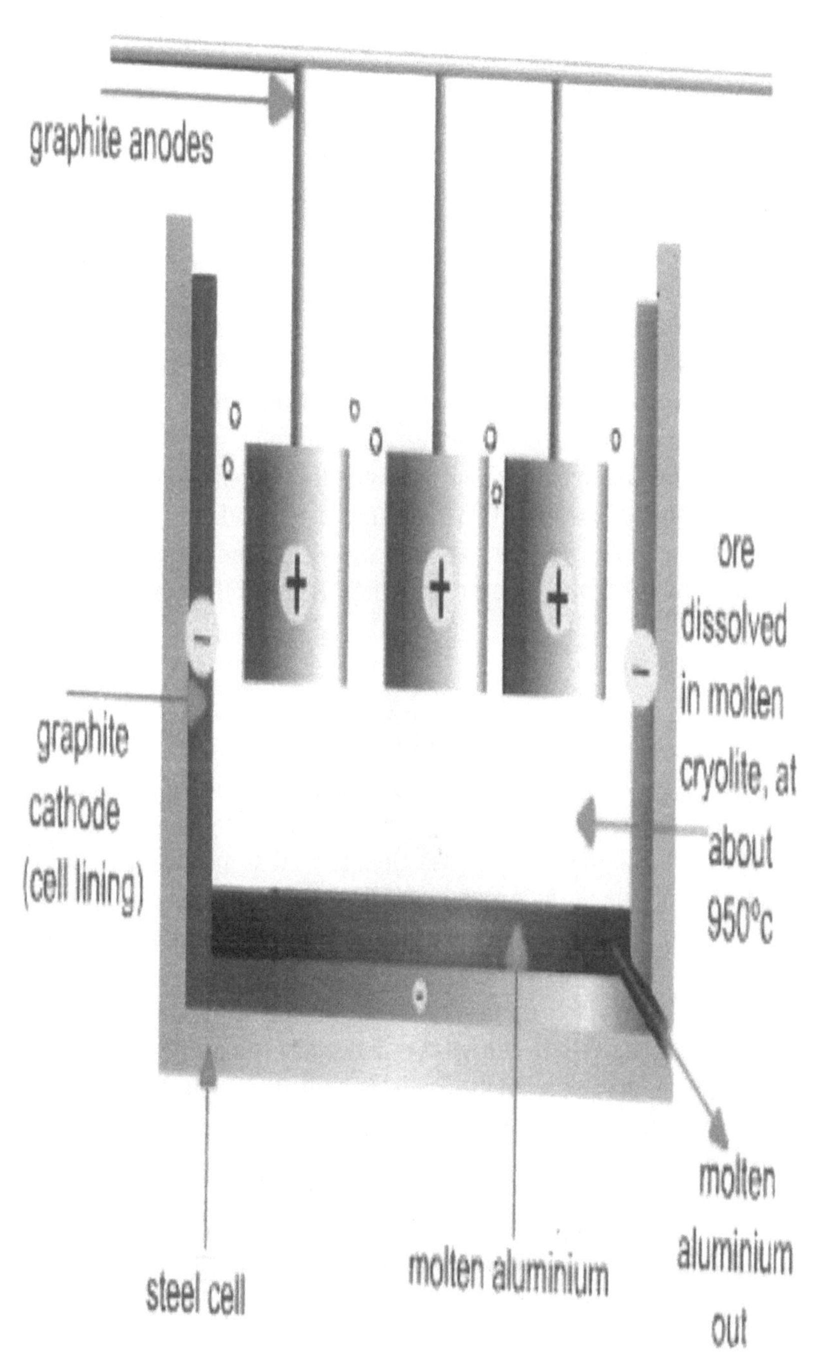

graphite anodes
graphite cathode (cell lining)
+
+
+
−
−
ore dissolved in molten cryolite, at about 950°c
steel cell
molten aluminium
molten aluminium out

Figure 10: Electrolysis
Source: http://ts1.mm.bing.net/

Recycling of Metals

Virtually all types of metals can be recycled into new metal that can be used
to make new products. Recycling metals protect the environment and saves
on energy consumption. Using second-hand raw materials means that less
natural resources are being depleted such as iron ore for steel production,
nickel for making stainless steel and alumina for making aluminum. There is
only so much metal available on earth and the more we strip the ground of
these natural resources, the more scarce and valuable these metals will
become. Carbon dioxide emissions are also reduced dramatically with metal
recycling. For example, when new aluminum is made using recycled metals it
results in an energy savings of 95 percent. Copper made from recycled metals
saves 85 percent in energy consumption while steel produced from recycled
metals adds up to 70 percent energy savings. Alton, J. Trevino (2012).

Applications

Some metals and metal alloys possess high structural strength per unit mass,
making them useful materials for carrying large loads or resisting impact
damage. The strength and resilience of metals has led to their frequent use in
high-rise building and bridge construction, as well as most vehicles, many
appliances, tools, pipes, non-illuminated signs and railroad tracks. The two
most commonly used structural metals, iron and aluminium, are also the most
abundant metals in the Earth's crust (Kreith and Yogi Goswami, 2004).
Metals are good conductors, making them valuable in electrical appliances
and for carrying an electric current over a distance with little energy lost.
Electrical power grids rely on metal cables to distribute electricity. Home
electrical systems, for the most part, are wired with copper wire for its good
conducting properties.

The thermal conductivity of metal is useful for containers to heat materials
over a flame. Metal is also used for heat sinks to protect sensitive equipment
from overheating. The high reflectivity of some metals is important in the
construction of mirrors, including precision astronomical instruments. This

last property can also make metallic jewelry aesthetically appealing (John Fernandez, 2006).

Source of Metals in Kenya

The main sub-sectors in Kenya's metal industry are steel smelting and hot rolling and the manufacture of wire and wire products, galvanized and cold-rolled steel products and pipes. These subsectors are interrelated, as they depend upon each other for the supply of inputs. Kenya does not mine structural metals e.g. steel, Aluminium etc. but simply import the finished products from countries like china and then fabricates them.

There were over 1,000 scrap metal companies registered with the Kenyan scrap dealer's association. It is estimated there are upwards of 150,000 people throughout Kenya who get income from sales of scrap metal to scrap metal dealers. The little scrap metal that is collected is mostly exported at very low prices for new use. Source: CDC Case Studies Athi River Steel, Kenya Scrap steel recycling.

Kenya's mining industry is dominated by production of non-metallic minerals such as soda ash, fluorspar, kaolin and some gemstones. Mining accounts for a very small part of Kenya's annual GDP. Gold is produced primarily by artisanal workers in the west and south western parts of the country, on several small greenstone belts. Iron ore is mined from small localised deposits for use in the domestic manufacture of cement (*www.SBMchina.com/Limestone-Mining*

CHAPTER FOURTEEN

DESIGN MATERIALS AND PROCESS

PAINT
INTRODUCTION

History of Paint

From cave paintings to modern high tech architectural coatings, paint has been used to decorate and protect buildings, to create works of art and to coat any number of things from ocean liners to toys. Until the nineteenth century and mass production, the history of paint mirrored local materials.

Paint has been used since pre-history. Cave paintings dating back an estimated 40,000 years feature artwork made with soot, colored earth and animal fats. The early Egyptians formulated paint that has remained brilliantly colored to this day, using ground glass and semi-precious stone, lead, colored earth and even animal blood mixed with oils, glues and fats. Over the centuries, other colors were formulated and perfected. Artists devised their own paint recipes, which were often jealously guarded. Paint as a method of decorating buildings did not become common until the nineteenth century. Prior to that, it was expensive and time consuming to make, and decorating was more often done with stone, mosaic tile and colored plaster. Stevie Donald

PAINTS

S.K Duggal (2007) defines paint as a liquid surface coating. On drying, it forms a thin film on the painted surface. He further classifies paint as oil paints, water paints, cement paints, bituminous paints and special paints.

Duggal also gives the following as the functions of paint: to protect the coated surface against possible stresses i.e. mechanical and chemical; deterioration- physical or environmental; decorate the structure by giving a smooth and colorful finish; check penetration of water through R.C.C; check the corrosion of metal; check the formation of fungus and bacteria, which are unhygienic and give ugly facades; check the decay of woodwork and to varnish the surface to display it to better advantage.

Components of Paints

Paints consist of a blend of components, each with their specific function. Commonly, these include the binder (medium or vehicle), solvent or thinners, base, extenders, pigments and driers, although other additives may be incorporated into specialist paints. The pigments give the paint color; solvents make it easier to apply; resins help it dry; and additives serve as everything from fillers to antifungicidal agents. Hundreds of different pigments, both natural and synthetic, exist. The basic white pigment is titanium dioxide, selected for its excellent concealing properties, and black pigment is commonly made from carbon black. Other pigments used to make paint include iron oxide and cadmium sulfide for reds, metallic salts for yellows and oranges, and iron blue and chrome yellows for blues and greens.

Solvents are various low viscosity, volatile liquids. They include petroleum mineral spirits and aromatic solvents such as benzol, alcohols, esters, ketones, and acetone. The natural resins most commonly used are lin-seed, coconut, and soybean oil, while alkyds, acrylics, epoxies, and polyurethanes number among the most popular synthetic resins. Additives serve many purposes. Some, like calcium carbonate and aluminum silicate, are simply fillers that give the paint body and substance without changing its properties. Other additives produce certain desired characteristics. Duggal (2007)

Design

Paint is generally custom-made to fit the needs of industrial customers. Changes in legislation and environmental concerns have led to the development of paints with reduced levels of volatile organic compounds (VOCs). Mainly this has been through the increased use of water- borne rather than solvent- borne paints. In some respects, waterborne paints have the advantage. They have low oduor emissions, brushes can be cleaned with water and they tolerate damp surfaces. However, they are not ideal for external use in cold and wet conditions. Other developments have been towards high solids paints, which have low solvent content and therefore very low VOC emissions (Auther Lyons,2008). Lyons also explains that a further trend is towards the use of natural paints based on plant oils, casein, and mineral positons.

Coats within a paint system perform specific tasks. Usually, a complete system would require primer, undercoat and finishing coat, although in the case of new external materials four coats may be appropriate See Figure 6.

Primers

A primer is a preparatory coating put on materials before painting. Priming ensures better adhesion of paint to the surface, increases paint durability, and provides additional protection for the material being painted. In practice, primer is often used when painting many kinds of porous materials, such as wood, plastic, metal, gypsum board, concrete stone etc.

 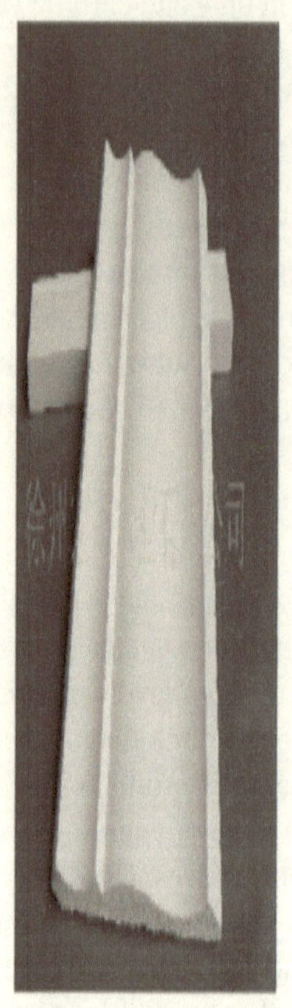 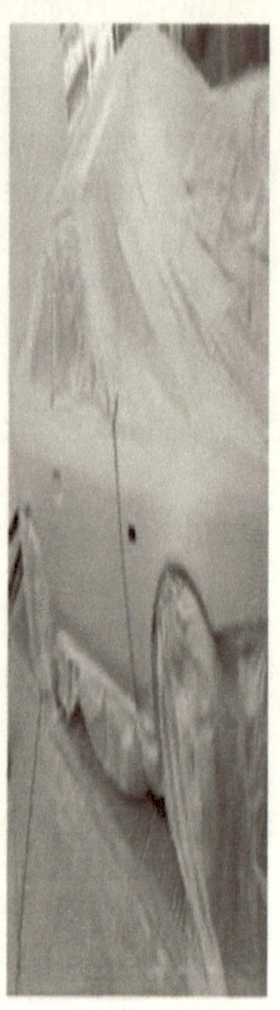

Primedwall *Primedwood**Primedcar*

Figure 2: Primed surfaces
Source: http://www.trianglehoneymoon.com/

Undercoats

Undercoats provide cover and a good base for the finishing coat. Most undercoats are based on alkyd resins or acrylic emulsions.

Finishing Coats

Finishing coats provide a durable and decorative surface. Some gloss, egg shell and satin finishes are still based on oils and alkyd resins, although waterborne products are increasingly becoming predominant.

Some water borne gloss finishes tend to be visually softer and are more moisture permeable than the traditional solvent – borne hard glosses. However, they have the advantage of quick drying without the evolution solvent odour; generally they are more durable and do not yellow on ageing. Matt and silk finishes are usually vinyl or acrylic emulsions.

Figure 3. Gloss finish
Source: http://ts3.mm.bing.net/th?id=H.4699704330027578&pid=1.9

Figure 4. Cream Eggshell finish (left) and Figure 5. Green Eggshell finish (right) Source: http://ts4.mm.bing.net/

Marble effect Graining Crackle effect Tortoiseshelling

Figure 6: An example of a paint system, comprising of 3 coats of paint, being applied on a wallform the 1_{st} coat to the 3_{rd} coat.

SPECIAL PAINTS

During the last few years a great many substances have been proposed as bases for paint instead of white lead. The paints made with these substances are called by special names, Figure. 7 Special Effects and often have peculiar qualities which adapt them for use under particular circumstances for example Special Effects Paints which have been discussed in the paragraph below.

Other special paints include: Heat resistant paint, Fungicide paints, Enamel paints that give highly durable, impact resistant, easily cleaned hard gloss surfaces see figure 8. Masonry Paints that give Smooth and sand textured finishes see figure 9. Water Repellent and Water Proof Paints, Anti - graffiti paints to aid in the easy removal of graffiti etc. DUGGAL, S.K. (2008).

Special Effects Paints

Special Effects Paints, reflecting the traditional process of graining, marbling, ragging and stippling, are popular see figure 7. Most Special Effects Paints require a base coat, applied by brush or roller, which is then patterned or distressed to create the desired effect. One proprietary system uses a special rag roller, which flails the wet finish coat giving random partial exposure of the darker first coat. Alternative finishes include metallic, pearlescent and graining effects. Water based acrylic glazes are virtually odour free and are touch dry within two hours. Edwards, L and Lawless, J. (2007).

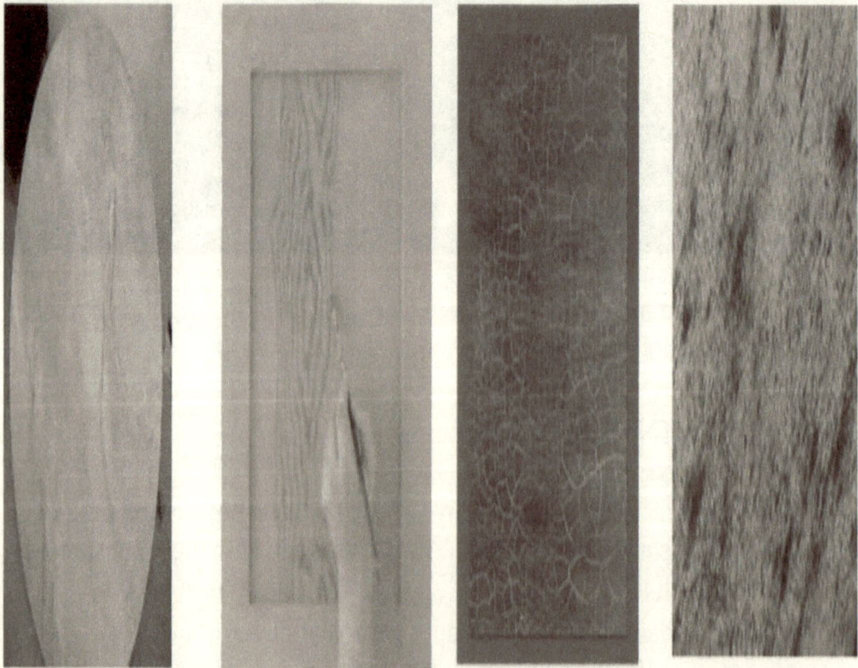

Source:http://www.bing.com/images/search?q=paint+effect+techniques

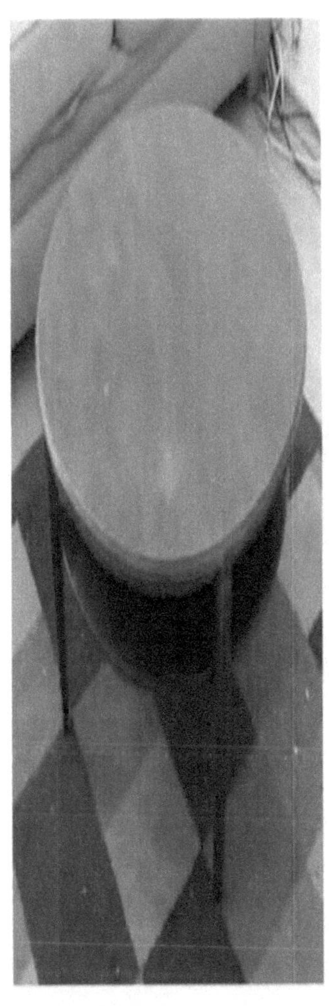

Enamel Paint

Figure 8: Coffee table with Enamel finish givinghighly durable, impact resistant, easily cleaned hard gloss surface

Masonry Paints

Figure 9: Smooth and sand textured Finishes forapplication to exterior walls of brick, block, concrete, stone or renderings. Where fine cracks are present,

Source: http://ts1.mm.bing.net/

NATURAL WOOD FINISHES

Natural wood finishes include wood stains, varnishes and oils.

Wood Stains

Wood stains are pigmented resin solutions which penetrate into the surface and may then build up a sheen finish. Most wood stain systems for exterior use include a water
– based or solvent based preservative basecoat which controls rot and mould growth. See figure 10 and 11. Allan, Everette (1998).

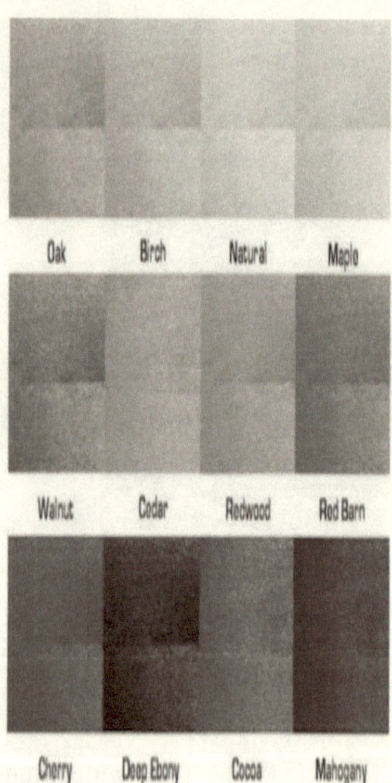

Figure 10: Woodstain (left) and Figure 11: Showing different types of (right)
Source: http://ts3.mm.bing.net/

Varnishes

Varnishes are unpigmented resin solutions which are intended to create a surface film see Figure 12 and 13 below.

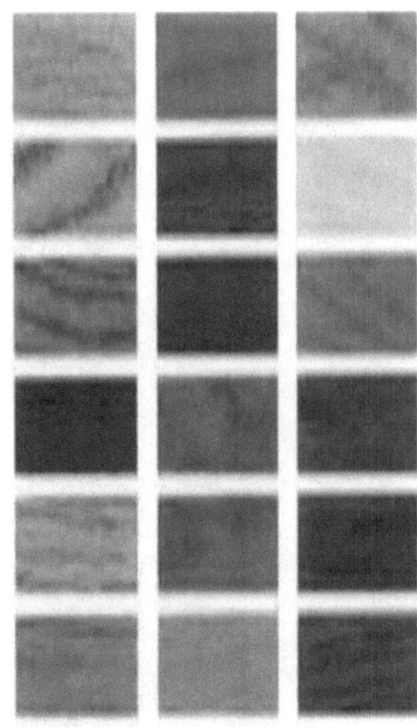

Figure 12: Shows floor being varnished (left) and Figure 13. Shows Variations in color of Varnishes (right) Source: http://ts1.mm.bing.net/

Oils

Oils such as teak are used mainly for internal applications. Formulations based on natural oils for exterior use are high in solids, producing an ultraviolet- resistant, microporous finish which may be transparent or opaque. The finish which should not flake or crack, may be renovated by the application of a further coat. See figure 14 below.

Figure 14: A wooded surface being oiled.
Source: http://images.meredith.com/wood/images/p_oil_varnish_blend.jpg

Wood finishes entirely composed of natural products are also available. These are based on blends of beeswax, larch resin, vegetable oils, and may incorporate minerals and earth pigments for colour and opacity.

Paint companies in Kenya

In the past few years, the paints industry in the country has been thriving on an upbeat construction and growing economy. As a result of the construction boom being experienced in most parts of the country, the market for paints and coatings continues to maintain a relentless upward march.

The leading paint manufacturers and painting companies locally include Sadolin Paints, Basco Paints and Crown Berger. Each of these companies manufactures its own specialized product – with some also offering professional paint services and training. Patrick, Thuita. (2010).

Lead levels in Paints Manufactured in Kenya

Paints produced in Kenya have high levels of lead that exceed international accredited limits, a report has revealed. A research carried out by an international NGO, iLima, in conjunction with International Persistent Organic Pollutants Elimination Network, (Ipen) revealed that the concentration of all paints sampled was 14,000 parts per million lead which is 165 higher than the US limit.

In 2009, an International Conference on Chemicals Management – in which the Government of Kenya was a participant – agreed by consensus to identify lead in paint as an international priority issue of concern. In response to the above, the Kenyan paint companies introduced Eco friendly paint in to the Kenyan market from 2011 in abid to curb the above concerns. Anthony Aisi (2012).
CONCLUSION

Changes in legislation and environmental concerns have led to the development of paints with reduced levels of volatile organic compounds (VOCs). Mainly this has been through the increased use of water- borne rather than solvent- borne paints.

CHAPTER FIVETEEN

DESIGN MATERIALS AND PROCESS

ECO MATERIALS

Definition

Environmentally friendly (also eco-friendly, nature friendly, and green) are ambiguous terms used to refer to goods and services, laws, guidelines and policies claimed to inflict minimal or no harm on the .environment (www.greenliving.nationalgeographic.org).

Ecodesign is an approach to design of a product with special consideration
for the environmental impacts of the product during its whole lifecycle. In a
life cycle assessment the life cycle of a product is usually divided into
procurement, manufacture, use and disposal.Life cycle assessment helps
companies measure the environmental impact of their products and services
across all life cycle stages; from extraction of raw materials, through to
manufacturing, distribution, use and disposal (www.presustainability.com).

Criteria for assessment of an eco material

According to Avril Fox in the book Green design, she points out five
guidelines which are used to assess on the _greeness' of a material. First and
foremost, a fundamental principle is the use of renewable raw materials (Fox,
pg 6).

These are resources that have a natural rate of availability and yield a
continual flow of services which may be consumed in any time period
without endangering future consumption possibilities as long as current use
does not exceed net renewal during the period under consideration
(www.eionet.europa).

The second guideline is the process of extracting the raw material from the
source. If the process is destructive and it leads to ecological imbalance, it
means that substitutes must be devised in order to protect the earth (Fox, pg
7). The third guideline used is the true cost of the material. The amount of
energy consumed in the manufacturing, transportation, installation and
maintenance of a material must be justified by the final use of the material
(Fox, pg 7). Another guideline used in the potential lifespan of a product.
Any artifact which is constructed to last is more environmentally friendly
than an object with a limited shelf life (Fox, pg 8).

The fifth guideline used is the ability of the material to be recycled if it
cannot last indefinitely. (Fox, pg 9).According to the United States
environmental protection Agency, recycling is the process of collecting and
processing materials that would otherwise be thrown away as trash and
turning them into new products. The benefits with recycling are that it
reduces the amount of waste sent to landfills and incinerators. It also
conserves natural resources such as timber, water, and minerals as well as

preventing pollution caused by reducing the need to collect new raw materials. In addition it reduces greenhouse gas emissions that contribute to global climate change and it helps sustain the environment for future generations. Moreover, it helps create new well-paying jobs in the recycling industries, (www.epa.gov/recycle.html).

History and Development

According to the American Marketing Association, green marketing is the marketing of products that are presumed to be environmentally safe. The term Green Marketing came into prominence in the late 1980s and early 1990s when The American Marketing Association held the first workshop on "Ecological Marketing" in 1975, the goal of that meeting being discussion of maintaining a balance on environmental issues while meeting primary customer needs (www.ama/historyofgreenmarketing.html).

The Corporate Social Responsibility (CSR) Reports started with the ice cream seller Ben Jerry's where the financial report was supplemented by a greater view on the company's environmental impact. In 1987 a document prepared by the World Commission on Environment and Development defined sustainable development as meeting —the needs of the present without compromising the ability of future generations to meet their own need‖. This became known as the Brundtland Report and was another step towards widespread thinking on sustainability in everyday activity.
The past decade has shown that harnessing consumer power to effect positive environmental change is far easier said than done. The so-called "green consumer" movements in the U.S. and other countries have struggled to reach critical mass and to remain in the forefront of shoppers' minds. One of green marketing's challenges is the lack of standards or public consensus about what constitutes "green,‖. Despite these challenges, green marketing has continued to gain adherents, particularly in light of growing global concern about climate change. This concern has led more companies to advertise their commitment to reduce their climate impacts, and the effect this is having on their products and services, (www.ama/historyofgreenmarketing.html). In the area of art and design, recycling has been happening since the early part of the 20th Century, when cubist artist Pablo Picasso and Georges Braque created collages from newsprints, packaging and other found materials.

(www.metmuseum.org/cubism/html)
Material Properties

According to the Hitachi group, Eco-products are defined as products that meet eight assessment criteria, including weight reduction, resource recycling, energy efficiency, and environmental conservation. The whole product life cycle should be regarded in an integrated perspective, with environmental aspects being analysed for every stage of the life cycle. These are, consumption of resources like energy, materials, water or land area. In addition, emissions to air, water, and the ground as being relevant for

the environment and human health and other factors like noise (www.hitachi.com/).

Applications of Eco Materials in Building Design

Ecodesign concepts currently have a great influence on many aspects of design; the impact of global warming and an increase in CO_2 emissions have led companies to consider a more environmentally conscious approach to their design thinking and process. In building design and construction, designers are taking on the concept of ecodesign throughout the design process, from the choice of materials to the type of

energy that is being consumed and the disposal of waste (www.slideshare.net/).

One way of practicing eco design is the use of local raw materials is less costly and

reduces the environmental costs of shipping, fuel consumption and CO_2 emissions generated from transportation. Also, materials that have been reclaimed such as wood/timber at a construction or junkyard can be given a second life by re-using them as support beams in a new building or as furniture, or stones from an excavation can be used as a retaining wall. The re-use of these items means that less energy is consumed in making new products and a new natural aesthetic quality is

achieved (www.slideshare.net/ecofriendlyinteriormaterials).

Solar power is a widely known and used renewable energy source that can be used in a wide variety of applications. There are two types of solar panels that generate heat into electricity; Thermal solar panels and Photovoltaic Panels. Thermal solar panels

reduce or eliminate the consumption of gas and diesel, and reduce CO_2 emissions.

Photovoltaic panels convert solar radiation into an electric current, which can power any appliance (Fernandez, pg 3). Green Roof is a partially or completely covered roof with plants or other vegetation. The covered roof creates insulation that helps regulate the outside temperature and controls how much goes in the building, it also retains water providing a water recycling system and provides sound proofing, which is ideal for noisy areas (www.greenroofs.org).
Eco Friendly Case studies in Kenya

Eco-Jeneza

As we learnt earlier, one of the guidelines is the use of renewable raw materials. It is with this backdrop that the Eco Jeneza has been chosen as a case study. The Eco Jeneza is a coffin made from recycled corrugated cardboard manufactured by the East Africa packaging industries. The reason for such an invention is the alarming rate of tree felling in the country. Statistics show that Kenya loses 616,000 trees every year to the coffin industry as 80% of bodies are buried on wooden coffins.

Fig1:Greenofficeblock
Source:www.roofrocket.com

Fig2:Solar panelled roof, Source: ises.org

For this initiative, EAPI has received thumbs up from the Mational Environment Management Authority, NEMA. However, their product is a hard sell to many Kenyans, who believe that their loved ones should receive a proper send off and that usually means a wooden coffin. (www.eapi.co.ke).

Fig3:Ecojeneza
Source: www.eapi.co.ke

Flipflop Recycling Company
As the name suggests, this is a company whose core business is to manage
and protect oceans resources, ecosystems and habitats by cleaning up oceans
and using the waste products innovatively. The main target waste material
picked collected from the ocean is rubbers sandals popularly known as
flipflops or slippers. The waste rubber is then handcrafted to produce
beautiful functional and decorative products.

Fig4:Productsmade from flipflops
Source: www.ffrc.org

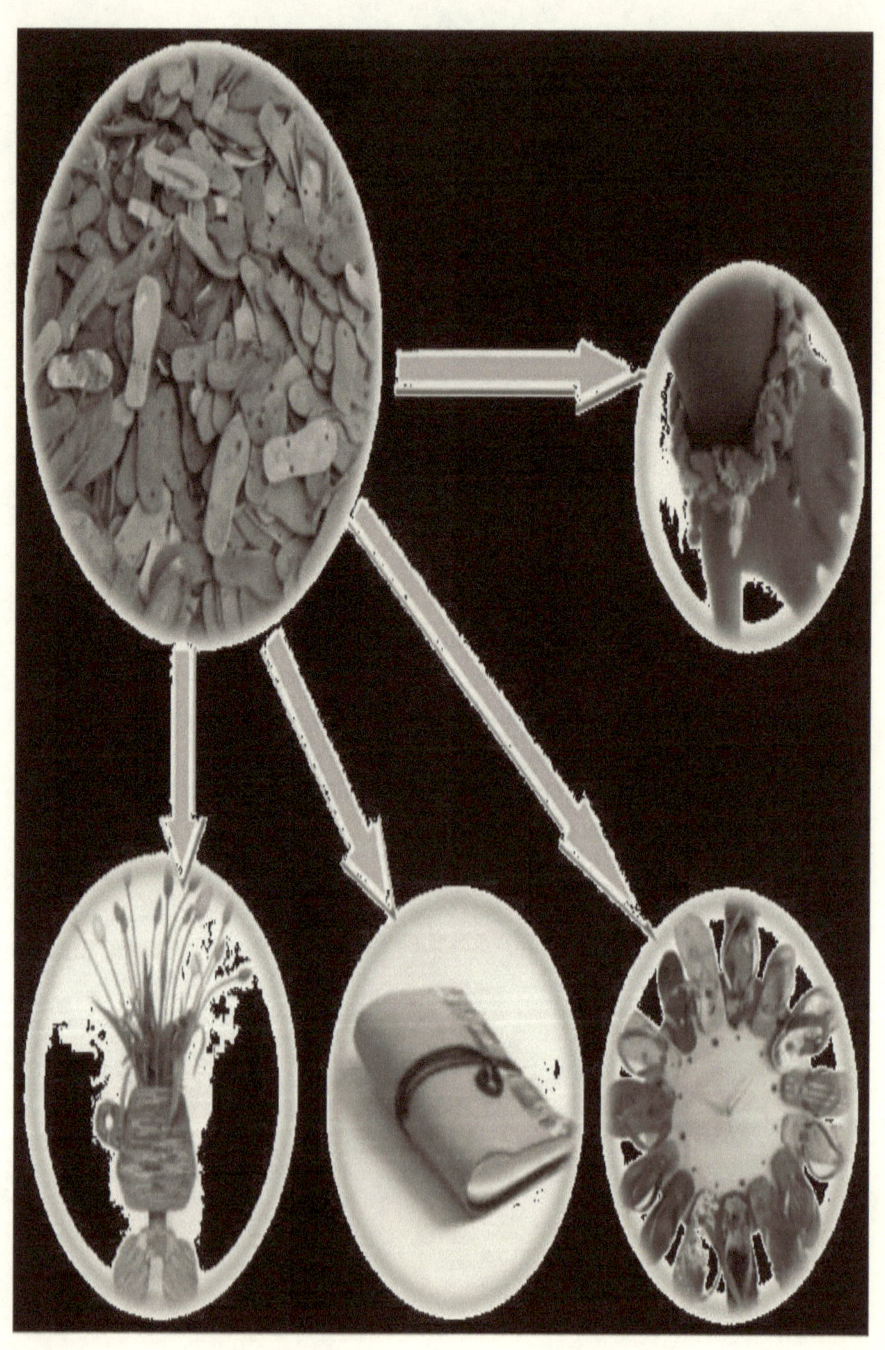

CHAPTER SIXTEEN

SMART TEXTILES

INTRODUCTION

Smart Textiles trace their origin from when man first set foot on the moon in the 1960s, Researchers' started seriously treading in the murky waters of smart materials in the 1990s. That is the time that many designers started incorporating the language of smart materials into their designs, the textile industry was not left behind. This is

according to Addinton and Schodek, 2007. Shanmugasundaram (2008) on the other hand, further explain that one of the main reasons for the rapid development of

intelligent textiles is the important investment made by the military industry. This is because smart textiles are used in different projects such as extreme winter condition jackets or uniforms that change colour so as to improve camouflage effects.

Intelligent textiles represent the next generation of fibres, fabrics and articles produced from them. They can be described as textile materials that think for themselves, for example through the incorporation of electronic devices or smart materials. Many intelligent textiles already feature in advanced types of clothing, principally for protection and safety and for added fashion or convenience. F. Boussu, G. Bailleul, J. L. Petiniot, H. Vinchon, (2002)

Definition ofSmartTextiles

Smart textiles are defined as textiles that can sense and react to environmental conditions or stimuli from mechanical, thermal, chemical, electrical or magnetic sources Gregory, Samuel, Hanks 2001). Modern and Smart Fabrics are designed to maximise characteristics such as lightness, breathability, waterproofing etc or to react to heat or light. They are usually manufactured using microfibers. Smart materials can change their properties in response to an external stimulus. Materials such as Lycra®, Thinsulate®, and Carbon fibres, Kevlar®, Teflon® and Gore-Tex® have different special properties that make them suited to particular uses. bbc.co.uk/gcsebitesize/smartfabrics

Componentsand General methodsof incorporatingsmartnessintotextiles

Three components may be present in smart textiles (materials), sensors, actuators and controlling units. The sensors provide a nerve system to detect signals. Some of the materials act only as sensors (passive smart textiles) and some as both sensors and actuators (active smart textiles). Actuators act upon the signals and work in coordination with the controlling unit (for very smart textiles) to produce an appropriate output.

These components may be fiber optics, phase change materials, shape memory materials, thermo chromic dyes, miniaturized electronic items, Piezo-resistive yarns etc. These components form an integrated part of the textile structure and can be incorporated into the substrate at any of the following levels: Fiber spinning level, Yarn/fabric formation level and finishing level. Matilda, McQuaid. (2005).

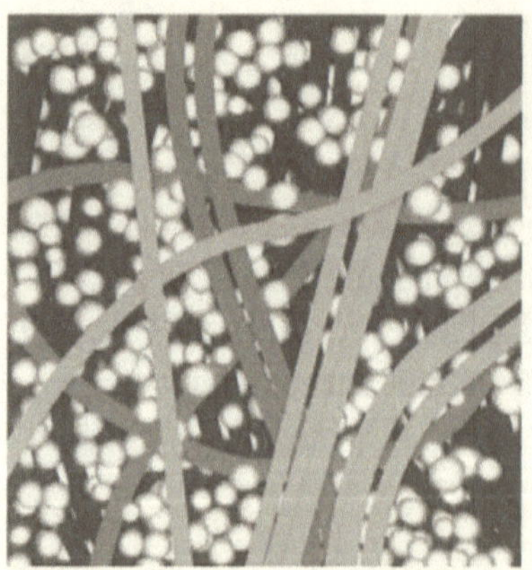 

Figure 1. Magnified image of PCMs Figure 2. Gore-Tex® contains a layer of plastic incorporated into fabric, based on Polytetrafluoroethene Source: http:/ bitesize gcse.school.uk.smartfabrics

Figure 3: Chromic textile
Source: http.//metallurgy for dummies.com/smart materials
Some ImportantApplication Areasof Smart Textiles

Smart textiles find a wide spectrum of applications ranging from daily usage to hightech usage. Below are some of the various important applications of such textiles. Textiles are considered used for the following broad categories. Comfort wear, sportswear, Heat protection, Medical applications, Military applications, Computing textiles, Fashion, Aviation Space research. M.M.

Farid, A.M. Khudhair, S.A.K. Razack, S. Al-Hallaj, (2004)

Figure 4, Shows two kinds of smart clothes. One group involves smart clothing with sensors located in close proximity to the skin, and which are used for biomedical applications. The sensors are generally enclosed in the layers of fabric or on its surface. In some cases, the fabric itself is used for the sensors. The second group of smart clothing involves the use of sensors and devices simply housed in pockets and not directly in contact with the skin. A wide range of exciting new functions can thus be added to clothing, including micro radios, microcomputers, flexible TV screens, microcellular phones, solar cells, energy-recovery systems (in shoes, generally see fig 6), and flexible keyboards. These devices are used mainly for communication purposes, displaying color and pictures, indicating moods, and sending messages. However, some devices or sensors used for monitoring purposes can also be placed in special pockets (GPS devices, fall detectors, data loggers, accelerometers, and activity detectors). These two main kinds of smart clothing are compatible and complementary. G. Troster, (2004)

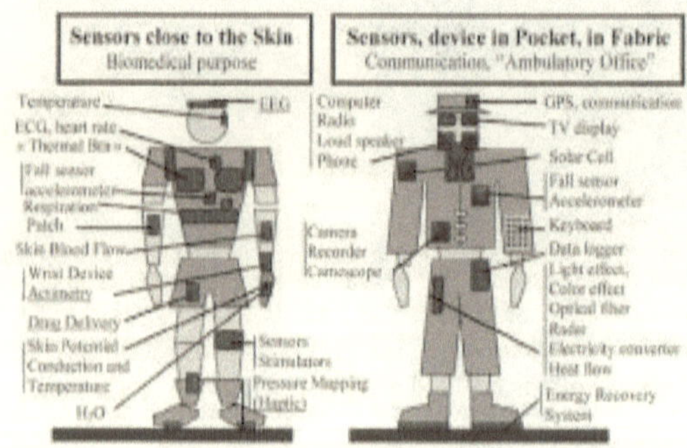

Figure 4: Two kinds of smart clothes.

Source: http://tectexntu.files.wordpress.com/

Figure 6: GTX GPS Xplorer Smart Shoes, Source:
http://www.geekabout.com/wpcontent/uploads/2007/02/shoes.jpg

GTX GPS Xplorer Smart Shoes, see Figure 6, are a good way to keep track
of anyone. These shoes come with a built-in small GPS tracking device
which provides the location of the shoe to a central location tracking service.

Market ofSmartTextiles

Marketoverview

The market for smart textiles is relatively small, but it is growing quickly,
according to Smart and Interactive Textiles, an August 2007 report published
by US-based research firm BCC Research. Smart or Interactive Textiles is a

new market segment resulting from the miniaturization of electronics and the fall in price of components and manufacturing costs for both electronics and textiles. A simultaneous trend in the clothing industry toward manufacture of specific products for dedicated uses i.e. for running, skiing, golf and extreme sports has created a niche where smart and interactive textiles enable new functions and features that can enhance a garment's performance and it's wearer's experience. Ahsan (Administrator)

Some Manufacturers of Smart Textiles

Companies with such products on the market include US sports apparel firm O'Neill, which markets a ski jacket with built-in keypads controlling an MP3 player, and US apparel firm Nike, which has teamed with electronics company Apple, to offer a shoe containing a pedometer that can communicate with Apple's iPod nano music player. Apparel companies Adidas and Rosner, both of Germany, the UK's Burton and USbased The North Face are also active in this area. Ahsan (Administrator), (2010).

Delaware-based Textronics has developed the NuMetrex heart-rate sensing sports bra. UK-based CuteCircuit designed a shirt that expands and contracts in response to Bluetooth commands. One product targeted for medical applications is the Lifeshirt, from California-based VivoMetrics, which monitors a number of vital signs.

C ONCLUSION
The textiles of tomorrow are stronger, faster, lighter, safer, and smarter. Our landscape, our buildings, our vehicles, our clothes, and our bodies all benefit from these highly engineered performance textiles. Understanding and controlling the composition and microstructure of any new materials are the ultimate objectives of research in this field, and is crucial to the production of good smart materials. The insights gained by gathering data on the behaviors of a material's crystal inner structure as it heats and cools, deforms and changes, will speed the development of

new materials for use in different applications.

CHAPTER SEVENTEEN

MANUFACTURED BOARDS

Definition

Manufactured boards are timber sheets which are produced by gluing wood layers or fibres together. They often make use of waste wood materials and they are developed mainly for industrial production as they can be made in very large sheets of consistent quality. The table below is a summary of the different types of boards. (Everet, pg 68)

Manufactured Image Description
Board Type
Plywood panel
Blockboard
Chip Board manufactured

Plywood is a manufactured wood

Made from thin sheets of wood veneer that is glued together with adjacent plies having their wood grain at right angles to each other.
It is a compound wood board onsisting of nearly square strips of softwood placed side by side and

sandwiched between veneer panels often of hardwood.
A composite wood material

from wood chips, sawmill shavings, or

even saw dust, and a synthetic resin or other suitable binder, which is pressed
and extruded.
MDF
hardwood

Hardboard
Sterling Board A wood product formed using

or softwood fibres, combining it with wax and a resin binder, and forming
panels by applying high temperature and pressure.

Hardboard is a composite wood roduct made out of exploded wood fibers
that have been highly compressed.

Sterling board is made from softwood strands compressed and glued together
with exterior grade,water-resistant resins. It has an irregular pattern.

Fig1:Summarytable of Manufactured Boards Source: www.thewarren.org/manufacturedboards.html

PLYWOOD

Definition

Plywood is a manufactured wood panel made from thin sheets of wood veneer. The veneers are glued together with adjacent plies having their wood grain at right angles to each other. There are usually an odd number of plies so that the sheet is balanced. (Lyons 1997,pg 95).
A three ply has three plywood veneers combined; a stout heart has three plies combined with the middle one being thicker, while multi ply plywood has many plies combined (Everett, pg 69).

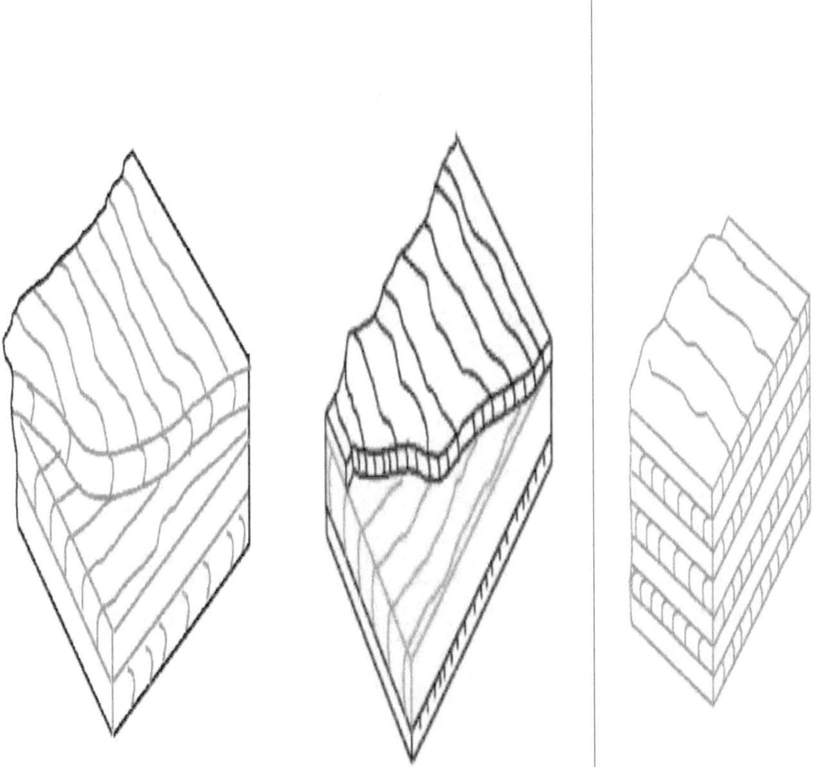

Fig2:Three Ply Fig3:Stout HeartThreePly Fig4:Multi ply Source: www.learning.covcollege.ac.uk,2012
Structural Characteristics

Cross-graining has several important benefits: it reduces the tendency of wood to split when nailed at the edges, it reduces expansion and shrinkage equating to improved dimensional stability, and it makes the strength of the panel consistent across both directions. For this reason, Plywood is preferred instead of plain wood because of its resistance to cracking, shrinkage, splitting and warping, and its general high degree of strength. (www.designtechnology.org/plywood.html)

History

Plywood was invented around 3400 B.C. by the Ancient Mesopotamians, who attached several thinner layers of wood together to make one thick layer. They originally did this during a shortage of quality wood, gluing very thin layers of quality wood over lesser-quality wood. Modern plywood was invented by Immanuel Nobel, father of AlfredNobel. Nobel realized that several thinner layers of wood bonded together would be stronger than one single thick layer of wood (www.thewarren.org/manufacturedboards/plywood.html).
Production

Plies are made by peeling pre-boiled log by rotating it against a knife (Everett, pg 68). The process requires a good log, called a peeler, which is generally straighter and larger in diameter than one required for processing into dimensioned lumber by a sawmill. The log is laid horizontally and rotated about its long axis while a long blade is pressed into it, causing a thin layer of wood to peel off. In this way the log is peeled into sheets of veneer which are then cut to the desired dimensions, dried, patched, glued together and then baked in a press at 140 °C to form the plywood panel. (Everet, pg 69) The woods commonly used to make plywood are gaboon, douglas fir, sapele, beech and birch. The thickness range of the sheets is between 0.36cm to 7.6 cm while the sheets are 1.2m by 2.4 m or 0.91m by 1.8 m. (Everett, pg 70). The grade of plywood is determined partly by the adhesive used and the durability of the timber (Lyons, pg 96).

Applications

Plywood is used in many applications that need high-quality, high-strength sheet material because it is has high resistance to cracking, breaking, shrinkage, twisting and warping. For this reason, it is used as an engineering material for stressed-skin applications. In addition, plywood is used to create curved surfaces because it can easily bend with the grain for example in making skateboard ramps. Different varieties of plywood exist for different applications.

Fig5:Furniture

madefromPlywood
Source: www.wikipedia.org
Softwood Plywood

Softwood plywood panel is usually made either of cedar, Douglas fir, spruce, pine, fir or redwood and is typically used for construction and industrial purposes like vehicle internal body work, packages and boxes and for construction of floors, walls and roofs.
(www.designtechnology.org/plywood.html)

Hardwood plywood

This type of plywood is used for demanding end uses because of its excellent strength, surface hardness, stiffness, resistance to creep and damage- and wear- resistance. It has a high planar shear strength and impact resistance, which make it especially suitable for heavy-duty floor and wall structures. For this reason, it is used for panels in formwork, scaffolding materials and container floors. In addition, because of its smooth surface it is used for musical instruments, sports equipment and furniture (www.designtechnology.org/plywood.html)

Special-purpose plywood

These are plywoods that do not have alternating plies which are designed for specific purposes like aircraft plywood which is made from mahogany or birch, and uses adhesives with increased resistance to heat and humidity. Plywood used for marine purposes is manufactured from durable face and core veneers, with few defects so it performs longer in humid and wet conditions and resists delaminating and fungal attack (www.designtechnology.org/plywood.html)

Drawbacks of Plywood

The adhesives used in plywood, urea formaldehyde and phenol formaldehyde are carcinogenic in very high concentrations. The WHO warns against use of them. (www.thewarren.org/manufacturedboards/plywood.html).

BLOCKBOARD

Definition

It is a compound wood board consisting of nearly square strips of softwood placed side by side and sandwiched between veneer panels often of hardwood. The sandwich is then glued under high pressure (Everet, pg 71) History

Blockboard is one of the oldest composites ever conceived. In accordance to research, furniture built with this material was in fact found in the Egyptian

Pyramids. (www.thewarren.org/manufacturedboards/blockboard.html).

Structural Characteristics

Blockboard panels are easy to cut and reclaim, are light in weight, stable and have high mechanical features. Besides its traditional use in joinery works, the great dimensions of the boards make it advantageous for factories manufacturing modern and quality furnishings, in particular doors and furniture, as the light weight exerts less stress onto hinges, improving furniture life. Blockboard is sold in sheets of 2440 x 1220mm and are normally 30mm thick (www.designtechnology.org/).

Manufacture of Blockboard

Block board is made up of a core of softwood strips. These strips may be up to about 25mm wide. The strips are placed edge to edge and sandwiched between veneers of hardwood. These are bonded with resin under controlled pressure and temperature to get perfect bonding. The sandwich is then glued under high pressure using Urea formaldehyde resin. (www.authorsteam.com/kanagaraj/blockboard.html)

For finishing, a variety of applied finishes such as wood veneers and plastic laminate surfaces may be used. If both sides are treated in the same way, the board has a good resistance to warping. In addition, because the edges of blockboard do not clean up well and are not very attractive, they are covered with a decorative strip of softwood, paint or veneer called lipin (www.authorsteam.com/).

Application

Blockboard is used to make shelves, furniture, kitchen cabinets, bank counters, ship counters, wardrobes, doors, paneling and partitions. When using blockboard to make such things as doors or tables, it is important to ensure that the core runs lengthways in order to achieve maximum strength. In addition, the screws and nails used to attach the blockboard must make contact with the strips of softwood and not the gaps between the softwood strips, otherwise the object made will not be firmly joined.

Drawbacks of Blockboard

Exposure to thermal variations and/or to humidity leads to thermal and mechanical stress and in the long run it leads to cracks in the finish or protective melaminic resin layers. These cracks on the surface of board allow humidity to penetrate to layers made of wood strips that become impregnated with humidity. That causes the beginning of rottenness or decay processes of wood material quickly making the board useless. In addition, blockboard is not suitable for outdoor use because the glues used are interior glues (www.designtecnology.org/blockboards.html)

Laminboard

This is a board similar to blockboard consisting of thinner strips (5-7mm) of softwood placed side by side and sandwiched between veneer panels. (www.musterkiste.com, 2012). This results in a particular even surface with high material stability. Because of this, they are considered to be of a higher quality than blockboards and they are an excellent base for high quality veneers or for high gloss paint. (Everett, pg 71). Lamin Boards are used for furniture, shop fittings, interior finishings, wall cladding, ship imteriors, theatre stages and motor manufacture. (www.musterkiste.com).

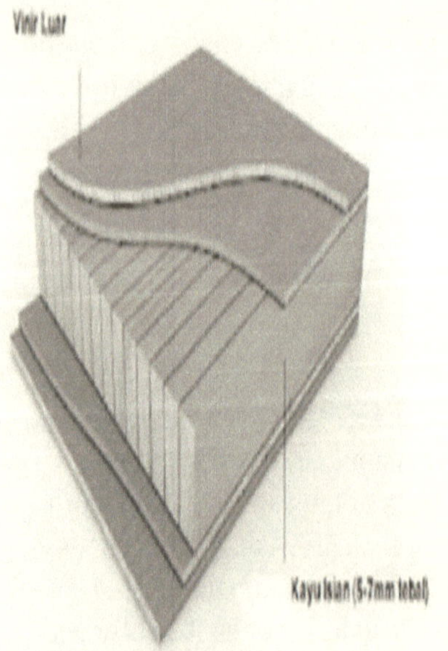

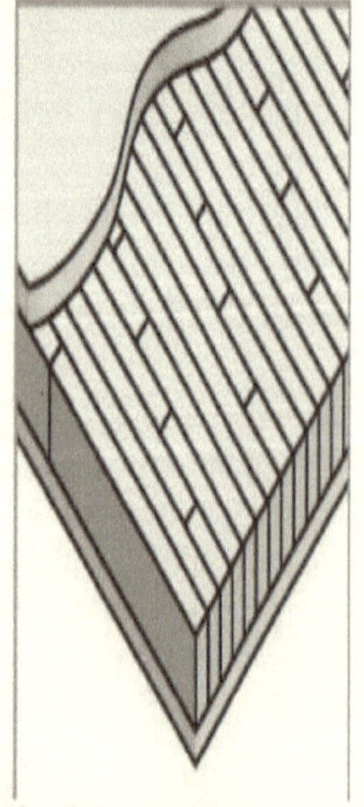

Fig6:Lamin board Fig7:Lamin board Source: www.jualtiplek.com Source: www.musterkiste.com

Battenboard
This is also similar to blockboard, but it has core strips which are wider than
those of blockboard; they are more than 30mm wide (Everett, pg71).

CHIPBOARD

Definition
Chipboard also known as particleboard is a composite wood material
manufactured from wood chips, sawmill shavings, or even saw dust, and a
synthetic resin or other suitable binder, which is pressed and extruded
(Lyons, pg 97).

History and Development

Modern plywood, as an alternative to natural wood, was invented in the 19th
century, but by the end of the 1940s a shortage of lumber made it difficult to
manufacture plywood affordably. Particleboard was intended to be a
replacement. Its inventor was Max Himmelheber of Germany. The first
commercial piece was produced during WorldWar II at a factory in Bremen,
Germany. It used waste material such as planer shavings, offcuts or sawdust,
hammer-milled into chips, and bound together with a phenolic resin.
(www.designtecnology.org/particlboard.html)

Physical Properties

Chipboard is cheaper, denser and more uniform than conventional wood and
plywood and is substituted for them when appearance and strength are less
important than cost. However, particleboard can be made more attractive by
painting or the use of wood veneers that are glued onto surfaces that will be
visible. However, portions of the chipboard may "blow out" when subjected
to excessive tension stress. In part, this arises from the lack of elasticity in
particleboard resins as compared to the long strands and compressible voids
contained in solid wood, a feature that, while preserved in the manufacture of
plywood, is compromised in particleboard. Furniture makers often cover
chipboard with real or imitation veneers, in an effort to simulate the look of
solid wood. Particleboard's selling points as compared to solid timber are its
low cost, its availability in large flat sheets, and its ability to be decorated

with all kinds of overlays
(www.thewarren.org/manufacturedboards/particleboard.html).

Manufacturing Process

Chipboard is manufactured by mixing wood particles or flakes together with a resin and forming the mix into a sheet. The raw material to be used for the particles is fed into a disc chipper for shredding. The particles are first dried, after which any oversized or undersized particles are screened out. Resin, in liquid form, is then sprayed through nozzles onto the particles. Once the resin has been mixed with the particles, the liquid mixture is made into a sheet. A weighing device notes the weight of flakes, and they are distributed into position by rotating rakes. The sheets formed are then cold-compressed to reduce their thickness and make them easier to transport. Later, they are compressed again, under pressures and temperature. This process sets and hardens the glue. The boards are then cooled, trimmed and sanded. They can then be sold as raw board or surface improved through the addition of a wood veneer or laminate surface (Lyons, pg 98).

Application

Chip board is used extensively in the making of furniture. It is also used in the construction of cabinet boxes and shelves. Whereas plywood has the potential to feather off in sheaves when extreme weight is placed on the hinges, chipboard in contrast, holds the screws in place under similar weight. In addition chipboard is favored for cabinet shelves that need to span a long width, like 30 inches or more since it will not bow under the weight like plywood. Moreover, chipboard is used in making speaker boxes (Lyons, pg 99).

Drawbacks of Chipboard

A major disadvantage of chipboard is that it is very prone to expansion and discoloration due to moisture, particularly when it is not covered with paint or another sealer. Therefore, it is rarely used outdoors or places that have high levels of moisture. In addition, during its production it causes a lot of air pollution because a large quantity of fine wood dust is released in the air. The other concern is with the release of formaldehyde because of the resin used.

Formaldehyde is classified by the WHO as a known human carcinogen. Another drawback is in application. When chipboard is used, unless it is adequately braced or built with thick material, chipboard shelves will visibly sag over time (or snap near the fasteners). In addition, when chipboard is damaged, it is difficult to repair. This is because, it is typically faced with by a non-wood veneer, which is practically impossible to match the original finish (www.thewarren.org/manufacturedboards/particleboard.html).

MDF
Definition

Medium-density fibreboard (MDF) is an engineered wood product formed by breaking down hardwood or softwood residuals into wood fibres, combining it with wax and a resin binder, and forming panels by applying high temperature and pressure. Large-scale production of MDF began in the 1980s, in both North America and Europe. (Lyons, pg 101)
Physical properties

MDF is denser than plywood. It is made up of separated fibres, but can be used as a building material similar in application to plywood. It is stronger and much denser than normal particle board.
MDF does not contain knots or rings, making it more uniform than natural woods during cutting and in service. Like natural wood, MDF may split when woodscrews are installed without pilot holes. MDF may be glued, doweled or laminated. Typical MDF has a hard, flat, smooth surface that makes it ideal for veneering, as there is no underlying grain to telegraph through the thin veneer as with plywood (Lyons, pg 101).

Application

MDF is used in the furniture industry to make kitchen cabinets, wardrobes and cupboards. It is also often used in loudspeaker enclosures, due to its increased weight and rigidity over normal plywood. It may be used to make display cabinets and interior fittings for shops and showrooms. MDF is used instead of plywood or chipboard because it is dense, flat, stiff, has no knots and is easily machined. Oil, water-based paints and varnishes may be used on it as well as veneers and laminates as surface finishes.
(www.thewarren.org/manufacturedboards.html).

Fig8:Furniture madeby MDF
Source: www.alibaba.com
Drawbacks of MDF

When MDF is cut, a large quantity of dust particles are released into the air causing air pollution. Moreover, Formaldehyde resins are commonly used to bind MDF together, and testing has consistently revealed that MDF products emit urea-formaldehyde and other volatile organic compounds that pose health risks at sufficient concentrations, for at least several months after manufacture.

HARDBOARD
Definition

It is a composite wood product similar to particle board and medium-density fiberboard, but is denser and much stronger and harder because it is made out of exploded woodfibers that have been highly compressed. It differs from particle board in that the bonding of the wood fibers requires no additional materials, although resin is often added. Unlike particle board, it does not split or crack. Unlike solid wood, hardboard is very homogeneous with no grain. A wood veneer can be glued onto it to give the appearance of solid wood. Other overlays include Formica, laminated papers, ceramics, and vinyl. (Lyons, pg 102)

History

A product resembling hardboard was first made in England in 1898 by hot pressing waste paper. In the 1900s, fiber building board of relatively low density was manufactured in Canada. In the early 1920s, improved methods of compressing wet wood pulp at high temperatures resulted in a higher density product. (www.designtechnology.org/hardboard.html).
Application

It has many uses, such as a substrate. It is used in construction, flooring, furniture, homeappliances, automobiles and cabinetry, and is popular among acrylic and oil painters as a painting surface due to its economical price .Hardboard has often been used as the surface material in clipboards, especially older models. It is also used as the final layer in many skateboard ramps and the half-pipe.Tempered hardboard is hardboard that has been coated with a thin film of linseed oil and then baked; this gives it more water resistance, impact resistance, hardness, rigidity and tensile strength. Tempered hardboard is used in construction siding. Perforated hardboard, is tempered hardboard that has a uniform array of holes in it, into which tool-hanging hooks or store fixtures can be placed. (www.designtechnology.org/hardboard.html)

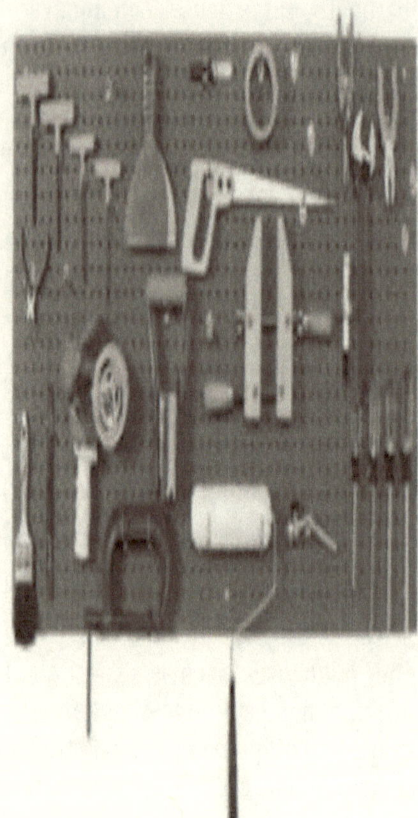

Fig9:Clipboard from hardboard Fig10:Perforated hardboard Source: www.inallbiz.com Source: www.alibaba.com

Sterling Boards

Definition

Sterling board is made from softwood strands compressed and glued together with exterior grade, water-resistant resins. It is easily recognisable because of the irregular pattern of flattened, softwood strands that make up the surface. The appearance of the surface is not very attractive. Sterling board is used where the appearance of the surface is unimportant (Lyons, pg 99).

Production

The softwood timber flakes are tangentially cut and measured approximately
75X35mm. These are dried and coated with wax and 2.5 % of either phenol
formaldehyde or melanine-urea formaldehyde resin. The mix is laid up in
three or occasionally five layers, with the grains running parallel to the sheet
on the outer faces and across or randomly within the middle layer. The
boards are then cured heat and pressure, sanded and packaged (Lyons, pg 99).

Application
It is used to protect windows of empty buildings or to make products that
need to be protected against the elements e.g. fishing boxes
(www.thewarren.org/).

DESIGN MATERIALS AND PROCESS

STEEL

INTRODUCTION

Steel is a finely crystalline ferrous metal derived from iron. It is produced by
removing impurities, principally sulphur and phosphorous from pig iron and
then accurately adjusting proportions of all ingredients including manganese
and silica. The first form of steel was produced in 1856 due to the invention
of the Bessemer Converter, which oxidized the high carbon, manganese,
silicon and phosphorous in molten pig iron. Ferrous metals, mild steel being
one of them, produced annually exceeds ninety percent of the total metal
produced. Some of the desirable qualities in steel are that it has high tensile
strength and high resistance to corrosion. (Everet, pg 94)

THE STEEL MAKING PROCESS
Oxidation of Pig Iron

In making steel, the carbon, phosphorous and other elements in pig iron are
reduced in quantity by oxidation through the converter process, open hearth
furnace, electric furnaces or spray steelmaking (Lyons, pg 111)

The Converter Process

This was the first method of making steel in large scale. Converters oxidize the high carbon, manganese, silicon and phosphorous contents of molten pig iron by blowing oxygen into the melt. In about twenty minutes, phosphorous reached an acceptable level. After this, a controlled amount of carbon was added to the melt and residual oxides and gases were removed by addition of ferro-manganese. Though this method was what was principally used, it had one major disadvantage which was that ores with high phosphorous content could not be converted until 1878 when a scientist, Sidney Gilchrist used furnace linings with lime flux which reacts with acids. Today, LD converters are used. They use low cost tonnage oxygen combining good scrap consuming capacity with a high production rate. Through this process, steel ingots are produced. (Lyons, pg 111)
Open Hearth Furnace

Though this process is now obsolete, it was developed in 1861. In this case, Gas and preheated air, together with oxygen and oil heated a charge of pig iron and steel scrap. Some carbon and most of the silicon was oxidized by the flame and the remaining impurities were removed by addition of iron ore, mill scale and lime. Steel ingots are the by- product of this process (Lyons, pg 112)

Electric Furnaces

In this process, electric and high frequency induction furnaces are used to produce alloy steels from molten steel and selected scrap. Shorter refining periods are possible by injection in oxygen. The high temperatures attainable allow both the melting of alloy additions and the removal of impurities, leaving steel ingots. (Lyons, pg 112).

Spray Steel making

In this process, molten pig iron is finely atomized by a blast of oxygen and converted to steel as it falls through a reaction chamber. However, in this case steel ingots are not produced (Everet pg 96)

Reshaping Steel Ingots

The ingots produced are reshaped into sections by rolling, extrusion, forging and casting. Forging is physical hammering the ingots into desired shapes. Rolling involves mechanical smoothing of the steel to form sheets. Cold rolling that follows the hot rolling gives clean surfaces and increases the metals strength. In making of complex shapes like hollow sections, extrusion is used. In the case of casting, only high carbon steels are suitable. In this case, the molten metal is poured into moulds to take up the desired shapes. The steels used in this case tend to be more brittle than those shaped by pressure. (Everet, pg 96)

CARBON CONTENT OF STEELS

All steels contain carbon in varying proportions and are subdivided in different categories depending on this. The carbon content gives varying properties which determine how the steel is used. Low carbon steels contain up to 0.15 percent carbon and are soft hence suitable for making wire and thin sheets. Mild steel contain 0.15 to 0.25 percent carbon and are strong, ductile and suitable for rolling into sections, strips and sheets. They are easily worked and welded thus they are mainly used as structural steels. Medium carbon steels contain between 0.2 to 0.5 percent carbon and are suitable for forging and general engineering purposes. High carbon steels contain between o.5 to 1.5 percent carbon. Because of this, they have high tensile strength and hardness. However, their ductility reduces, they are too brittle for structural work and they are difficult to weld. Due to these qualities, they are suitable for casting, making files and cutting tools. (Lyons pg 113)

TYPES OF STEELS

Structural Steel

The type of steel used in this case is mild steel which is strong, ductile and easily welded. It is mainly used in making the frames of multi-storey buildings especially because it is less costly than reinforced concrete. There are many types of these steels, all differing in tensile strength, yield stress and ductility. As a result of this unique properties, each type has different preferred uses. However, the strengths apply only at normal temperatures. At about 550°C, there is loss of strength and considerable expansion, meaning

that they must be protected if they are to survive building fires.
(www.worldsteel.org)

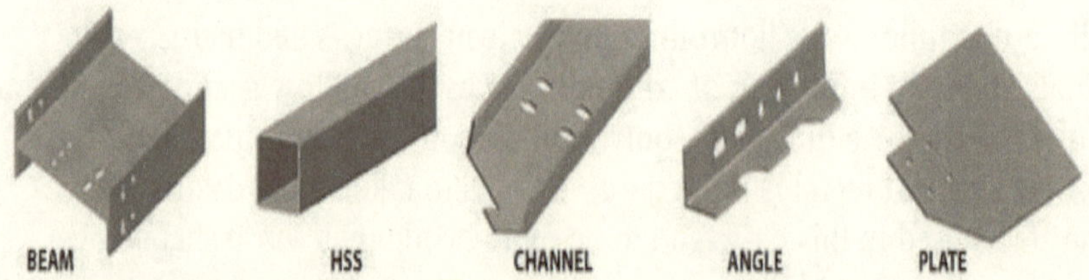

Fig1:Various structural steelshapes

Sourc e: steelconstruction.org

F ig2:ASteel Structure
Source: (www.ivfab.com)

Weathering Steel
This is plain carbon steel containing 0.2 percent copper. It has better
resistance to corrosion, but it is greatly affected by elements of weather.
(Everet, pg 97)
Cor-Ten

This is a type of steel that contains 0.25 to 0.55 percent of copper. As a result it develops an oxide coating, russet-copper dark to purplish brown in colour. It most desirable qualities are its high tensile strength and slow rusting properties and therefore it is used in the manufacture of sections, plates, sheets and coils. However, due to corrosion of the oxide with weather elements, it stains adjacent walls or pavings. (Everet, pg 97)

Sheet Steel

This is a type of steel that is rolled to be not more than 3mm thick. However, mild steel can be cold formed to be up to 5mm to 6.3mm thick. Sheet is available in mild steel, low alloy high strength steels, Cor-Ten, and in stainless steels. However, when sheet steel is uncoated, it corrodes easily. To protect it from corrosion, they must be galvanized, vitreously enameled or get decorative pre-finishes like paint, PVC coating and laminates in a wide range of colours and textures. Because of their different unique properties, Sheets are used for wall and roof cladding, curtain wall panels, floor and roof trough decking, lintels, metal door frames, steel condit and fittings for electrical wiring, corrugated steel sheets, demountable partitions and furniture, ducting and rainwater goods. (Everet, pg 97)

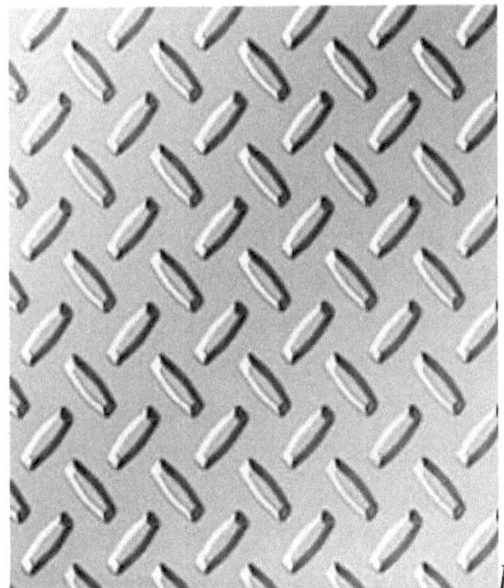

Fig3:Etched StainlessSteel.
Source: www.isaacbutterworth.co.ke
Alloy Steels

Fig4:Roof steel sheets

Source: www.indiamart.com

This type of steel formed by combining steel with at least five percent of alloying elements with the aim of providing special properties like ultra-high strength, corrosion or heat resistance. In addition, alloy steels can be heat treated through a process known as annealing to get the required degrees of hardness, and strength throughout their thickness and not just on the surface. Hot rolled and processed high tensile alloy steel bars are mainly used for concrete pre-stressing. (www.worldsteel.org)

Stainless Steel

Stainless steel is the most common type of steel, its development dating back to 1913. It is formed by combining Steel with Chromium. Some of the desirable qualities it has are that it is resistant to high temperatures, it is hard, strong and has a good appearance. In addition, it develops an invisible corrosion resistant film in air and has high resistance to organic and weak mineral acids. It is also compatible with nonmetals and other metals and it does not stain materials adjacent to it. Moreover, because of the hard, smooth, corrosion free surface of stainless steel, it does not hold dirt easily, and when it does, the dirt can be washed off easily. (www.worldsteel.org)

Stainless steel is available in many forms, either as rolled, extruded and drawn forms. They can be forged and cast and fabricated by normal methods including soldering, brazing and welding. For finishing, there are five standard mill finishes and four polished finishes. Polishing means creating a lustrous surface and this can be done by mechanically grinding with fine abrasives and a mirror polish. For complex shapes which cannot be mechanically polished, electro plating is used to give the desired bright or dull matt finish. In this case of electro plating, the oxide coating used can have a varying colour range from gold to dark brown. (Everet, pg 97)

There are different classifications of stainless steel depending on the amount of Chromium present. There are martensitic stainless steels which have about 13 percent of Chromium. The second category is known as Ferritic, with about 17 percent of Chromium while the third is Austenitic, usually with 16-19 percent of Chromium in combination with 6-14percent nickel. This third category is non-magnetic, with high tensile strength, ductility, and with good welding and soldering properties. Due to these properties this type of stainless steel is suitable for normal internal uses and for uses where good appearance is important. (Everet, pg 98)

Because of the distinct unique properties of stainless steel, it has varying uses while it is in different forms. First and foremost, light gauge stainless steel tubes that are between 5mm to 42mm in diameter are suitable for plumbing, hot water heating and for connection by capillary or compression fittings. The advantage with these stainless steel tubes is that they are cheaper, stronger and more resistant to corrosion than copper tubes. Secondly, stainless steel sheets are used to make roof and wall coverings, urinal slabs, hospital equipment, sink tops and kitchen and restaurant equipment. In addition, they are used for window frames, sandwich panels and for insulation cladding. Thirdly, because of the high tensile strength, they are used in structures as reinforcement for concrete, for cramps, wall ties, sole plate anchors, dowels and other fixings for securing precast concrete and stone wall claddings. (www.worldstainlesssteel.org/pdf/stainlesssteelfamily)

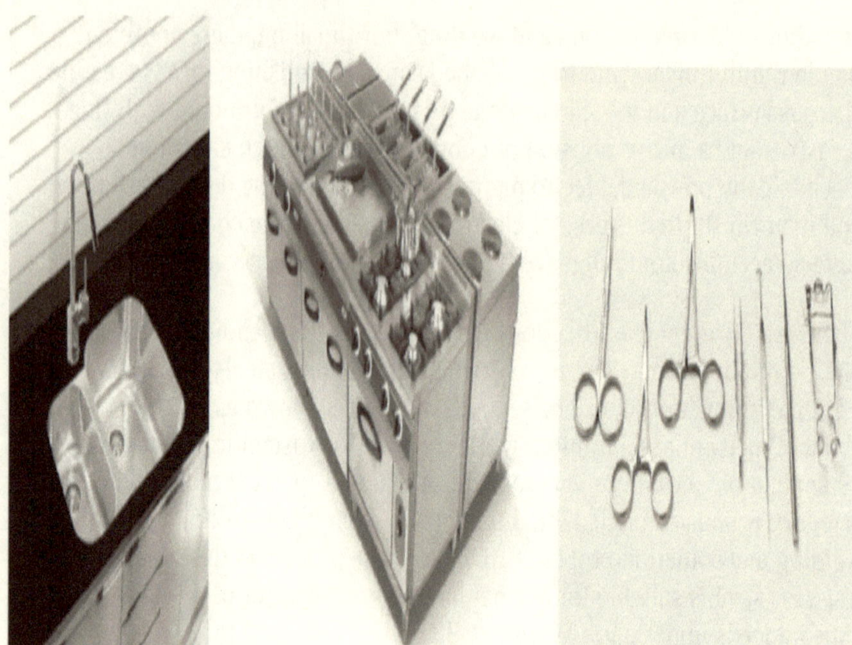

Fig5:Sink Fig6:Catering Equipment Fig7:SurgicalInstruments Source: www.Alibaba.Com

HEAT TREATMENTS FOR STEEL

Steel is heated to modify its mechanical properties so as to obtain a wide range of properties. This is because; subjection to temperature cycles alters the shape and sizes of the constituent grains, thereby altering different properties. The first type of heat treatment is known as hardening. It is a type of heat treatment whereby the steel is heated above a critical temperature and then rapidly cooled. The resultant effect is hardening of the steel but reduction of ductility. The second type of heat treatment is tempering. In this case, the metal is reheated below the hardening temperature followed by cooling at any rate. What results in this case is greater ductility but loss in strength. In the case of low carbon steels, hardening and tempering cannot be directly applied. The surfaces are first carbonized through a heat treatment known as case hardening where the steel is heated while it is surrounded with a carbonaceous material. (Everet, pg 98)

Moreover, steel can be annealed. This is a type of heat treatment where the

steel is heated to a critical temperature above 600°C, held at this temperature
for a period in relation to the thickness of the metal and then cooled slowly at
a controlled rate in the furnace. This process softens the steel and removed
internal stresses. Normalizing is another heat treatment alike to annealing.
However, in this case, the steel is heated above a critical temperature and
then it is cooled more rapidly. This results in an alteration in grain size and
acquisition higher tensile strength. (Everet, pg 98)

PRODUCTION OF STEEL IN THE WORLD

Metal and steel industry is considered the backbone of the economic
activities of any given country. The per capita steel consumption is an
internationally recognised indicator of the level of development of that
country. The table below shows the production of steel in the world.

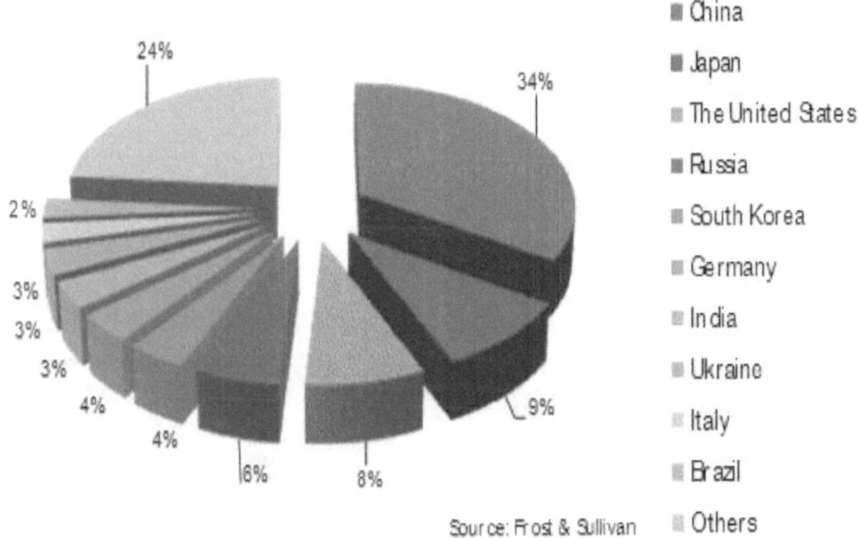

Fig8:Piechart indicating Steel Production
Source: www.frostandsullivan.com

THE STEEL INDUSTRY IN KENYA

Kenya has a basic metal sector making a variety of downstream products
from local and imported steel scrap, steel billets and hot rolled coils. Kenya

imports steel billets, coils, wire rod and wires, steel plates, sheets, steel scrap and pig iron. The country possesses a broad- based metal products sector with various independent engineering, foundry and metalwork workshops. The main sub-sectors in Kenya's metal industry are steel smelting -rolled steel products and pipes. These subsectors are interrelated, as they depend upon each other for the supply of inputs. Statistics by the Trade ministry show that metals and steel products are currently Kenya's largest manufactured goods exported within the Comesa and EAC regions. www.kam.co.ke.

The industry is heavily dependent on imported raw materials, since no local sources have been developed to date. From the basic metal and allied industry, a diversified network of downstream industries have emerged, which include motor vehicle and auto-ancillary, a range of fasteners, reinforcement bars for construction, furniture, agricultural tools, kitchenware, drums and containers, wheelbarrows, structural and fabrication, electrical panels, and supply of raw material to the jua kali sector. www.kam.co.ke.

CHAPTER NINETEEN

DESIGN MATERIALS AND PROCESS

STONES
Introduction

A stone is a portion of a rock used as building and decorative material They are used in building as blocks, slabs, flags, setts, roofing slates and damp-proof courses. (Everet, pg 71)

Fig1:Stoneblocks Fig2:Stone slabs
Source: www.shutterstock.com www.pambobora.com

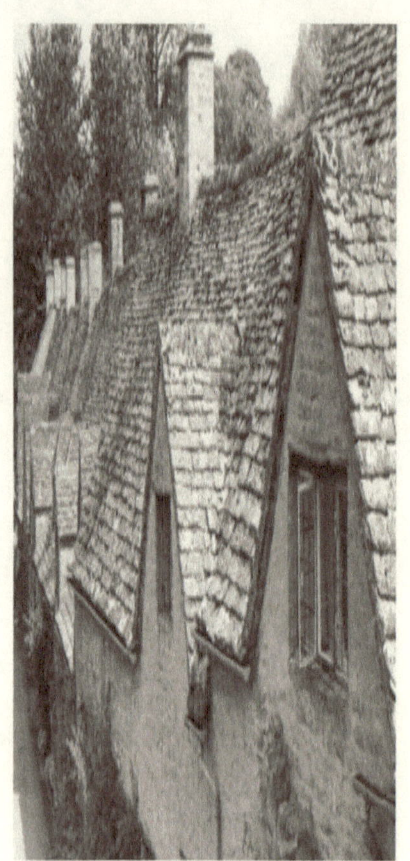

Fig3:Stone roofingslates Fig4:Stone setts
Source: www.englishheritage.org.uk www.wrightofcampden.com

History and Development

Stone Age

The period where our ancestors used stones for tools is known as the Stone Age. Obsidian and flint were used for knives and spears. River rocks were used to break other things. Caves were used as places to live and rocks and boulders were used to sit on and to build fire pits.
(www.rocksforkids.com/uses.html)

Fig5:Stone agetools

Source: www.xtimeline.com
Modern Age
In Modern Times, stones are used for building stone, in production of
artifacts, for decorations and jewellery. (www.rocksforkids.com/uses.html).

Properties of Stones

Strength and Durability

Durability is the ability of a stone to endure and maintain its essential and
distinctive characteristics i.e. resistance to decay, strength and appearance.
Physical properties such as density, compressive strength and porosity are
measured in order to determine its durability. Durability is based upon the
stones natural physical properties, characteristics and the environmental
conditions to which it will be or is subjected too. (www.aboutcivil.org)
Porosity and Permeability

Porosity is the ratio of pores in the stone, to its total solid volume. Pores and
the capillary structure develop differently in the three stone groups, with
sedimentary rocks having the most porosity. However, very high porosities
may allow excessive volumes of corrosive fluids such as acid rainwater to
enter and cause severe damage to the rock. For this reason, most durable
sedimentary stones have moderate porosity. (www.aboutcivil.org)

Associated with stones porosity is its permeability. This is the extent to which pores and capillary structures are interconnected throughout the stone. These networks, their size, structure and orientation affect the degree and depth to which moisture, vapors and liquids can be absorbed into the interior of the stone. Permeability is increased when a stone is highly fractured or the veining material is soft or grainy (www.aboutcivil.org).

Hardness and Weathering

Hardness is the property of a material to avoid and resist scratching. It is determined by comparison with the standard minerals of the Moh's scale, with the hardest being diamond, and the least hard being talc. (www.aboutcivil.org)

Weathering, on the other hand is dependent on the mineral composition, textural differences, varying degrees of hardness and pore or capillary structure of the stone. In addition, the tntensity and duration are the two key elements that govern to what extent weathering reactions will have on stone. (www.aboutcivil.org)

TYPES OF STONES
Introduction

All rocks fall into one of three classes depending on their geological formation. The three broad categories are Igneous, Sedimentary and Metamorphic Rocks. (Campagna, pg 12)

Igneous Rocks

Igneous rock is formed through the cooling and solidification of magma or lava. They may form with or without crystallization, either below the surface as intrusive rocks or on the surface as extrusive rocks. Intrusive igneous rocks are formed from magma that cools and solidifies within the crust of a planet. Since the magma cools slowly, the result is that these rocks are coarse grained, for example granite stone. Extrusive igneous rocks are formed at the crust's surface as a result of the partial melting of rocks within the mantle and crust. Extrusive rocks cool and solidify very quickly, and as a result they are fine grained, for example obsidian stone. (www.fi.edu/igneousrocks)

 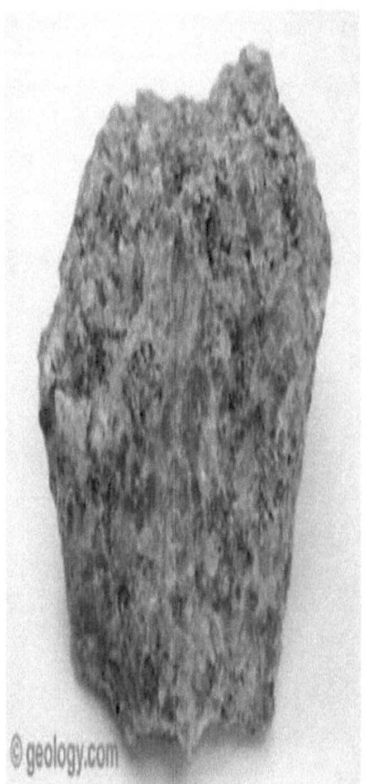

Fig6:Obsidian Stone Fig7:Granite Stone
Source: www.geology.com Source:www.geology.com

Sedimentary Rocks

Sedimentary rocks are types of rock that are formed by the deposition of material at the Earth's surface and within bodies of water. The particles settle and accumulate or minerals to precipitate from a solution. Before being deposited, sediment was formed by weathering and erosion in a source area, and then transported to the place of deposition by water, wind, ice, mass movement or glaciers which are called agents of denudation. Based on the processes responsible for their formation, there are three basic types of sedimentary rocks: 1) clastic sedimentary rocks such as breccia, conglomerate,quartz, mica, sandstone and shale, that are formed from mechanical weathering debris; 2) chemical sedimentary rocks such as rock salt, gysum and limestones, that form whendissolved materials precipitate from solution; and, 3) organic sedimentary rocks such as coal and coral limestones which form from the accumulation of plant or animal debris.

Fig8:Cream Quartz stone Fig9:Mica Source: www.quartzstone.org
Source:www.esrf.eu

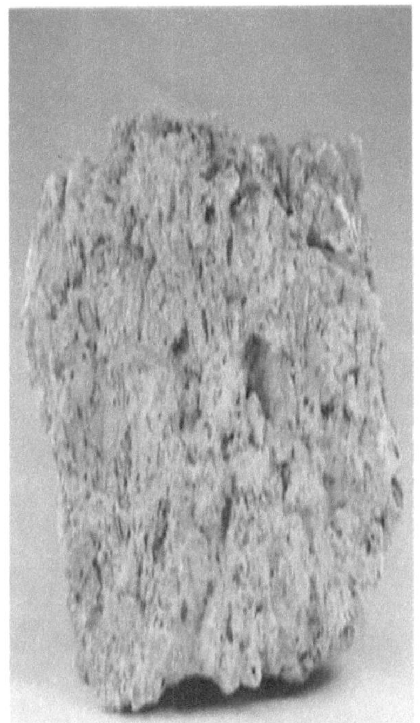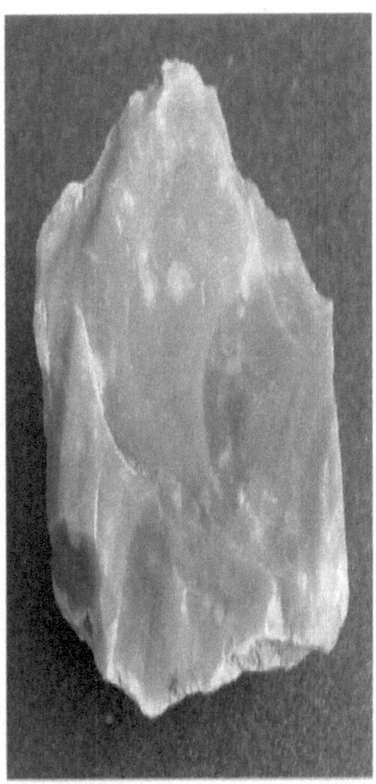

Fig10: Lime stone Fig11: Chert Source: www.geology.com
Source:www.geology.com

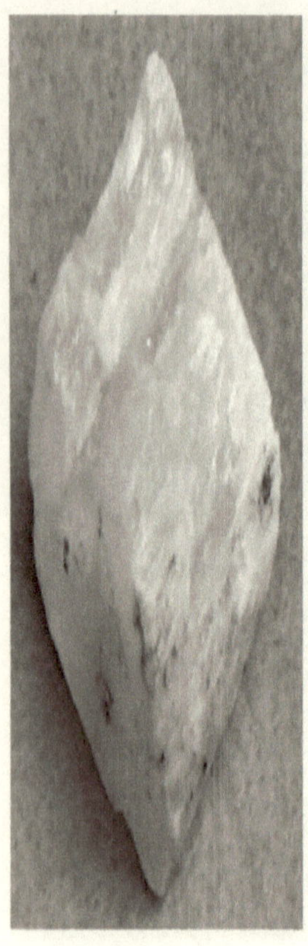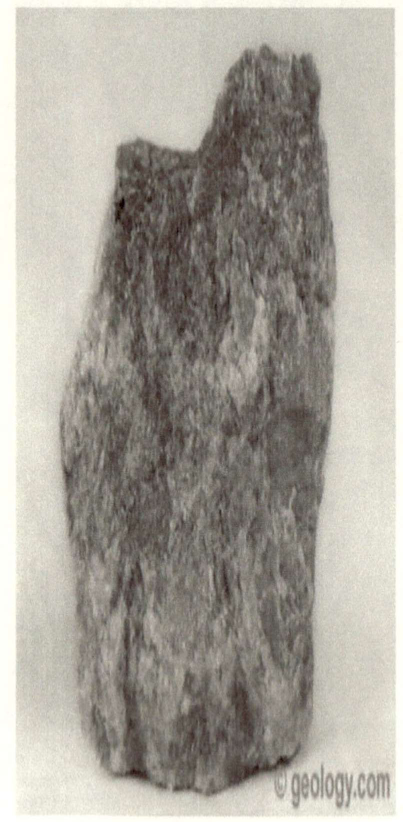

Fig12: Gypsum Fig13: Barite
www.shivamchemicals.in Source: www.geology.com

Metamorphic Rocks

Metamorphic rocks arise from the transformation of existing rock types, in a process called metamorphism, which means "change in form". The original rock, which may be sedimentary, igneous or another older metamorphic rock, is subjected to heat and pressure causing profound physical and/or chemical change. They may be formed simply by being deep beneath the Earth's surface, subjected to high temperatures and the great pressure of the rock layers above it. They can form from tectonic processes such as continental collisions, which cause horizontal pressure, friction and distortion. They are

also formed when rock is heated up by the intrusion of hot molten rock called magma from the Earth's interior. Some examples of metamorphic rocks are gneiss, slate, marble,schist, and quartzite.
(www.fi.edu/metamorphicrocks.html)

Fig14:Marble

Source: www.Deviantart.com

QUARRYING AND PROCESSING

TECHNIQUES Quarrying

Fig15:Slate www. geology.com

Natural stone comes from a quarry from where it is excavated as blocks. There are two type of quarries; open pit and tunnel, both of which have particular problems during excavation (Campagna, pg 24).

Fig16:Open pitQuarry
Source: www.wikipedia.org

Sawing

This is the process whereby the blocks coming from the quarry are transformed into slabs or strips using either of the three types of sawing methods which are; diamond wire, gangsaw or diamond disk. (Campagna, pg 26)

Surface Finishing
This is the treatment that brings out the aesthetic features of the material. The three kinds of finishing are mechanical, impact and chemical as explained below. Mechanical Finishing

In this type of finishing, the stone is put into contact with an abrasive to reduce the original surface roughness. In this case, the stone will have a rough, honed or polished surface depending on the size of abrasive used (Campagna, pg 28).

Impact Finishing

In this type of finishing, a strong external force is applied on the stone surface in order to alter and enhance the original surface roughness. In this case, the stone can either be brushed, bush-hammered, tooled, sandblasted or flamed. (Campagna, pg 29)

Fig17:Chiselledstonework
Source:www.castiastone.com

Fig18:Sandblastedstoneused as signage
Source: www.macdonaldsons.com
Chemical Finishing

In this case, chemicals are applied to stone in order to produce reactions that transform the material surface so as to improve their characteristics. The stone can be corroded by acid washing to obtain different effects dependent on the material, chemical and the processing time. This finishing can be used to reduce the ruggedness of stone, remove oily or dust spots on the material or induce oxidation which changes material colour. (Campagna, pg 30).

USE OF STONE AS A DESIGN MATERIAL

When one thinks of stone, its use in famous buildings probably first comes to mind, but few people probably realise that stone in some form enters our lives probably a hundred times even before we leave the house each day. Five main groups of uses can

be identified. (www.bgs.ac.uk/stoneuses.html).

Use Physical Property Application and Example

Building and decorative Stone is used because of its stone resistance to weather or its aesthetic appeal.
Buildings made from
natural stone last a long
time. In the case of the
ancient Egyptians, their
pyramids still stand as
testimony to a remarkable
building period back on the
edge of history.
It is used for buildings, walls, paving slabs. The used more stones include limestone, sandstone and marble.
Granite countertops are Used in kitchens. Granite is a hard wearing, volcanic stone that doesn't react with acidic foods. In ddition granite is not sensitive to heat, and very difficult to scratch or chip.

popular granite,

Marble has a pleasant pattern and it is used for decorative surfaces. Slates are used as roof tiles Sandstone, which is not so hardwearing or beautifully patterned is used for garden walls and and paths in landscaping.

Aggregates Stone used for its strong physical properties – crushed and sorted into various sizes for use in concrete, coated with bitumen to make asphalt or used 'dry' as bulk fill in construction.

Industrial Purposes limestone can be used for its chemical (mainly alkaline) properties as Calcium carbonate $(CaCO_3)$

Mostly used in roads, concrete and building products.

Murrum is used for
covering and flooring road surfaces.

Used in farming and manufacturing industry. Ground limestone is used

for soil conditioning in agriculture, animal feed supplements poultry grit)

Cement if limestone (or its variety chalk) is mixed with clay or sandstone
before firing, it can
produce Portland cement When mixed with aggregates,it makes concrete.

Lime burning (Calcining) Limestone when heated to a high temperature
breaks down into lime (calcium oxide) and carbon dioxide gas. It can then be
used as a more powerful alkali than limestone It is used as a cement with
sand, to make mortar, or as a soil improver in agriculture. It is also used for
latex treatment and as flux in steel making

Fig19:Building Stone

Fig20:Granite countertop

Fig21:Taj Mahal-marble

Source:www.geology.com

MAINTENANCE OF STONEWORK

Moisture from rain, snow or other environmental conditions penetrates the wall leading to cracks, efflorescence, rust staining, paint peeling and darkening of masonry works. (www.aboutcivil.org)

For this reason, stonework must be maintained so as to keep a good appearance, to minimize the likelihood of decay and to prevent defects. An example is the use of water repellants, like resin which are applied on the stones. These treatments prevent capillary absorption without sealing surfaces. They also inhibit water movement inwards (Everet, pg 74).

STONE PRODUCTION IN KENYA

One of the biggest stone suppliers in Kenya is Ndarugo Stone suppliers, located in Juja, Kiambu County. They mine and market natural machine cut building stones for construction (www.alibaba.com/KE/stoneproduction.html).
In addition, in Western Kenya there is large scale granite stone production. The granites are divided into two groups based on the coloration i.e., light coloured (leucocratic) and dark coloured (Melanocratic). The types of granite stones are black, red, green, yellow and vihiga granite. (www.kesaba.org/kenyastoneproduction.html)

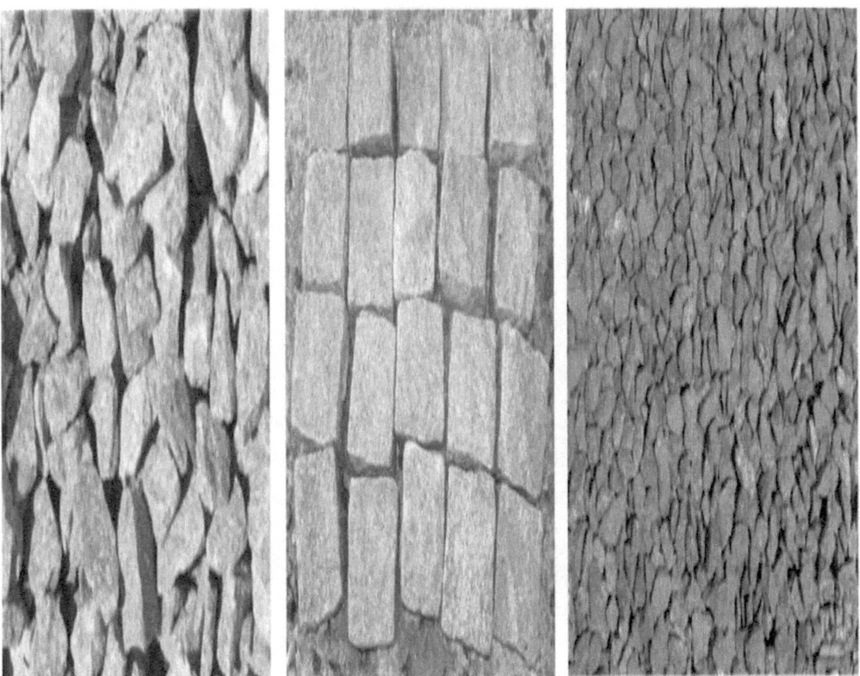

Fig22:Red granite Fig23:Yellow granite Fig24:Green Granite Source: www.selectstoneohio.com

CHAPTER TWENTY

DESIGN MATERIALS AND PROCESS

ALUMINIUM

ABSTRACT

The Future of the Aluminium Industry (2010) is that Aluminium's future remains bright, with increased demand, increased production and improved industrial environment structures. The properties of the various aluminium alloys has resulted in aluminium being used in industries as diverse as transport, food preparation, energy generation, packaging, architecture, and electrical transmission applications. Depending upon the application, aluminium can be used to replace other materials like copper, steel, zinc, tin plate, stainless steel, titanium, wood, paper, concrete and composites. The properties of aluminum that make this metal and its alloys the most economical and attractive for a wide variety of uses are appearance, light weight, fabric-ability, physical properties, mechanical properties, and corrosion resistance.

Like many industries today, the building and construction industry is faced with many environmental challenges. As the world looks towards a more sustainable future, there are many issues that need to be considered, including: impact on climate change; the materials used; and methods of waste disposal. As the world grows to recognize the importance of the lifecycle of the building and its fittings and that that must be balanced against the realities of design, function and economy, aluminium has increasingly become the material of choice. The good news is that Aluminium is 100% recyclable and uses only 5% of the energy used to make the original product. The recyclability of aluminium is unparalleled. When recycled there is no degradation in properties when recycled aluminium is compared to virgin aluminium. The role of recycling in the aluminum industry cannot be overstated.

INTRODUCTION TO ALUMINIUM

Aluminium is included with steel, stainless steel and reinforced concrete as a structural -metal of construction. Aluminium in its commercially pure state is a soft, ductile metal too low in strength to be of interest to a structural engineer. According to Bowen (1966) it is essential to study the details in properties and characteristics of Aluminium to maximis on its use. After iron, aluminium is now the second most widely used metal in the world. This is because aluminium has a unique combination of attractive properties. Low weight, high strength, superior malleability, easy machining, excellent corrosion resistance and good thermal and electrical conductivity are amongst aluminium's most important properties.

According to the East African Association of Engineers, on their book on Aluminium Alloys, The semi-manufactured products of Aluminium have been in existence in the form of a pure metal which is ductile and soft and cannot be used in highly stressed material of construction. Thanks to the improvements effected in the technique of alloying, several excellent aluminium alloys have been created which possess mechanical properties very little inferior to those of structural steels. The addition of small amounts of other elements like copper, magnesium, silicon, manganese, zinc, nickel and chromium have had more significance. The properties of an alloy are determined by the proportions of these alloying elements and by the fabrication process methods employed.

According to Kissel and Robert (1995), they sate the fact that Aluminium is the metal of choice as a structural metal. Its most common structural alloy (6061-T6) has a minimum yield strength which is virtually equal to that of steel. This strength coupled with its light weight (a third that of steel), makes aluminium advantageous for structural applications where dead load is concerned. Its high strength to weight ratio has favored the use of aluminium in diverse applications as large clear span dome roofs, tractor trailer frames, and crane booms.in each case, the reduced dead load, as compared to conventional materials, allows a higher live or service load.
Aluminium is indeed a metal of choice because it is corrosion resistant. Carbon steel, on the other hand has a tendency to self-destruct over time by virtue of the continual conversion of the base metal to iron oxide, commonly known as rust. Alluminium alloys are also rendered inherently corrosion resistant by the formation of a protective oxide film. While stainless steel and

aluminium both have corrosion-resistant properties, cost considerations often favor the use of aluminium. The competitive cost of aluminium is another of its advantages. Furthermore, aluminium is often used without any finish coating or painting. The cost of the initial painting alone may result in steel being more expensive than aluminium. Coatings also have to be maintained and periodically replaced. The costs of maintaining steel, then, give aluminium a further advantage in lifecycle cost. When corrosion resistance, a high strength toe weight ratio and competitive cost are significant design parameters, then several aluminium alloys merit serious consideration.

ALUMINIUM HISTORY

The history of Aluminium has been handled candidly by Weidlinger (1956). He goes on to state that, In 1807, Sir Humphrey Davy suspected the presence of aluminium in clay but despite great efforts and elaborate experiments was unable to obtain it in any form. In 1833, the basic raw material, Bauxite was discovered south of France in the village of Les Baux and in 1825, Hans Christian Oersted a professor of physics in Denmark, produced what appears to have been the first metallic aluminium. In 1827, Friedrich Woehler, a German scientist, produced aluminium as a grey powder. It was not until 1845 that he was able to transform the powder to solid particles. Friedrich Woehler, discovered aluminium's amazingly light weight property, easy to shape, stable in air,and could be melted with a blowtorch. In 1854, a French scientist, Henri Sainte-Claire Deville and Robert Von Bunsen, discovered how to isolate aluminium by using sodium instead of potassium and obtained 96% to 97% purity. In 1886, Charles Martin Hall in Ohio, discovered that metallic aluminium could be produced by dissolving alumina in molten cryolite and then passing an electric current through the solution. He patented his discovery in the United States of America in 1889. Heroult in France secured patent rights in 1889. In 1989, the first aluminium hull for a yacht was built in Switzerland and from here on aluminium spread to practically all industries. At the present time, aluminium is a basic material of the building industry.

ALUMINIUM PROPERTIES

Aluminium has a unique combination of attractive properties as stated by Canon Aluminium Fabricators Ltd (1959).

DURABLE: Aluminium building products are made from alloys that are weather-proof, corrosion-resistant and immune to the harmful effects of UV rays, ensuring optimal performance over a very long lifetime.

FLEXIBLE: Aluminium's combination of properties mean that it can be easily shaped by any of the main industrial metalworking processes, including rolling, extrusion, forging and casting, guaranteeing virtually unlimited design potential.
LIGHT-WEIGHT: Aluminium's light weight makes it cheaper, easier to transport and handle on site.Aluminium is light with a density one third that of steel,

HIGH STRENGTH TO WEIGHT RATIO: Aluminium combines low density and high strength.
THE METAL THAT IS EASY TO FABRICATE So it is easy, for instance, for flashings of any
shape, colour, and size. Joining and connecting of sections is very easy and simple, as aluminium welds, brazes, solders and responds well to adhesives.
CORROSION

RESISTANT: Aluminium has excellent corrosion resistance which can be enhanced by anodizing, painting or lacquering. Aluminium reacts with the oxygen in the air to form an extremely thin layer of oxide coating providing an effective protective barrier that wears other metals.
INSULAR : A layer of insulated aluminium siding is four times more effective than un-insulated wood siding, four inches of brick, or ten inches of stone masonry.

RECYCLABLE: Aluminium is 100% recyclable and uses only 5% of the energy used to make the original product.
DUCTILITY: Readily formed by folding, pressing, rolling, forging and die-casting well. MACHINING Aluminium is easily worked using most machining methods–milling, drilling, cutting, punching, bending, etc. Furthermore, the energy input during machining is low. HIGHTHERMAL CONDUCTIVITY: Aluminium is an excellent conductor of heat and electricity. Analuminium conductor weighs approximately half as much as a copper conductor having the same conductivity.
EASY JOINING: Features facilitating easy jointing are often incorporated

into profile design. Fusion welding, Friction Stir Welding, bonding and taping are also used for joining. LINEAR EXPANSION: Compared with other metals, aluminium has coefficient of linear expansion. This has to be taken into account a relatively large in some designs.

REFLECTIVITY: Aluminium is a good reflector of both visible light & radiated heat. SCREENING EMC‖Tight aluminium boxes can effectively exclude or screen off electromagnetic radiation.The better the conductivity of a material, the better the shielding qualities.
ALUMINIUM HAS EXCELLENT RESISTANCE IN NEUTRAL AND SLIGHTLY ACID ENVIRONMENTS: Aluminium isextremely durable in neutral and slightly acid environments In environments characterised by high acidity or high basicity, corrosion is rapid. NON-MAGNETIC MATERIAL: Aluminium is a non-magnetic (actually paramagnetic) material. To avoid interference of magnetic fields aluminium is often used in magnet X-ray devices. ZERO TOXICITY: Aluminium is not only non-toxic but also does not release any odours or taint products with which it is in contact making it suitable for use in packaging for sensitive products such as food or pharmaceuticals where aluminium foil is used.
DUCTILITY MALLEABILITY: HIGH: Aluminium is both very malleable, and very ductile, it means that it is possible to roll it into sheets, and if it is ductile it can be drawn into wires. RECYCLING: The recyclability of aluminium is unparalleled. When recycled there is no degradation in properties when recycled aluminium is compared to virgin aluminium. Furthermore, recycling of aluminium only requires around 5% of the input energy required to produce virgin aluminium metal

ALLUMINIUM & ALUMINIUM ALLOYS

Aluminum alloys are normally classified into one of three groups: wrought non-heattreatable alloys, wrought heat treatable alloys, and casting alloys.

I) WROUGHT NON-HEAT-TREATABLE ALLOYS cannot be strengthened by precipitation hardening; they are hardened primarily by cold working. The wrought non-heat-treatable alloys include the commercially pure aluminum aluminum-manganese series, the aluminum-silicon series, and the magnesium series.

series, the aluminum

II) WROUGHT HEAT TREATABLE ALLOYS: can be precipitation hardened to develop quite high strength levels. These alloys include the (Al-Cu and Al-Cu-Mg), the (Al-MgSi), (Al-Zn-Mg and Al-Zn-Mg-Cu), and the aluminum-lithium alloys. which develop the highest strength levels, are the main alloys used for metallic aircraft structure.

III) CASTING ALLOYS include both non-heat-treatable and heat treatable alloys. The major categories include the (Al-Cu), (Al-Si + Cu or Mg), (Al-Si),(Al-Mg), (Al-Zn), (AlSn). The alloys can be strengthened by precipitation hardening, but the properties obtained are not as high as for the wrought heat treatable alloys.

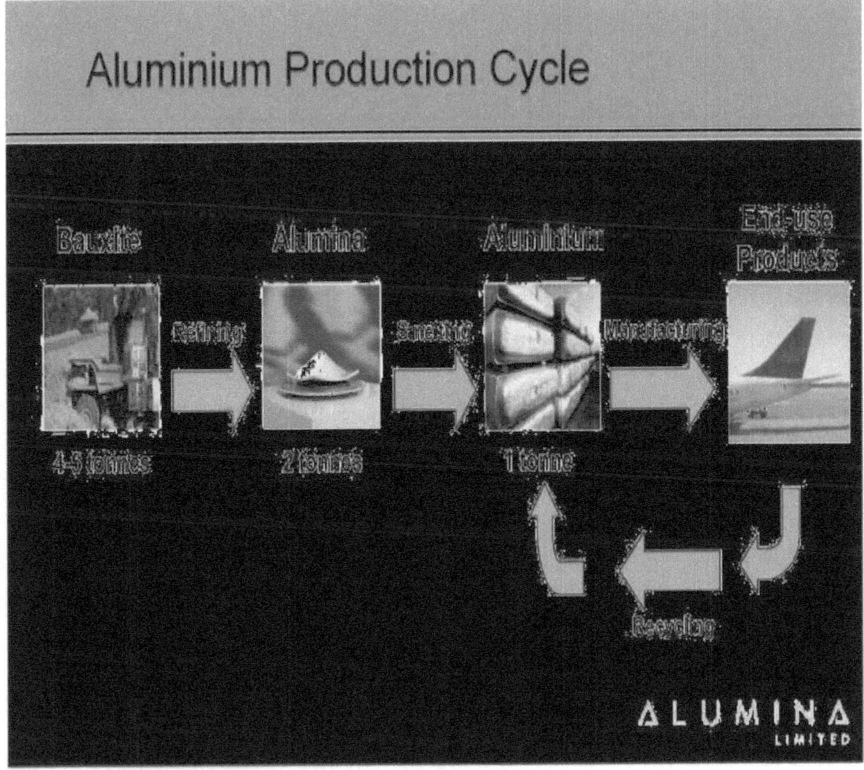

Figure: 1: Aluminium Production Cycle

ALUMINIUM MINNING & PROCESSING

According to Weidlinger (1956), the aluminiumproduction cycle is explicitly shown in figure 1. Aluminium is commercially obtained only from Bauxite ore, named after the French town of Le Baux where the first high grade aluminium deposits were found. See Figure 2A and 2B for the chemical composition of Aluminium.

High grade Bauxite contains 50%-60% alumina (aluminium oxide) chemically combined WITH 15%-32% water to forma hydrated oxide.The ore also contains 2%-7% silica, 2%20% iron oxide and 2%-4% titanium oxide, in addition to other trace materials. Bauxite deposits occur near the surface and are mined in open pits with clay, sand and free moisture. After crushing the clay is removed by washing, screening then dried in rotary kilns at temperatures of 200_0c-250_0c to reduce transportation costs.

REFINNING: is commercially done by the Bayer process.

Dried ore is ground to a powder and fed into a mixer with soda ash, crushed lime and hot water forming caustic soda. The mixture is pumped into large digesting tanks and converted to sodium aluminate while other impurities form insoluble substances, unaffected by the caustic solution. The sodium alluminate is passed through pressure reducing tanks, pumped into filter presses where it runs through heavy cotton cloth while the solid impurities called ─red mud‖ are filtered out and then washed off.

Next the solution is pumped into precipitators and the mixture is then pumped into thickeners which separate the precipitated alumina (aluminium hydrate) from the caustic soda solution which is fed back to the digesters for reuse.

CALCINNING: is the last step in the refining process done in rotary kilns at a temperature of $2,000_0F$. This converts the aluminium hydrate to alumina by eliminating the chemically combined water of hydration. After cooling, the alumina is shipped to the reduction plant. A carbon-lined vessel contains molten cryolite which dissolves the alumina. An extremely large current is passed throughsolution, breaking down the alumina into metallic aluminium and oxygen. The Aluminium accumulates at the bottom of the reduction pot.

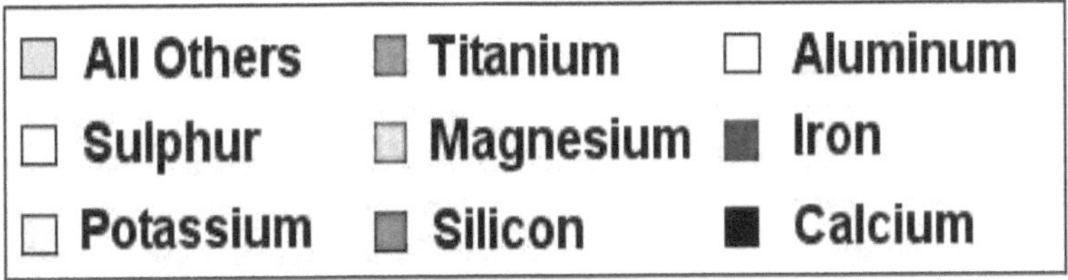

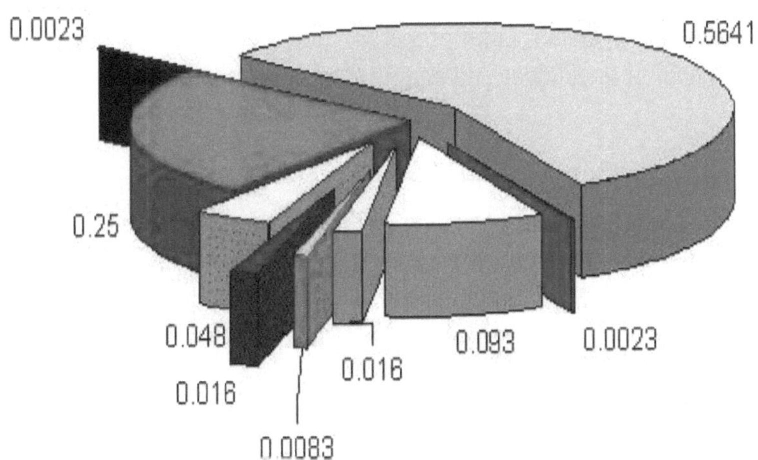

FIGURE 2A: chemical composition of aluminum ore in decimals

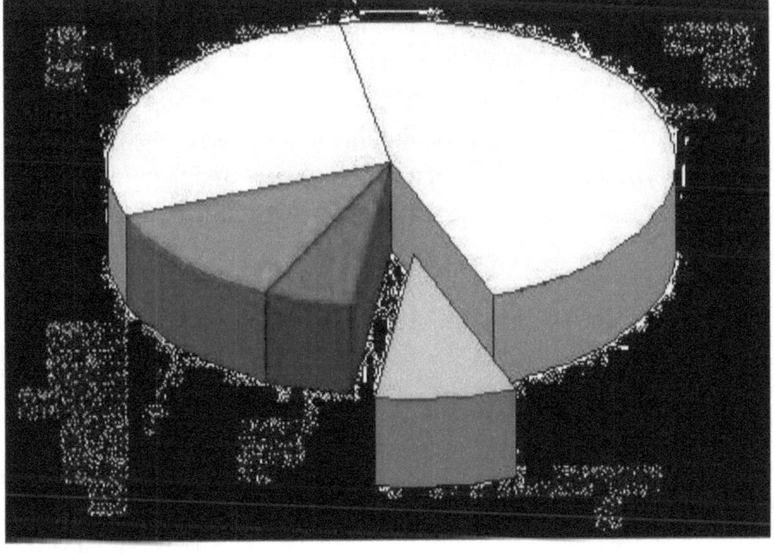

FIGURE 2B: chemical composition of aluminum ore in percentages Source:

WORKING WITH ALUMINIUM

Aluminium is a versatile material that lends itself to many production methods, which in turn means that there are a range of different products that can be made out of aluminium. Common aluminium forming processes include: I) Extrusion II) Rolling III) Sand casting 4) Die casting. Add to this its ability to be heat treated to tailor properties and its ability to be joined using any number of techniques and aluminium becomes a material with real potential.

I) EXTRUSIONS: Extruded products comprise over half the aluminium products available. The largest consumer of these products is the building industry, which uses aluminium extrusions in window and door frames. Other applications for extruded aluminium products include bicycle frames, structural automotive components, pipes and tubes, furniture etc.

II) FLAT ROLLED PRODUCTS: Rolled aluminium products consist of plates, sheet and foil, which may vary in thickness from several millimetres think to tens of microns thick.

III) SAND CASTING: is a versatile technique that is generally used for high-volume production. IV) DIE CASTING: The automotive industry is the largest market for aluminum castings, and cast products make up more than half of the aluminum used in cars. Cast aluminum transmission housing and pistons have been virtually universal in cars and trucks throughout the world for years. Die casting differs from sand casting in that it utilizes re-usable moulds.

ALUMINIUM EXTRUSION ALUMINIUM EXTRUSION

ALUMINIUM DIE-CASTING ALUMINIUM FLAT ROLLED

ALUMINIUM SAND-CASTING FLAT ROLLED PRODUCTS

WORKING WITH ALUMINIUM
APPLICATION & USES OF ALUMINIUM

PACKAGING (FOOD & JUICE CANS): Corrosion resistance and protection against

UV light combined with moisture and odour containment plus the fact that aluminium is non-toxic and will not leach or taint the products has resulted in the widespread use of rolled aluminium for packaging has been in aluminium beverage cans. Rolled aluminium goes into making beverage cans, food containers and foil wrappings, which take advantage of properties such as strength, lightness, impermeability and its odourless nature.

ALUMINIUM COOKING EQUIPMENT

IN HOUSEHOLD ALUMINIUM FOIL ALUMINIUM FOIL CONTAINERS: Aluminium also has further end uses in products used more readily around the home. The material is used to make saucepans, kitchen utensils, golf clubs, tennis bats, indoor and outdoor furniture, fridges, and toasters.

Figure 3: aluminium in aircraft construction
Source: http://www.google.co.ke/imgres?q=aluminiumin+aircraft&um
ALUMINIUM USE IN TRANSPORTATION: Aluminium's unbeatable strength to weightratio gives it many uses in the transport industry. Figure 3, shows aluminium use in aeroplanes. Trains, boats and cars aluminium is useful for this lightweight property (which gives fuel efficiency) but not essential, in planes however maintaining a relatively low weight is vital (in

order to level the ground), and aluminium allows planes to have to this. In modern planes aluminium makes up 80% of their (unladen) weight. Its corrosionresistance is an advantage in transport as it makes painting planes unnecessary saving some hundreds of kilograms of further weight

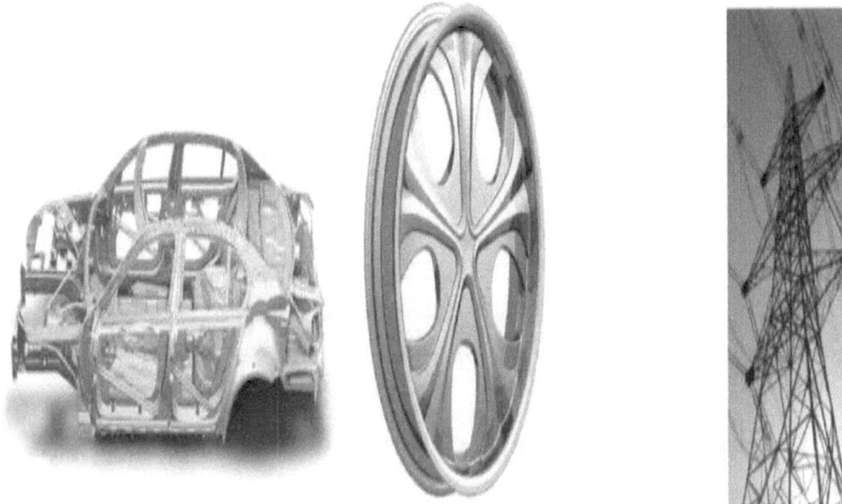

FIGURE 4: aluminium in the aviation industry-chasis & wheel rims Source: http://www.google.co.ke/imgres?q=aluminium+in+automobile&um

FIGURE 5: aluminium in power lines Source:
http://www. Google .co. Ke/imgres? q=aluminium+in+power+lines&um
MOTOR VEHICLE INDUSTRY: Figure 4 shows the use of aluminum for car parts such as cylinder heads, pistons, radiators and wheel rims makes cars lighter, which reduces fuel consumption and pollution levels.

ELECTRICAL USE: Because of its light weight and electrical conductivity, aluminum wire isused for long distance transmission of electricity, See Figure 5. Weight is also important in aluminium's electrical uses, where it's low density makes it the first choice for long distance power lines despite having just 63% of the electrical conductivity of (much denser) copper. In fact 1 kg of aluminium conducts almost twice as much electricity as 1 Kg of copper.
Aluminium is also more ductile than copper, so it is easier to draw it into wires to produce these power lines, its corrosion resistance completes

aluminium's profile as the perfect choice for long-distance electricity distribution. Aluminium has other electrical applications too including TV aerials, satellite dishes, and being the standard base for bulbs.
CONSTRUCTION INDUSTRY: Siding, roofing, gutters, window frames, hardware, paint are made from aluminum. Aluminum materials are also used for farm and highway construction, door frames, windows, skylights, cladding, gutters and roofing. Figure 6: shows aluminium cladding where a single layer of insulated aluminium cladding is equally effective as four inches brick or stone wall.
FIGURE 6: aluminium cladding in building construction

Source: http://www.google.co.ke/search?
hl=en&q=aluminium+use+in+cladding
FIGURE 7: aluminium domes are an excellent alternative for steel roofs, source: http://www.google.co.ke/search?
num=10&hl=en&site=imghp&tbm=isch&source

DOMES AND CANTILEVERS – Figure 7, shows lightweight structures: Aluminium has anincredible strength to weight to ratio. What this means for designers is that major cantilevers and open span structures are possible.

CONCLUSION

According to a statement made by John (1958), he interviewed an accomplished architect, Mr. Victor Gruen, famous for building shopping centers and city plans, and he had this to say….— Aluminium has a highly advantageous place in modern architecture with very attractive and durable qualities. It is shiny when polished, elegant when satin finished, and cheerful when left in its natural appearance or coloured. Apart from that it is one of the few building materials which lend to a building exterior gaiety and interest, not only on the first day but permanently.‖
Further more, more compliments on aluminiumm are made by an architect with a deep sense of beauty and delight, Mr. Minoru Yamasaki, that ―I believe aluminium has a very important place in modern architecture as it allows me to stretch our horizon in creativity and because it is a very pliable material in extrusion, when shaped in other words it takes the form of architecture, or what you want very easily‖ he goes on to add ―Aluminium is a wonderful material because it has a lasting quality in good finishes and it is

more plastic than steel‖

CHAPTER TWENTY ONE

DESIGN MATERIALS AND PROCESS

GLASS

ABSTRACT

Glass is indeed highly appreciated in many applications for its inert nature and its contributions to safeguarding people's health and well being. According to GlobalSpec, (2006), the primary reason for the popularity of glass is that its properties can be varied according to requirements. Glass can be made as strong as steel or more delicate than paper. It can be woven like the web of a spider or it can be molded into a mirror that would weigh in tons. According to Mr. Phillips (1950), the author of —Get acquainted with glass‖, he further explains that the role of glass in the home, is indeed vital and an indispensable commodity in modern day civilization, As an inert material, it guarantees that food, medicines and beverages placed in glass containers are not stained by the packaging. Glass is a resource efficient material which is made of abundant natural raw material such as sand and glass waste (cullets). Glass is a fully recyclable material that can be recycled in close loop over and over again. Thanks to glass recycling, significant amounts of raw materials are saved and natural resources are preserved saving on energy as cullets melt at a lower temperature than raw materials. Studies show that glass in buildings, through all these benefits, contribute to people's well-being and improved health conditions. The future of Glass is an unlimited material whose number of applications is constantly evolving and which is more and more use in combination with other material for high-tech applications.

Key Words: Glass, Sand, Silica, Recyclable, Cullets,

INTRODUCTION

According to Phillips (1950), Glass is one of the most useful and versatile commodities, having important applications in every field of human activity. Glass is by definition an amorphous solid material made by fusing silica with a basic oxide. Glass is called amorphous because it is neither a solid nor a liquid but exists in a vitreous, or glassy, state. Jones G.O. (1971), goes on to explain that the term —glass‖ refers to a class of materials of great practical usefulness. With a number of characteristic properties such as transparency, brittleness, and it tends to soften progressively and continuously when heated. Doremus R. (1973) introduces glass as an amorphous solid. He goes on to say, —A glass… is a material, formed by cooling from the normal liquid state, which has shown no discontinuous change … at any temperature, but has become more or less rigid through a progressive increase in its viscosity‖ or more succinctly, —glass is an organic product of fusion which has been cooled to a rigid condition without crystalisation‖

A BRIEF HISTORY OF GLASS

According to Doremus (1973), he goes on to summarise the history of glass by noting down that natural glasses has been used by man from the earliest times of which there is archeological evidence. Phillips (1950) continues to note that glass can occur in nature when lightning strikes loose sand or rocks. The heat of flash causes a certain amount of fusion resulting in the formation of thin glass of crust not more than one eighth of an inch on the surface of the rocks or the sand itself may be fused into long, slender tubes measuring up to a half inch in diameter, which run downward into the sand for several feet. According to Sir W.M Flinders Petrie as quoted by Morey (encyclopedia Britannica, pg4), the earliest known glaze dates from 12000BC. And the earliest pure glass from about 7,000B.C both were found in Egypt, and were probably brought there from Asia at first glass was used for decorative objects, but later it was molded or pressed into vessels. The invention of glass blowing in about the first century B.C greatly increased the use of glass for practical purposes in Roman times, mainly for vessels but later for windows.

THE CHEMICAL COMPOSITION OF GLASS

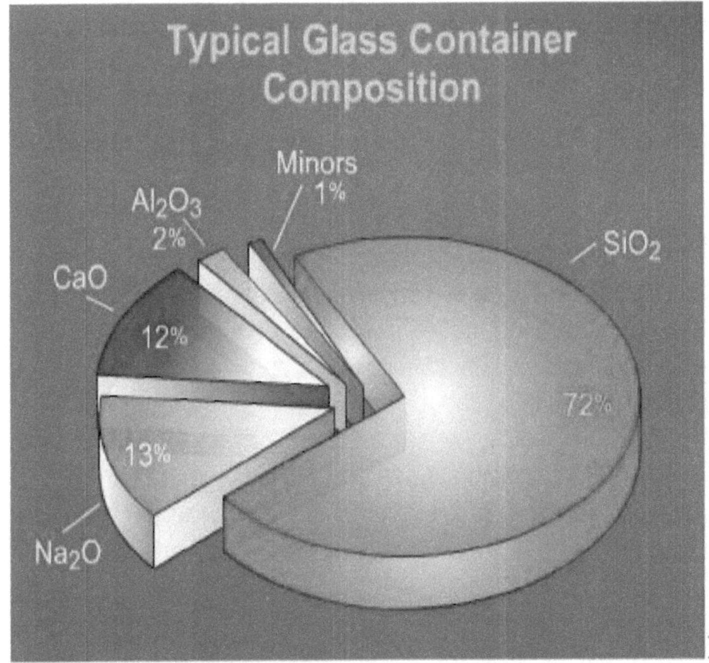

FIGURE 1: (2010), Glass Packaging Institute

Source:
http://gpi.org/glassresources/education/sustainabilityrecycling/s
24-glass

composition.html

Figure 1: graphically shows the composition of glass as follows:(i) Sand (SiO2 silica – 72%) In its pure form it exists as a polymer, (SiO2) (ii) Soda ash (sodium carbonate Na_2CO3 – 13%) (.iii) Limestone (calcium carbonate or $CaCO_3$ - 12%)

PHYSICAL PROPERTIES OF GLASS

APPEARANCE: Ordinary glass is transparent and more or less colourless. transparent, translucent and opaque glasses can be coloured in four ways:1) Pot Colour is uniform throughout its thickness, 2) Flashed Glass has an extremely thin layer of transparent coloured glass applied to one surface during blowing 3) Ceramic pigment may be fused to one side 4) Painting

DENSITY: Glass weighs $2.5kg/m_2$ per/mm thickness, Aluminium 2,771, Steel $7,850kg/m_3$ DURABILITY: Glass is extremely durable in normal conditions.

GLASS IS THE MOST ASTOUNDING BUILDING MATERIAL. A typical piece of 6mm-thick clear float glass is 87 percent transparent to visible light and yet strong enough to fulfill a number of building roles that provide protection, security and comfort. Glass strength is highly variable and deliberately modified for differing applications.

STRENGTH IN TENSION: To improve its resistance to impact and breakage, glass can be either toughened or laminated. In the case of breakage, fragments adhere to the flexible "interlayer" between glass layers, reducing the chance of injuries.

CHEMICAL RESISTANCE: Glass resists most acids with the exception of hydrofluoric, at high temperatures phosphoric acid.

WEIGHT: Glass, like water, can be deceptively heavy even in relatively small physical sizes. Glass has a density of 2,500 kilograms per cubic meter, making it approximately 2.5 times heavier than the equivalent volume of water and heavier for its size than many other building materials. The weight aspect of glass means that window frames and other structural elements need to be specifically designed for their glazing role.

STRENGTH: Glass in building is required to resist including wind loads, impact by persons and animals and sometimes thermal and other stresses.

COMPLETELY BRITTLE, so there is no permanent set which in ductile materials gives warning of impending failure. Another characteristic is that RESISTANCE TO SHOCK LOADS is about twice that of static loads which can be withstood indefinitely.

CONDUCTIVITY - FIRE RESISTANCE: Fire resistant glass, increases levels of protection, which is measured in defined time periods (30, 60, 90, 120, 180 minutes).

NOISE CONTROL.; The acoustic glass in a double-glazed unit uses a special interlayer that acts as a dampening core so that sound energy is effectively blocked from passing from the outside to the inside pane of glass.

CONDUCTIVITY: Glass is generally a poor conductor of electricity, with volume

electricalresistivity of 310,000,000,000 Ωm. VISIBLE LIGHT TRANSMISSION & SOLAR HEAT TRANSMISSION & ULTRA-VIOLET LIGHT TRANSMISSION:

DECORATIVE INTERIOR DESIGN: Glass can transform living spaces and work environments, see figure 2 showing an interior with glass accents. Glass can be combined with stone, wood or metal for a strong visual and tactile effect. In offices and other professional settings, glass offers a fresh, light yet serious aesthetic and has the advantage of being a material that wears exceptionally well and is impervious to moisture and most cleaning products.

FIGURE 2: white marble living room with white accents
Source: http://www.google.co.ke/imgres?q=glass+in+interiors

SOLAR CONTROL GLASS is glass designed to reduce or prevent solar heating of buildings, eithertinted (coloured) throughout the material (called a "body tint"), or else it has a microscopically thin and transparent coating on one side.

TEMPERATURE PERFORMANCE: Glass products made for fire protection are enhanced with theaddition of substrates, laminates and other technologies to maintain rigidity at high temperature.

SELF-CLEANING GLASS: is glass that has been coated with a special dual-function layer thatharnesses the elements windows and facades are exposed to - namely, sun, and rain - to break down and wash away dirt.

SECURITY / ANTI-VANDAL: Toughened glasses can be regarded as anti-vandal glasses. Laminated anti-vandal, anti-bandit and bullet resistant glasses

Glass Manufacturing process or Glass-making

Kumar S, (1980), in his book titled —The Story of Glass‖, gives an in depth analysis of glassmaking in modern times (pg22-58). Glass-making can be categorized into 5 different functions as follows. i) Hand Glass Manufacture, ii) Sheet glass Manufacture, iii) mechanical sheet glass Manufacture, iv) Float glass Manufacturing process, v) Bottle Manufacture. Figure 3 below, shows float glass manufacturing process.
Glass industries are characterised by a multitude of production processes depending on the final product manufactured and its end-applications. However, all these manufacturing processes have a common origin: There are three (3) basic operations involved in all of these forming methods depend upon the peculiar characteristics of glass as a material. First, silica sand is heated to a temperature of $2,000_0c$ extremely red-hot to white- hot, the mass will melt to form a thick syrupy liquid depending upon method and composition. On subsequent cooling the melt would form a rigid glassy mass. Secondly, this very hot, syrupy liquid must somehow be transferred from the pot or tank and into the air or a mold, so that further work can be done on it. Thirdly, at these temperatures glass cools rapidly by radiation and by contact with cooler air or metal. In a matter of a few seconds at most this cooling has so increased the viscosity that the glass has become, to all intents and purposes, a solid.

FLOAT GLASS MANUFACTURING PROCESS

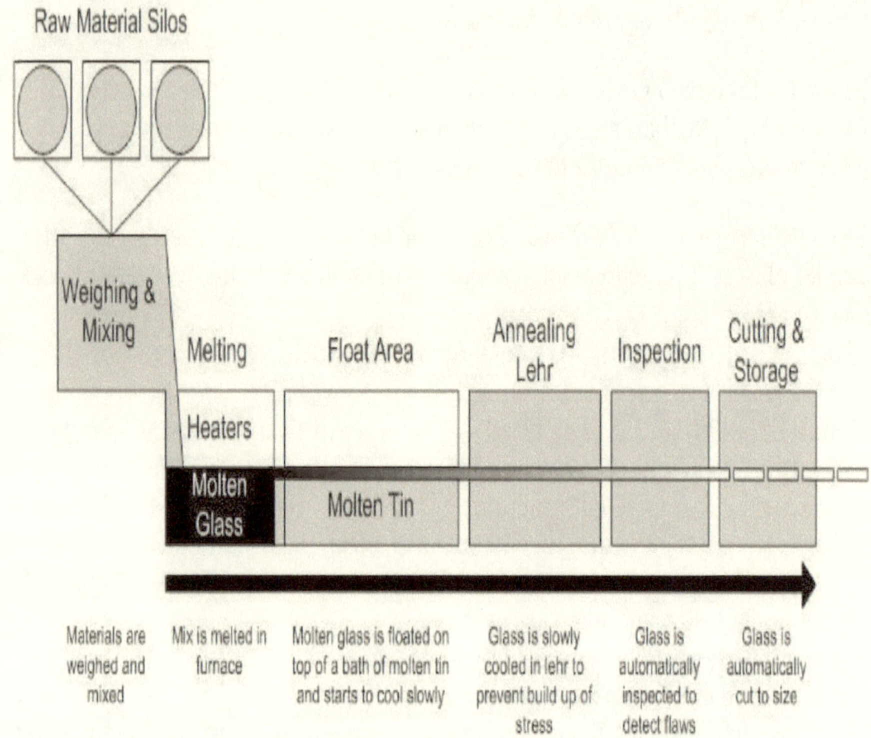

Figure 3: source: (11$_{th}$march 2010), —float glass production‖, tangram technology ltd, Source:
http://www.tangram.co.uk/ti-glazing-float%20glass.html
COMMON CHALLENGES IN THE GLASS INDUSTRY 2010 (NORTHERN EUROPE

- Overcapacity
- Competition from low-quality companies
- Maintaining quality and service
- The economy
- Government regulations
- Obtaining loans/financing
- Taxes
- Worker morale
- Finding qualified employees

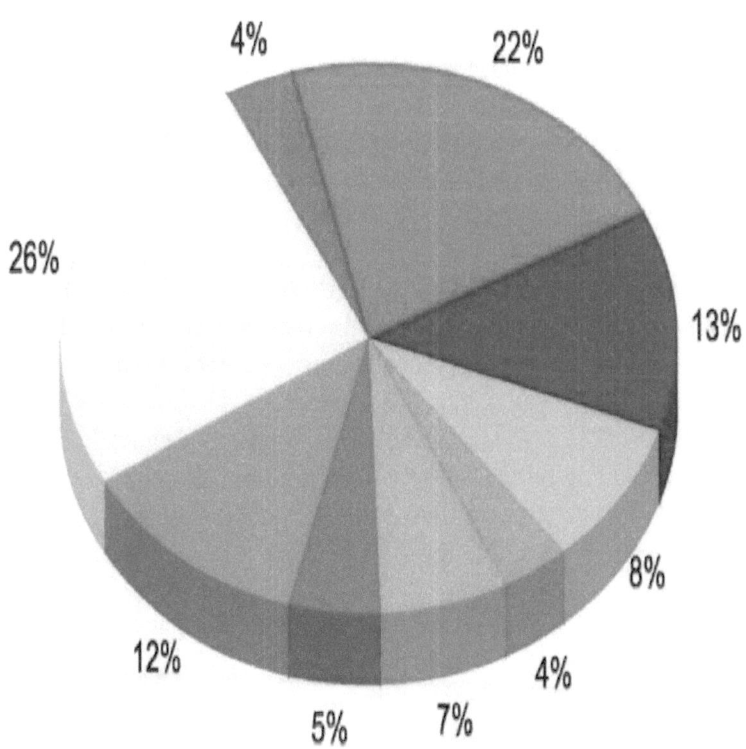

Figure 4: Source: http://www.glassmagazine.com/glassblog/ Source: what-are-greatest-challenges-facing-fabricators-next-year-107147

According to Chase Jenni, Figure 4 shows that, in the economy, competition from low-quality companies, and overcapacity are among fabricators' greatest obstacles going into 2011, according to respondents to Glass Magazine's ongoing survey of North American fabricators of glass, metal and related products. Glass Alliance Europe, (December 2009), reports that, the common challenges are to share expertise, knowledge and best practice in order to remain sustainable and competitive. Glass manufacturing is a high-temperature, energy-using activity which constitutes a constant economic and environmental challenge for the glass industries to keep energy use to a minimum. Promoting recycling, ensuring access to raw materials and managing chemicals in the most responsible manner: Glass making requires sand and recycled glass as raw materials.

QUALITIES OF GLASS MATERIAL

I) GLASS PROTECTS THE PRODUCT: Glass has an excellent shelf-life since it can be pasteurised, sterilised, microwaved, reduces food waste, and maintains high levels of carbonation and vacuum and maintains the true taste of the contents. Glass protects against the effects of light and temperature for longer than most other materials.

II) GLASS PROTECTS THE ENVIRONMENT: Glass is a pure and sustainable material capable of being 100% recycled indefinitely. Its structure does not deteriorate through the recycling process. Recycled glass reduces energy consumption for melting.
III) GLASS PROTECTS THE CONSUMER: Glass is chemically inert: Glass needs no protective coating inside and does not leach harmful chemicals into the product. For the consumer there is an association of quality with glass products.

IV) FROM NATURE TO GLASS: Glass is comprised mainly of natural minerals (sand, limestone and soda ash), glass is an ecological material that is desired for its purity and elegance. The natural quality of glass is enhanced by its stability, easily withstands extreme temperatures of heat and cold.

V) FROM GLASS TO PACKAGING: The impermeable nature of glass makes it a safe form of protective packaging. In addition to being an excellent barrier against the external environment, glass containers do not interact with or alter the taste, smell or composition of the products they contain.

FROM STANDARD PACKAGING TO UNIQUES DESIGNS: The flexibility of glass in its molten state during the forming process allows for a wide variety of products an infinite array of potential forms with a broad palette of colors (bottles, jars, etc.) to be manufactured.

VI) GLASS – THE CLEAR CHOICE : As a fully and infinitely recyclable material, combined with its purity, glass is the packaging material of choice when it comes to sustainable development. Natural, strong, neutral, respectful of its contents, capable of the most promising innovation and infinitely recyclable: glass withstands the test of time.

VII) GLASS – AESTHETICALLY BEAUTIFUL & A NATURAL MATERIAL: The aesthetic quality of glass enhances the desire for the product.

TYPES & VARIETIES OF GLASS

Phillips. J.C, (1950) in his book —Get Acquainted with Glass – Material: industry: Uses‖, has extensively highlighted the varieties of glass (pages 34-61) as shown below.

I) SHEET GLASS: Glass windows and partitions can withstand adverse weather conditions like rain, heat, cold, for generations if not centuries assuming that they are not accidentally broken. Uses are in lantern slides, microscope slides, X-ray plates, picture framing glass, mirrors, showcases, shelving, desk-tops, cabinet doors.

II) PLATE GLASS: Plate glass is made by rolling-casting and is subjected to the additional operations of grinding and polishing. Plate glass is used wherever highest quality glazing is desirable. The show windows of large stores, automobile windshields, fine mirrors. HEAT ABSORBING PLATE: Glass with special chemical composition that has the property of excluding much of the heat in the sun's rays while transmitting most of the visible light.

Plain corrugated reinforced with wire mesh used in air conditioned buildings. ROLLED GLASS: Available as fire-polished chemically etched or sandblasted. III) TEMPERED PLATE GLASS: 3-4 times stronger than ordinary plate glass but Tempered plate glass is made by reheating plate glass and then rapidly cooling the surface by means of air jets. Tempered Plate glass cannot be cut once it has cooled. Tempered plate glass doors are used for building entrances and display stores, wire glass in sky-lights, showcase shelving and exhibitions.

IV) COLOURED STRUCTURED GLASS: has grown in importance as an architectural material, Stronger and cheaper than marble or tile.

V) ARCHITECTURAL GLASS: is glass with relatively deep surface patterns formed by pressing or casting and used primarily in the architectural field e.g. Pyrex Chemical Resistant glass, Crystal glass. The patterns include pressed panels that are flat on one side and ribbed on the other.

VI) BUILDING BLOCKS: Glass building blocks are made in two sections fused together at high temperatures to form a hollow, rectangular unit. The tight all glass joint permanently maintains a dead air space inside, thus giving maximum heat insulation and preventing condensation or —weeping‖ within the block. Building blocks used in food industries, dairies, butcheries and candy manufacturers.

VII) LAMINATED SAFETY GLASS: is made of two pieces of polished window glass with an inner layer of transparent plastic material. When the glass is broken by impact, the internal layer reduces splintering and scattering by holding the broken pieces together. Laminated glass also has good sound-insulating qualities for this reason it is used in hospitals, factory offices, telephone booths and broadcasting studios and modern automobiles.

VIII) BULLET RESISTANT GLASS: This glass is laminated plate plate glass designed principally for protection against firearms.
IX) BOTTLES & OTHER GLASS CONTAINERS: Bottles, jars and plain glass. A gathered fixed amount of molten glass by suction and forcing it automatically into a mold.

X) HEAT RESISTANT GLASS: expands and contracts less than ordinary glass when it is heated or cooled. Special heat absorbing properties of glass when used in the domestic oven contribute to oven efficiency and fuel economy. Glass coffee makers, infant's bottles are made from heat resistant glass.

XI) OPTICAL GLASS: The composition must be such that the correct optical characteristics are obtained and at the same time there must be a minimum of flaws or imperfections. Optical glass is used in telescopes, microscopes, binoculars, photographic lenses, motion picture projectors, spectacles, X-ray stereoscopes.

XII) LABORATORY GLASSWARE: Beakers, Flasks, thermometers, Barometers, Test tubes, Laboratory ware of borosilicate glass with excellent heat resistant properties. XIII) FIBRE GLASS: is useful in thermal insulation, electrical insulation, and sound insulation. Staple fibre is formed by causing molten glass to flow from extremely small orifices from which it is picked up by a high pressure steam or air blast and pulled into long, fine fibres, the thickness of human hair and about 9 inches in length. Each fibre is a tiny but solid rod of glass so that fibre glass has all the properties of glass in bulk. It is heat resistant and noncombustible, cannot absorb moisture therefore cannot decay, resistant to ordinary weathering and to acids, oils and corrosive vapors and an excellent electrical insulator.

XIV) FOAM GLASS: The foam glass is made by adding finely divided carbon to ground glass and heating the mixture to a high temperature in a mold. It amazingly weighs as much as cork and floats on water. Has heat insulating properties of cork yet unlike cork it is not affected by dampness and condensation because it does not absorb water, a property that leads it to its use in cold storage rooms and refrigerators.

USES & APPLICATION OF GLASS

I) ELECTRICAL INDUSTRY: *Phillips. J.C, (1950), explainshowglassisused*in the manufacture ofthe integral and irreplaceable incandescent lamp that is the ordinary light bulbs than for all other electrical purposes combined.

II) CHEMICAL INDUSTRY: Containers of milk bottles, jars, glasses, cylinders etc. Glass plumbing, Glass tanks, pumps.

III) GLASS IN TRANSPORTATION: Railroad uses production of signal glasses that would give strong, uniform, standardized colours in all kinds of weather. Aviation beacons, Course lights, Landing field lights, Plane running lights, laminated glass is used in airplane windshields. Automobile safety glass and tempered glass, headlights.

IV) GLASS RE-INFORCED PLASTICS IN INDUSTRY: The union of glass and plastics to form a new material of industry for the production of an extremely fine pliable glass fibre and the development of low pressure or contact resins eg washing machine parts made of glass reenforced plastic laminates.

V) THE ROLE OF GLASS IN THE HOME: *Phillips. J.C, (1950),*the home is a place where glass has a real creative opportunity in construction and decoration, cooking, utensils, containers, shelves, bath-tubs, shower stalls, windows (sheet glass). Our homes are bright and cheerful light, air, sunshine and colours of nature enter through the impressive expanses of clear glass, Interior furnishings, in the kitchen cupboards, sliding doors, worktops, glass doors. Fabrics made of fibre glass for shower curtains for decorative and utility fabrics available as large varieties of weaves designs and colours. These coloured glass fabrics can be dry-cleaned, washed, and ironed like ordinary cloth, machine made tumblers, goblets, cocktail glasses, wine glasses, containers, cooking utensils, paintings, sculptures, flower vases, plates, glass Jewelry and ornaments e.g emerald, ruby, sapphire and topaz. Glass home lighting in lamps, flood-lights, fluorescent lighting, television tubes, screens etc.
VI) GLASS ROLE IN SCIENCE & RESEARCH: *Phillips. J.C, (1950),*Fever thermometers, the impervious, easily cleaned surface of glass typifies the modern hospitals standards of cleanliness as glass meets the equally important requirements of economy and durability. Flat glass and building blocks are extensively used in the hospital construction. Glass cabinets for storing sutures, laboratory glassware, graduated cylinders, glass bottles, hypodermic syringes, ampoules, capillary glass tubes etc. Bandages and Casts flexible fibre glass bandage which has comfort and freedom of

movement to those who suffer fractures and injuries requiring immobilization. Optical instruments like eye glasses with no glare from light reflects are now an actuality. Glass Radiation, Sun Lamps in germicidal lamps. X-ray tubes are made from borosilicate glasses.

VII) GLASS IN THE BUILDING INDUSTRY: About Glass for Europe, (2007), states very clearly the numerous uses of glass in the building industry. The glass used in today's window and façades takes care of prime concerns like safety, security, and environmental protection to convenient functions like self-cleaning or practical qualities like scratch resistance or design aspects, the choices are many and varied;

Glass is used for THEMAL INSULATION: can be one of several desirable maintenance, solar control, noise reduction, decorative glass and enhanced safety and security.
SOLAR CONTROL; designed to reduce or prevent solar heating of buildings.

SAFETY & SECURITY: To improve its resistance to impact and breakage, glass can be either toughened or laminated, depending on where and how it is being used.
FIRE RESISTANCE, NOISE CONTROL: Acoustically insulating glazing can be a major contributor to comfort levels in buildings and houses. Its benefits are greatest for people living or working near busy high streets, urban traffic, motorways, railway lines and airports, or on a flight path.
SELF-CLEANING: Self-cleaning is glass that has been coated with a special dual-function layer that harnesses the elements windows and facades are exposed to - namely, sun, and rain - to break down and wash away dirt.

CONCLUSION

From all the findings in this term paper on glass, the study proves that glass will continue to remain important to our society, Even with the development of various kinds of glass-like substances, it seems unlikely that society will stop using glass during any time in the near future. Many glass alternatives only offer benefits as glass alternatives in certain, often limited, situations. Glass remains overall the best choice for most applications requiring a transparent solid. It seems unlikely that the near future will produce a glass alternative that matches the ability of glass to function in a variety of different situations. No matter how the future unfolds, glass has been and continues to remain one of the most useful discoveries in the history of mankind. With applications ranging from vision correction to the creation of dish ware, glass is a constant companion to humans across the world.

GYPSUM

ABSRTACT

It is aesthetically beautiful. Gives a smooth finish, rendering is orderly and even. Glossy or oil paint can be applied directly without absorbing the paint. See Figure 4 and 5. High performance dry walls. Neither does this plaster shrink so the plastered walls do not crack and fine details are achieved in mouldings. Gypsum….the preferred choice for interior décor in renders and finishes.

Products of the gypsum industry are plaster, plasterboards, gypsum fiberboards and gypsum blocks, which are all used in the building industry. Gypsum is also an essential ingredient in cement production, where it is used as a hardening retarding agent. Outside the construction industry, dried and grinded raw gypsum is called land plaster and used as a soil conditioning fertiliser. Furthermore, gypsum is used in the making of ceramic moulds, plaster cove and cornice, surgical and dental casts, as a water conditioner for beer-brewing and sugar-refining, as ingredients in flour, bread, ice-cream and pet food, and as an agent in pharmaceutical products. Demand for Gypsum is principally driven by activity in the construction sector. The value of construction output continues to increase in real terms. Demand for new and refurbished housing is increasing and in conjunction with the need for new schools, hospitals, offices and shops, there is likely to be increasing demand for Gypsum building products for the foreseeable future.

Introduction

According to the Eurogypsum Committee (2007/07/06), Gypsum is a naturally occurring mineral and it is an evaporate mineral, left behind in sedimentary rocks which settled through evaporation of sea water trapped in lagoons. Gypsum in absolutely pure form is white to grey or pinkish red. Crystals of gypsum can be extremely colorless and transparent. Gypsum is the most common sulphate mineral and is classified as a non-metallic mineral, found in rock form. It is composed of 79.1% calcium sulphate and 20.9% water, by weight. Chemists call it Hydrous Calcium Sulphate, and as there is one molecule of calcium sulphate combined with two molecules of water. It has the chemical formula $CaSO_42H_20$. By volume this works out to nearly 50% water in the mineral structure.

This water however, is perfectly dry, and is known as "water of crystalization". Gypsum is a natural insulator, feeling warm to the touch when compared to a more ordinary rock or quartz crystal. From a chemical point of view it is Calcium Sulphate Dihydrate ($CaSO_4.2H_2O$) deposited in sedimentary layers on the sea bed. Under high pressure and temperature Gypsum turns into Anhydrite (CaSO4). In nature, Gypsum and Anyhdrite occur as beds or nodular masses up to a few metres thick. Gypsum is formed by the hydration of Anhydrite. Anhydrite is often mined in conjunction with Gypsum.

The content of Gypsum in sedimentary rock varies from 75% to 95%, the rest being clay and chalk. There are four varieties of natural Gypsum, namely —Selenite‖, —Ordite‖, —Satin Spar‖, and —Alabaster‖. The Gypsum Industry is working towards building value for society by offering safe, economic and recyclable products for the home owner using substitutes to natural Gypsum whenever possible, in order to reduce the pressure on natural resources. USES & APPLICATION OF GYPSUM in interior decor

Figure 1A: GYPSUM CONSTRUCTION PLASTER Figure 1B: GYPSUM CEILING BOARDS

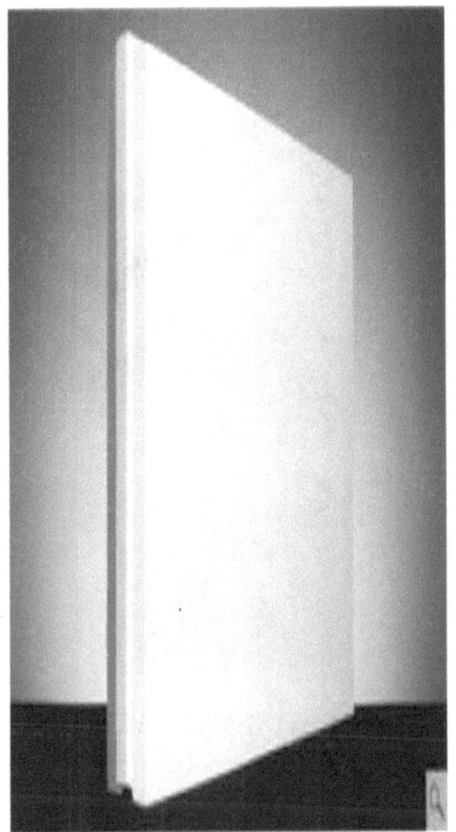

Figure 1C: GYPSUM BLOCKS Figure1 D: GYPSUM PLASTERBOARD

Figure 1E: GYPSUM WALL BOARD Figure 1F: GYSUM DRYWALL
Figure 1: gypsum use in building industry
BUILDING INDUSTRY: See Figure 1A,B,C,D,E,F, for the greatest use of gypsum plaster is in the building industry today is in renders and finish for interior design and including gypsum plasterboards. Most is used to make wall board, also know as sheet rock. PORTLAND CEMENT

& ROAD CONSTRUCTION; Gypsum is also added to Portland cement to strengthen the material, so it can be used in concrete for roads, bridges and sidewalks just to name a few. AGRICULTURE FARMAING: gypsum is used as a fertilizer by adding it directly to the soil. This increases the productivity of the land. PAINTING INDUSTRY: Gypsum can be added to paint as a filler, whereby gypsum must first be ground up into a powder and dried. SCULPTURES: labaster is a soft solid form of gypsum that takes carvings well thus it was able to be carved into many different sculputural shaped objects. WINDOWS: The transparent form of gypsum (selenite) was used for windows before glass was created. FIRE PROTECTION: Gypsum contains a large amount of water, and this gives it fire protection qualities. This is important because it will give some protection from house fires. It is also important because it can be used as molds, allowing melted metals to be poured and formed within. TILES: found in the bathroom are more often than not attached to the wall with a form of gypsum mortar. PLATES, CUPS AND SAUCERS FROM YOUR KITCHEN were most likely poured into a gypsum formed mold. The uses of gypsum are, as we can see nearly endless.

Gypsum Minning, Production, Processing

According to Spence Robin and Dudley Eric and Coburn Andrew, (1989), technologies used to produce gypsum plaster depend on i) the type and quality of the desired finished product, ii) the type and quality of the raw gypsum, iii) the size of the market and producer. Figure 2, shows the process technology of the plant. EXTRACTION OF GYPSUM : Gypsum is extracted from open air or underground mines, using specific drilling machinery and non-polluting explosives. Most rock gypsum deposits are relatively narrow seams and occur close to the earth's surface. 3 types of extraction processes can be carried out. i) Open Cast minning, ii) Drift minning iii) shallow shafts. PREPARING GYPSUM: Gypsum has to be broken down to get even sizes of gypsum particles. The process may involve several stages including drying (crushed, sieved), crushing, screening to remove impurities, grinding to achieve a fine powder. CALCINING OR HEATING: See Figure 2: Temperatures employed between 120_0C-180_0C and between 240_0C800_0C to produce different products. Gypsum is calcined either by direct heat, by mixing it with fuel and burning the two together within a container. Calcining is carried out either by direct heating, or the use of non-permanent kilns and permanent kilns.

A BRIEF HISTORY OF GYPSUM PLASTER: Throughout the centuries, expertise was gained in many parts of the world with gypsum calcinations. In the 1700's, Paris was already the —Capital of Plaster‖ (Plaster of Paris) since all the walls of wooden houses were covered with plaster, as a protection against fire. The King of France had enforced this rule after the big London fire literally destroyed the city in 1666. Large gypsum deposits near Paris have long been mined to manufacture … —Plaster of Paris‖

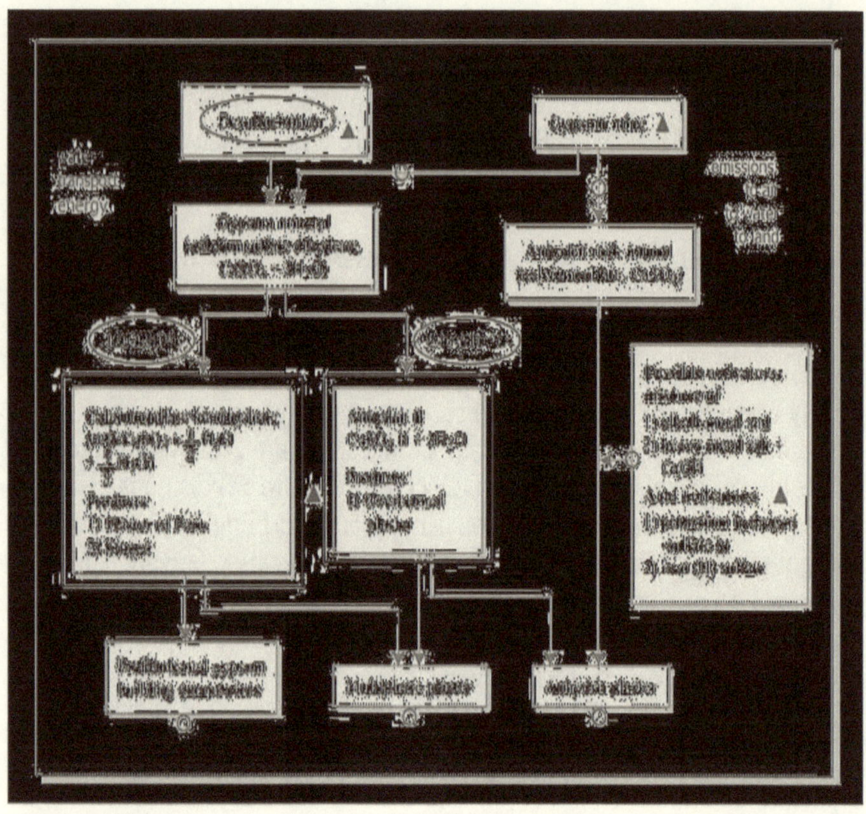

Figure 2: Gypsum Production flow Chart (2009)

Source: http://www.flickr.com/photos/mitopencourseware/3247212401/

Synthetic GYPSUM: —FGD Gypsum‖
According to the Eurogypsum Committee (2007/07/16), The Gypsum Industry is working towards building value for society by offering safe, economic and recyclable products for the home owner using substitutes to natural Gypsum whenever possible, in order to reduce the pressure on natural resources. An intelligent alternative is Gypsum that comes from the flue gas desulphurisation plant (FGD) of the power station industry. This FGD Gypsum is the end product of a wet purification procedure with natural lime that essentially forms according to

the same laws as natural Gypsum – but in a speeded-up process taking only a few hours. FGD Gypsum is an important supplement to the supply of natural Gypsum. This synthetic Gypsum has a higher purity (Gypsum content of 96%) than most natural Gypsum (80%). This means that lower quality Gypsum can be blended with high purity Desulphogypsum, allowing material that would not have been mined in the past to be classified as exploitable reserves. Gypsum Recycling Gypsum products are amongst the very few construction materials where —closed loop‖ recycling is possible, i.e. where the waste can be used to make the same product again and not merely recovered for use in other —downcycling‖ applications, such as are the case with some other construction materials, e.g. waste concrete and bricks used for aggregates in road construction. Furthermore, a major advantage of Gypsum is that it is eternally recyclable. Once collected, the plasterboards are broken down into a fine powder which is then re-introduced, in a controlled blend, into the manufacturing process. Tonnages derived from this source are increasing. Only a small quantity is currently recycled from demolition waste due to challenges surrounding contamination with other materials. This is an area of continuing research and development, according to the Eurogypsum Committee (2007/07/16),

ADVANTAGES OF GYPSUM PLASTER OVER ALTERNATIVE MATERIALS E.G PORTLAND CEMENT AND LIME

FIGURE 3: gypsum board – —good acoustics & sound control‖
Source: http://continuingeducation .construction .com/article.

DECORATIVE INTERIOR FINISH: Aesthetically beautiful with a smooth finish, rendering is orderly and smooth. Glossy or oil paint can be applied directly (gypsum material easily absorbs), See Figure 4 and 5.
HIGH PERFORMANCE DRY-WALLS: Gypsum plaster does not shrink when it dries, so plastered walls do not crack and fine details may be achieved in mouldings. CONSTRUCTION TIME IS 5-8 TIMES FATSER & IT IS NOT MESSY: Gypsum plaster dries and hardens quickly, so a second finishing coat of plaster may be applied promptly. It requires no curing.
ENERGY EFFICIENT: In the manufacturing process, the raw materials gypsum must be heated to temperature of only around 900_oc to $1,100_oc$ and Portland cement is formed at $1,450_oc$. This means gypsum plaster requires simpler technology and considerably less fuel.

ECO FRIENDLY IN NATURE: If applied in an air conditioned room, gypsum is faster to make the room cooler faster compared with other conventional material usage.

GYPSUM IS NOT FLAMMABLE-THERMAL PERFORMANCE: Gypsum plaster is naturally fire resistant, does not distribute heat. SOUND INSULATION: Figure 3, shows an interior with gypsum décor with good acoustics. GGYPSUM IS LIGHT WEIGHT & FLEXIBLE: Therefore reduces load on structure 8-10 times than a brick wall. GYPSUM HAS NO CHEMICAL REACTION ON PAINT. GYPSUM HAS IMPACT RESISTANT QUALITIES: Safe during earthquakes. Gypsum material does not fall abruptly so that residents have more time to save themselves.

F I GURE 4: gypsum suspended ceiling living room design Source:‖ http://designindoor.com/2012/04/six-advantages-of-gypsum-for-you-to-know/suspended-ceilingliving-room-design/

Limitations in the use of Gypsum Plaster

1. NOT SUITABLE FOR EXTERIOR FINISH:
2. CANNOT BE USED IN DAMP & MOIST AREAS

3. CEMENT CANNOT MIX WITH PLASTER OF PARIS
4. NON-HYDRAULIC SETTING BINDER: Slightly soluble in water
5. MORE EXPENSIVE THAN CEMENT

FIGURE 5: gypsum – smooth renders & fini shes in a living room Source: (April 2012)
—DESIGN INDOOR‖ http://designindoor.com/2012/04/six-advantagesof-

gypsum-for-you-to-know/suspended-ceiling-living-room-design/

Conclusions

Natural Gypsum will continue to cover the basic raw material needs of the
Gypsum industry, followed by synthetic Gypsum (FGD). As previously
stated, this study has led me to conclude that gypsum boards will remain the
preferred choice of material for interior decors because of its unique
characteristic compared with the traditional materials like blocks and bricks.
Gypsum is 9-10 times lighter than bricks, 3-4 times faster to install, and can
bear properties like fire resistance, acoustic insulation up to a level that
cannot be achieved with other substitute materials. Gypsum is flexible
ensures site cleanliness and is one of the most environment friendly materials
available in interior and architectural design. Gypsum improves the indoor air
quality and provides thermal insulation. The construction price of a wall
based on gypsum board is substantially cost efficient compared to
conventional materials like bricks and plywood. And indeed the greatest use
of gypsum is in renders and finishes for interior deco use. it is abundant,
economical, fire resistant, strong and versatile. It can also reduce the
transmission of sound. Although natural gypsum still dominates the market,
the use of synthetic gypsum has grown rapidly during the past decade in
particular.
Three factors are responsible for this major shift in the market; stricter
environmental regulations at coal-fired stations resulting in increased output
of flue-gas desulfurization (FGD) gypsum, the high cost of environmental
measures and resistance to accumulation of waste motivating power
companies to sell usable waste products, and the low cost of FGD gypsum
compared to natural gypsum. Furthermore, a major advantage of Gypsum is
that it is eternally recyclable. Once collected, the plasterboards are broken
down into a fine powder (Figure 6A) which is then re-introduced, in a
controlled blend, into the manufacturing process and the final product is seen
in Figure 6B.

Figure 6A: GYPSUM DRYWALL RECYCLING Figure 6B: RECYCLED
WALL BOARD WITH UPTO 25% RECYCLED GYPSUM POWDER
Source: http://www.google.co.ke/search?hl=en&q=RECYCLED+GYPSUM

CHAPTER TWENTY THREE

DESIGN MATERIALS AND PROCESS

LEATHER

ABSTRACT

Kenya Footwear Manufactures Association, Secretary Mr. Simon Nga'ng'a
has called on the government in the past to sensitise the public to appreciate
local leather products more over imports as the country has enough personnel
and skills to produce quality and durable products. Kenya manufactures
varied leather goods including footwear, handbags, belts, etc. Most of these

are exported to Uganda, Tanzania, COMESA, USA, EU, etc Kenya also has a thriving livestock industry and is exporting products in all the subsectors within the sector. The Export Promotion Council (http://www.epckenya.org/) goes on to state that Kenya has a thriving tanning industry with 12 functioning tanneries with an installed capacity of handling 3.3 million hides and 8.3 million skins. Products produced under this category include wet blue and tanned leather. Figure 1, is a display of very impressive footwear locally made. With such potential, it is indeed of utmost importance to study the leather sector and promote leather products.

Figure 1: an impressive display of leather boots locally produced by Kenya footwear manufacturers association Source:
http://www.google.co.ke/search?q=leather+products+in+kenya&hl
According to Leather Goods (6$_{th}$ Edition), (1990), reports that Synthetic Leather goods have grown over the years. This is as a result of the rise of the plastic industry and the development of new manufacturing techniques to add value and produce cheaper products to compete with the leather industry. Synthetic leather products of the same type are also included under leather goods, including items made from such materials as plastic, fabric, canvas,

and tapestry

in addition to items made from a combination of these with leather.
Using synthetics, manufacturers can produce a range of genuine looking
leather items. Synthetics such as PVC and polyurethane, used in conjunction
with leather, can contribute to smooth finishes impossible to achieve with the
use of the hide alone. Moreover, synthetics have an obvious cost advantage –
polyurethane is roughly half the price of leather, and indeed, products with up
to 50% synthetic content may be stamped with legend —Genuine Leather‖.

Key Words: Leather, Wet blue, Tanning, Livestock industry, Hides, Skins,
Livestock, AnimalHusbandry

INTRODUCTION

BASF, The Chemical Company (4_{TH} Edition), defines Leather as a
manufactured product that can be made from hides and skin of any living
creature after applying a variety of chemical and physical processes (namely,
tanning, tawing and chamoising), the aim of which is to preserve from
putrefaction the unique collagen fiber tissue which forms the middle layer,
for an intended purpose. Skins are those of small or young animals including
calf, pig, goat, sheep, birds, rabbits, reptiles etc Hides are those of larger
animals including cattle, horse, buffalo, ostrich etc. Leather is used in the
production of a variety of different Leather goods, for shoes, garments,
upholstery and increasingly the automotive sector. Leather is a very versatile
material and the various different applications in which it is used make very
varied demands on its performance. More than 90% of all the Leather
produced is used in the manufacture of shoes, automotive upholstery and
trim, upholstery for furniture and clothing.

Kirsten Jorgensen (1974), a fashion designer in leather wear, observed that,
despite the fact that Leather undergoes a number of refining processes,
Leather can be regarded as a natural material, and as such it has many good
qualities. It is virtually indestructible. It is warm in cold weather and as it is
also porous, comfortable to wear in hot weather. It is dirt resistant. It is also
pliable and soft. And of course, it has a character and beauty of its own.
Export Promotion Council (EPC) goes on in print, stating that, In Kenya, the

bulk of the conventional leather production is accounted for by just three species namely cattle hides or bovine material (accounts for 70% sheep skins (20%) and goat skin (10%). Other less significant sources include calf, lamb and kid skins, fish, buffalo hides, ostrich skin, and crocodile and pig skins.

THE HISTORY OF LEATHER

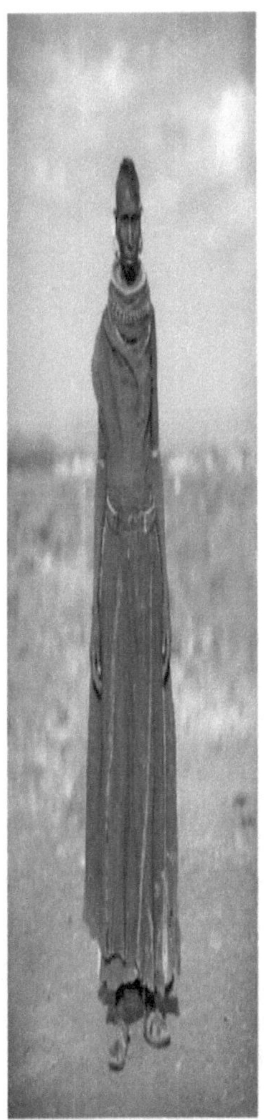
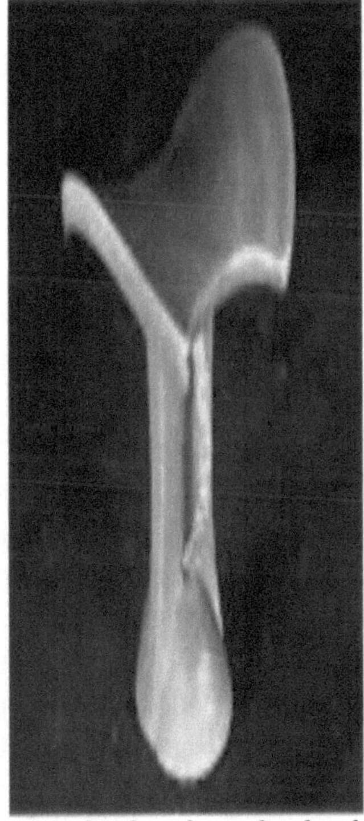

Figure 2a: Turkana woman in leather dress, leather headrest, 2 Djemebe leather drums Sources: http://www.google.co.ke/search?q=turkana+woman+in+leather+dress

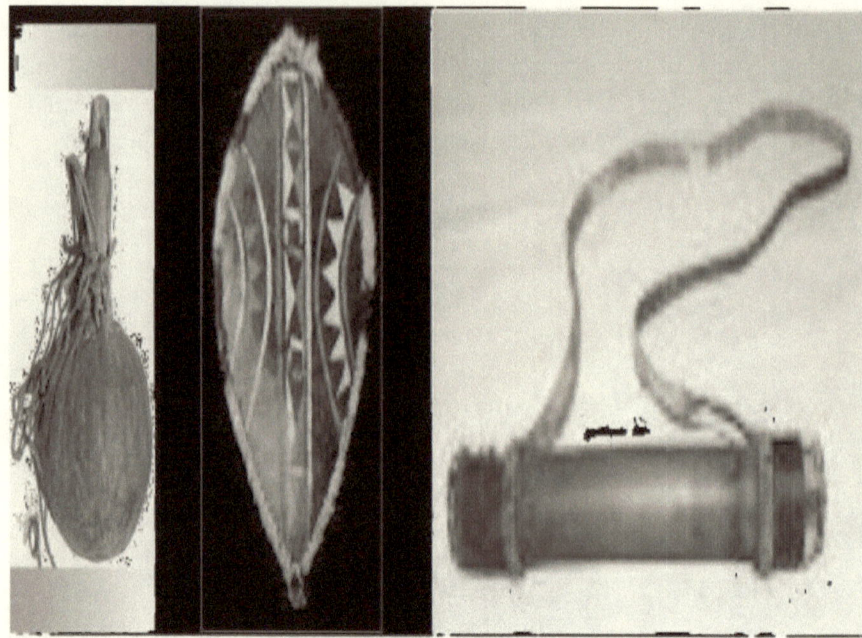

Figure 2b: 3 a leather turkana milk jug kenya * beaded leather container *
shields made from cattle hide Source: http://www.google.co.ke/search?
hl=en&q=traditional+leather+stool

According to Ley Xenia parker (1968), Leather, a unique and valuable
material, has played a very important role in the development of civilisation.
From prehistoric times man has used the skins of animals to satisfy his basic
needs, see figure 2A and 2B. The most valuable remaining part of the animal
after slaughtering is the hide. Traditionally, hides and skins were dried and
only the best hides were traditionally used for simple tanning. The resulting
leather is hard and not very durable. Out of hides, skins and leather the
women made traditional containers, covers for beds or clothing, see figure 2A
and 2B. Man turned to leather for clothing because it was bigger, stronger
and warmer. He has used hides to make clothing, shelter, carpets and even
decorative attire. From leather, man made footwear, belts, clothing,
containers for liquids, covering huts, or making tents, boats, tools, weapon
handles and even armour or shields. The early leathers were made from
cowhide, calfskin, pigskin, deerskin,

and goatskin leathers. The hides and skins coming from animals either
hunted or farmed for food purposes. The leather industry is one the oldest

industries known to mankind.

THE LEATHER TANNING PROCESS

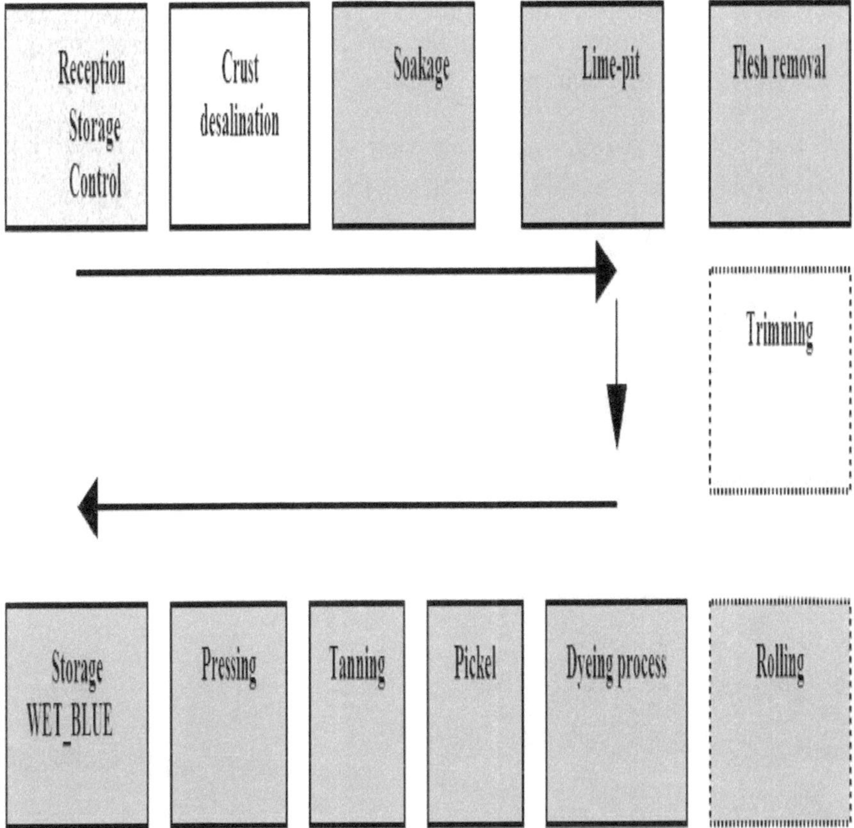

Figure 3: wet blue tanning process
Source: http://www.google.co.ke/search?

According to Waterer (1972), there are 3 different methods of Tanning that can be applied: Chrome Tanning or Wet Blue, Aluminium or Oil Tanning & Vegetable Tanning. Figure 3 above is a graphical chart showing the stages of the Chrome Tanning process of wet blue which is the most widely used, worldwide. The leather manufacturing process is divided into three sub-processes: Pre-Tanning stage, Tanning Stage and Crusting Stage. —Wet blue is the process of converting raw hides and skins to tanned leather using chromium salts‖ says Sub Committee Chairman Hanna Adel (2000), a Chemist. She goes on to say,‖ The hide becomes blue when chromium salts are added, —The trade terminology —wet blue‖ means the hide is free of hair and it is tanned. The hide is wet at that stage. Tanners buy wet blue stock to produce several types of products such as shoes, garments, leather and upholstery‖. The tannery extracts the moisture, oils and natural preservatives and removes the hair. At this stage, it's called "Wet Blue", see figure 4.

The wet blue hides are put into a giant drum with the new oils, preservatives and coloring and let it tumble for hours and hours. Depending on the thickness of the leather, it can take up to 10 hours for the new life giving liquids to penetrate all the way to the middle of the hide. Finally, the leather is pressed in heated presses, hung up to dry at a certain humidity level, sprayed with finishes and sealers and then pressed again.

Figure 4: chrome tanned leather or —wet blue —
Source: http://www.hiwtc.com/products/wet-blue-cow-leather-4643-68195.htm

Figure 5 shows a summary of all the stages of leather chrome tanning, from the leather manufacturing process is divided into three sub-processes: Pre-Tanning stage, Tanning Stage

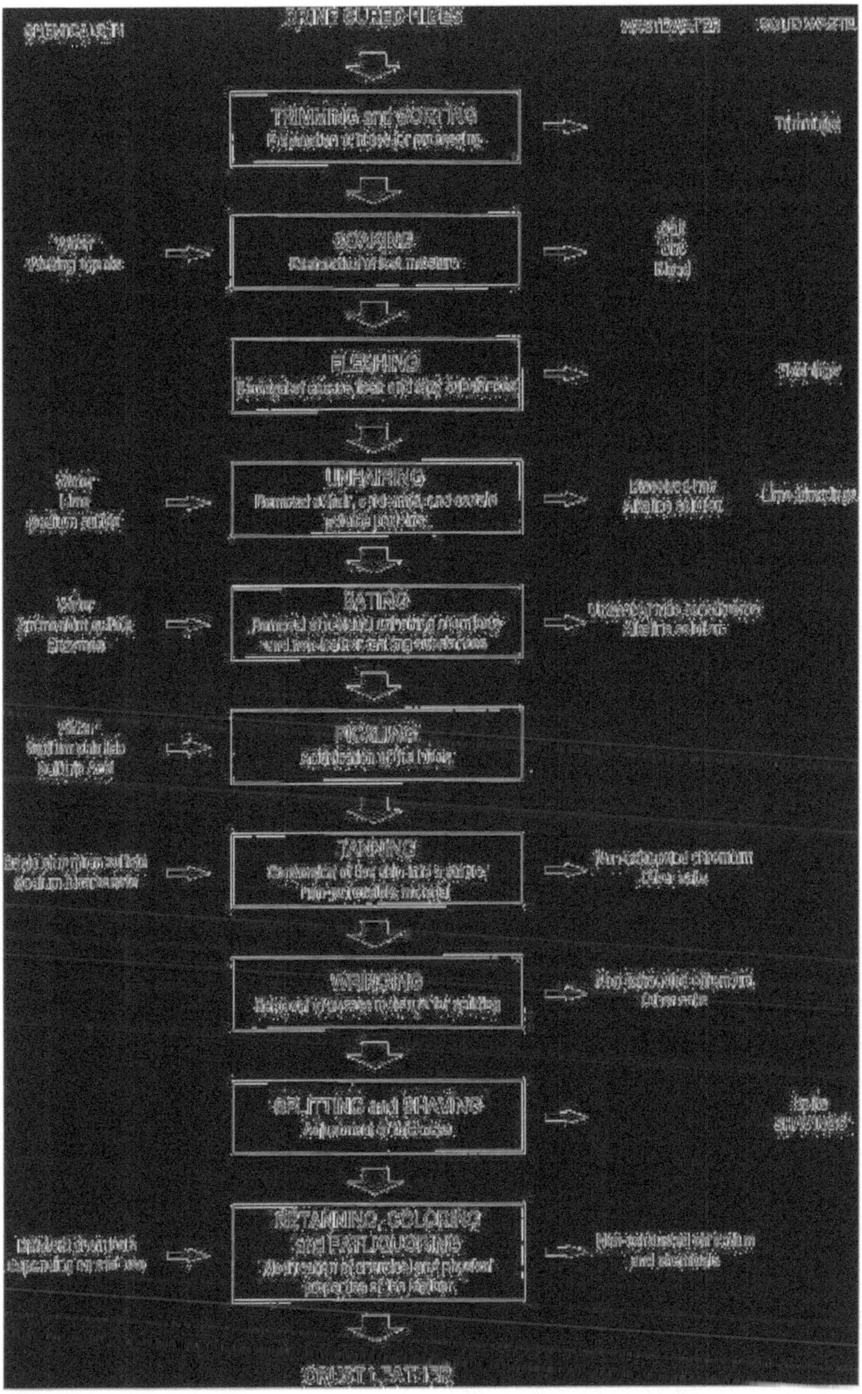

BRINE CURED HIDES

CHEMICALS IN   WASTEWATER   SOLID WASTE

TRIMMING and SORTING
Preparation of hides for processing
→ Trimmings

Water   SOAKING   Salt
Wetting agents   Rehydration of hide tissue   and
          Dirt

FLESHING   Fatty tissue
Removal of excess flesh and fatty subcutaneous

Water   UNHAIRING   Dissolved hair   Lime sludge
Lime   Removal of hair, epidermis, and keratin   Alkaline solution
Sodium sulfide   debris per hide

Water   BATING   Ammonia nitrogen
Ammonium salts   Removal of residual unhairing chemicals   Alkaline solution
Enzymes   and loosening of collagen structure

Water   PICKLING
Sulfuric acid   Acidification of hide tissue
Sodium chloride

Basic chromium sulfate   TANNING   Formaldehyde, chromium
Sodium bicarbonate   Combination of tan chemicals to stabilize   dyes, salts
          hide; non-metallic material

          WRINGING   Non-metallic chromium
          Removal of excess moisture by pressing   dyes, salts

SPLITTING and SHAVING   Splits
Adjustment of hide edge   Shavings

Natural dyeings   RETANNING, COLORING   Non-metallic chromium
depending on end use   and FATLIQUORING   and chemicals
          Adjustment of chemical and physical
          properties of the leather

CRUST LEATHER

Figure 5: leather chrome tanning: (June 1998)
Source:http://www.google.co.ke/imgres?
q=chrome+tanning+process+leather+in+a+diagram e &um, (volume 18,
issue 3, 1 pages 211–218), elsevier science ltd

The PHYSICAL properties of leather

Muirhead Andrew (1840) has been producing leather since 1840 and is the
largest supplier in the United Kingdom. Therefore, we quote them on stating
the physical properties which make leather a unique and valuable material for
upholstery purposes. Leather has high tensile strength combined with the
ability to resist tear, high resistance to flexing and Leather has a high
resistance to puncture. Leather contains a great deal of air, which makes it a
poor conductor of heat and this property is very important when it comes to
considering comfort.

Indeed Leather is a good heat insulator and it is permeable to water vapour.
Leather fibres will hold large quantities of water vapour. This property
enables leather to absorb perspiration, which is later dissipated. A significant
factor in comfort Indeed leather has unique thermostatic properties, whereby,
Leather is warm in cold weather and cool in hot weather An ideal property in
Leather is its ability to be moulded and tends to retain its new shape. It has
both elastic and plastic properties in wear. Leather has resistance to wet and
dry abrasion whereby the wear and maintenance, are controlled by the
tannage and surface finish. Furthermore, Leather is inherently resistant to
heat and flame, it is also resistant to fungi, mildew and chemical attack. The
atmosphere of modern cities is polluted from the burning of carbon fuels with
sulphur dioxide gas, which can accelerate the deterioration of leather. Modern
leathers are tanned and dressed to resist these harmful chemicals.

TYPES OF LEATHER, uses & application

Figure 6: an impressive display of leather boots by Kenya footwear manufacturers association Source: http://www.google.co.ke/search? q=leather+products+in+kenya&hl According to Mr. Mohammed Farouk (Technical Manager) of Leather Industries of Kenya Limited in Thika town, their distribution of Leather covers the Kenyan market and the Leather is sold according to the needs of use which determines the type, finish and gauge of leather supplied. The range of leather supplied are: i) Hair-On, (See Figure 6 for an impressive range of Safari Boots produce locally), ii) Pigmented Leather(Gents Shoes), iii) Aniline Finish (very good for Bags), iv) Suede Leather, v) Suede Split, vi) Nubuck Leather (Spongy finish), vii) Patent Finish (Shinny & very Expensive-Officers boots), viii) Fish Leather(Textured Finnish decorative sandals),

ix) Upholstery (car seats & sofa sets), x) Kips Leather (Goat skin), xi) Camel (cheapest), xii) Goat Leather, Sheep (Expensive & very Soft-its leather not exposed to branding), xiii) Fish Leather (decoration), xiv) Ostrich Leather (decoration), xv) Rabbits leather.

CHALLENGES FACING THE LEATHER INDUSTRY IN KENYA

According to Maina Moses the lead designer and trainer at the Training and Product Centre for the shoe Industry in Thika, and according to The Republic of Kenya, (June 2001), published a report on the —Position Paper on Leather & Leather Products‖, highlighting the Challenges facing hide, skin, leather good and leather footwear industry in Kenya are as follows:- LEATHER PRODUCTS ARE EXPENSIVE: Leather products like handbags, purses, wallets belts, sandals, bags are too are too expensive for ordinary Kenyans.

IMPORTS: Imported Leather Footwear from Ethiopia is sold at a lower price than the local leather shoe and Imported Cheap second-hand leather shoes and Bulk imports of Synthetic shoes from China. Countries like Egypt have a ―duty free‖ policy on raw materials for leather production, so their production costs are lower & products cheaper.

COST OF POWER is too high, & when a generator is used the production costs double. LOW SUPPLY OF RAW MATERIALS – Only 15% wet blue is consumed locally & 95% is exported. Orders can take up to one and a half months to be delivered. Export of Raw Materials ―wet blue‖ deprives locals of jobs and livelihoods.

LEATHER PROCESSING IS EXPENSIVE: Technology for processing leather to the finished stage is very expensive and thus inaccessible to most tanneries.

THE QUALITY OF KENYAN'S HIDE AND SKINS LEATHER IS NOT OF HIGH STANDARD due to defects such as flays marks, brand marks, scratches, ticks marks, pox marks, hair slip due to poor preservation. Poor Animal Husbandry, Declining Leather Production, ECONOMIC LIBERALIZATION in the 1990's made 11 tanneries close shop. LACK OF SKILLFULL DESIGNERS.

MECHANICAL: Branding: by use of a red hot iron to impose permanent marks on the animal remains visible in tanned leather.

CONCLUSION

Dr. Mwinyikione Mwinyihija, (2010) deputy director of Leather Development, Ministry of livestock Development summarized the future of the leather industry in Kenya. He goes on to say, ―It is possible to conclude with certainty that Kenya is introducing a comprehensive livestock development policy that will create a sound animal husbandry practice capable of increasing livestock productivity leading to high quality hides and skins. There is need for all the staff under the Hides, skins and leather development service to undergo total quality management techniques within the value chain. Funding of critical identified challenges in the value addition chain from peri and post slaughter is of paramount necessity for sustainable improvement of quality. The establishment of the Leather Development Council (LDC) has ensured a well coordinated and vibrant leather industry by